What Teachers Need

How the Education Community Can Promote Sustainable Well-Being and Help Heal the Profession

Edited by
Amanda Moreno and Jeanette Banashak

Published by Teachers College Press,® 1234 Amsterdam Avenue, New York, NY 10027

Front cover design by Geronna Lewis-Lyte. Photo of bowl by Chanchal/Adobe Stock; blackboard by Homo Studio/Unsplash; desk by Jivar Photo/Stock by Getty Images.

Library of Congress Cataloging-in-Publication Data is available at loc.gov

ISBN 978-0-8077-8403-7 (paper)
ISBN 978-0-8077-8360-3 (hardcover)
ISBN 978-0-8077-8404-4 (ebook)

Printed on acid-free paper

Manufactured in the United States of America

Contents

PART II: BEYOND CULTURAL AFFINITY: HEALING TEACHING BY AND FOR TEACHERS OF COLOR

PART III: EXPANSIVE SEL: HEALING LEADERSHIP AND HUMANIZING SYSTEMS

PART IV: HEALING TEACHING THROUGH INNER AND OUTER HARMONY: SELF, OTHERS, EARTH

Preface

The Embers of Change

Like all labors of love, the journey to this book's fruition has been winding. Despite many references to it, this is *not* a pandemic book (like we've all insisted to our friends that this is not a pandemic divorce, pandemic puppy, or pandemic-inspired urge to learn to play the ukulele!), but we don't deny that a collective clarity has been unearthed since 2020. For us, that clarity involved the knowledge that we did not possess the magic answers to the questions so many teachers were asking (How should we ensure that children's social–emotional skills don't suffer? How can I tell how well students are receiving the material when their screens are off? How can I help settle a crying child when I'm not allowed to get physically close to them?). And, along with so many other local, national, and global traumas coming fast and furious that do not stop at the schoolhouse door (e.g., decimation of education funding, youth mental health crisis, antitrans and other regressive policies, racial reckoning, geopolitical unrest), we couldn't be the all-knowing sages teachers hoped for in those crises either. Worst of all, we couldn't explain or make excuses for leaders or policymakers who, under the best of circumstances, wouldn't give teachers adequate time and resources to manage the school-based fallout of these harms, and under the worst circumstances would blame teachers for that fallout. Could a book bring some long-deserved relief to teachers, at the very least, by taking the heat of this world on fire *off of them* and putting it instead on those tasked with creating the conditions for their work?

We've been making attempts to lighten educators' burdens in what we call the "compensatory space." Schools don't have everything they need *inside* their walls, so they call us from the *outside*, and we do what we can together. This work happens in the context of professional development courses and consultation, higher education certificate and degree programs in early education and social and emotional learning (SEL), and schools-based program development, implementation, and research. We've learned that two things can be true: outsiders need to remain humble, but our perspective can feel miraculous to educators precisely *because* we're outsiders to the daily grind of the school. So, when they finally hear, "You're right, this (and there are so many *this*-es) is not OK," it seems to be the salve of affirmation they need to simply go on. However, we know that we're not the only ones trying to work a little bit of magic out there in the compensatory space, both in and outside of school buildings. (Educators compensate for the resources they don't have every single day.) Thus, the idea for an edited book was born.

We wanted to feature diverse individuals with different levels of experience and vantage points on the field who are using different approaches to creating healing and wellness—starting with the adults—in our education system. For example, we intentionally included junior authors who would be willing to tell us the hard truths about whether the teachers of the future are likely to buy what we are trying to sell them. We hope you'll want to read about what courageous educators and their supporters are doing to create healing transformations in their contexts, even if you might view their challenges, roles, or identities as very different from your own. We could all use a good dose of silo- and myopia-curing.

And speaking of breaking out of silos, there's a chapter on expanding our view of care and healing to include Earth others, the land, and the planet. We're confident it will be reparative and soul-nourishing to hear from the brilliant educators working under literal crisis conditions, nevertheless making headway toward healing teaching, giving us the gift known as *perspective*.

MEET THE EDITORS

The editors of this book have had the privilege of being in proximity to brilliant educators since early in their lives. Amanda Moreno decided to pursue "child studies" in college, and through a work study position at age 18, while bleaching tables (that's what they did in those days), rubbing backs at naptime, and setting up snack for kids at the university child care center, she watched agog as the teachers held the room with a perfect balance that's difficult to describe even now, thinking, "How do they know how to *do* that?" What's more, the teachers were treated as such professionals; there was no distinction of echelon in her mind between that vocation and doctor, lawyer, or any other esteemed career in our society. Amanda believes that ultimately, that brief period of believing in a utopian but inaccurate vision of the education system was more blessing than curse. Ever since, she has been confusing her Depression-era parents by talking about and researching children and feelings. Presently, she likes to say that her work takes place at the "nexus of cognition and emotion in the classroom," which means that feeling and learning and teaching are inseparable, and when students and teachers *want* to be at school, you've pretty much won the whole game. This book focuses on the teacher side of this equation, one part of which is reflected in a program we designed called "SELove"[1] (Moreno et al., 2025). The SELove program represents our efforts to

1. There is no chapter on SELove in this book because the program description and its findings were previously published in an open access journal, and we wanted to save all the precious space possible to platform others' approaches.

bring SEL and healing-centered education together through support of teachers' reflective insight and self-compassion.

Jeanette Banashak's first job in high school was planning and facilitating outdoor curricula as a summer day camp counselor for elementary-aged kids. Six years later, while teaching in the classroom for the first time, she would gaze out the window with the same longing for being outside as she did as a child. The monkey bars! The wall-less boundaries! The green grass! Recess still existed back then. As an early career teacher, though usually preferring to be outside, she learned to appreciate the indoor rhythms of the school day with the constant need for spontaneity, self-management, and understanding individual needs of her students. Her earliest colleagues became models for empathy, fostering supportive classroom environments, building something with zero budget, and squeezing every last learning and connection moment out of the day. Twenty-seven years later, with four degrees in education, if Jeanette can't get outside to teach SEL, she brings nature inside with plants, pets, aromas, and naturescapes of babbling brooks and birdsong. Her life's work is returning to foundational principles and practices with joy and curiosity, teaching contemplative pedagogy and andragogy to humans of all ages.

WHAT'S INSIDE

In the first chapter of *What Teachers Need*, Amanda lays out some of the main reasons for the crisis in teacher morale and retention that inspired our urgency for building this book, and provides an argument for why it is high time we put the adult educators first in our reform efforts. Every chapter thereafter describes a specific, innovative, implementable approach to helping to solve this crisis through the healing and well-being of the adult educators. The chapters within Part I focus at the intra- and inter-individual level, under a theme we deem "radical professional intimacy." Part II's chapters also focus on the interpersonal level, but from the vantage point of educators of color (i.e., Black, Native American, and Latine educators), so that they can each redefine what professional intimacy looks like on their own communities' terms. We suggest, however, that each of these chapters holds powerful wisdom and suggestions for educators of any identity, because they are all addressing how to repair the dehumanization that exists widely across the teaching profession. In Part III, the focus widens out to more concretely address leaders (e.g., principals and superintendents), systems, and policies. Each chapter describes innovative approaches to heal the teaching profession despite the difficult odds embedded in "scaling" solutions that are more broadly felt. Finally, each chapter in Part IV makes intriguing connections between the micro/individual and macro levels that impact teachers and education as a whole (e.g., nature and the planet, natural disasters and war, systemic racism and patriarchy, toxic work cultures as a result of capitalism). These chapters offer tangible ideas and strategies that help answer the question, "Where do we begin?" when a barrier to healing seems too vast to overcome.

What Teachers Need does not provide a complete answer to healing, but rather, embraces Akomolafe's (2023) concept of "emancipatory wholeness," which suggests that true liberation does not come from perfection or complete clarity but rather the uncertainty, patience, humility, relationality, and complexity that are part of the real world. Even if you don't believe in magic, whatever position you hold that touches the art and science of teaching, we hope that the myriad wisdoms in these pages provide the tinder and kindling your community needs to ignite a transformation of their own making.

REFERENCES

Akomolafe, B. (2023, January 24). *Dr. Bayo Akomolafe on slowing down in urgent times.* Atmos. https://atmos.earth/dr-bayo-akomolafe-on-slowing-down-in-urgent-times/

Moreno, A., Banashak, J., Kontoudakis, M., Evans, A., Bajet, R., & Laase, A. (2025). Giving to teachers what we ask them to give to others: Supporting adult SEL through reflective insight and healing. *Social and Emotional Learning: Research, Practice, and Policy*, *5*, 100086. https://doi.org/10.1016/j.sel.2025.100086

Acknowledgments

We would like to express our sincere gratitude to everyone past, present, and future who has contributed to this collaborative book and made it possible. Thank you to Erikson's Dean of Faculty Dr. Maxine McKinney de Royston; President (and author in this book) Dr. Mariana Souto-Manning; Vice President of Academic Affairs Dr. Pam Epley; and Vice President for Strategic Growth and Partnerships Dr. Ayanna Brown, for all their support and guidance. Thank you, Nashita Syeda, for administrative genius along the way. Thanks to Erikson Institute, for the financial support for Amanda's sabbatical and a faculty innovation fund grant for Jeanette.

Thank you to our wonderful editor, Sarah Jubar, who made the initial invitation to us to do a book, and to the entire publishing team at Teachers College Press for helping to make the book readable. Thank you to Matt Bourque, our generous and talented graphic artist.

Thank you to all of our authors for saying yes, and for the insightful, thoughtful, and hopeful ways you show up to improve the conditions in education.

Jeanette's personal acknowledgements: Thank you, Amanda, for the thousands of conversations about healing teaching and SEL that have served to challenge and develop my philosophy and practice of scholarship, teaching, and service, for affirming that love can cause learning in any context, and for your singing that brings harmony to my life. To my first teachers, my parents, and my siblings and niblings, for all you've taught and continue to teach me through the moments and years. To Sr. Virginia for your vision of extroverted me as a contemplative-true-to-myself educator. To all the Earth others, including our two kitties, who bring so much joy and wonderment into daily life. To our brilliant and creative adult children and their partners for cheering me on and looking out for all of us, all the time. And, to my true home, Beth, for your deep, soulful listening and intuitive responses to the surprises of life's unfolding.

Amanda's personal acknowledgements: Thank you, Jeanette, for taking that trip to Portland, enthusiastically taking this ride with me, engaging in deep conversations about things like whether the phrase "the common good" is actually good, and for helping me adopt a philosophy of reciprocity with the natural world. I couldn't have asked for a more steady, open, thoughtful, and reliable partner for this, the first book project for both of us. Thanks to Mom, for always engaging with everything I do, and for believing me when I said that yes, even an edited book does merit "a year off of work." Thanks to John for your partnership on our continued parenting journey with our adult children, and to those three amazing women for teaching me more about SEL, love, and repair than any degree ever did. Thanks to Julie and Scott for your encouragement and inside scoop on the entertainment world. Thanks to Erin and Jen—my "Brain Trust" sisters, for your unwavering presence, love, and support. Thanks to Suni for your expert consultation and friendship. Thanks to Tootsie Roll for being there for writer's block squishes and hikes to Calvert Cliffs. And last but certainly not least, immeasurable thanks to my sister Jillian, a gifted career elementary school teacher, and the ongoing inspiration for "the sis test"—the sniff test that all my ideas generated from the ivory tower must pass.

CHAPTER 1

They Didn't Start the Fire

Why It's Time to Focus on the Grown-Ups

Amanda Moreno

If you want to get a sense of the depth of the teaching crisis in America, look no further than "Teacher TikTok." This is where teachers on TikTok share content related to their teaching experiences, offer advice, share lesson ideas, engage in discussions about the profession, and more. But be warned—the content is not for the faint of heart, especially if you are someone who trains, supports, or prepares teachers. You will see yourself in bold relief—sometimes being ribbed with lighthearted humor, but more often than not, painful stories lurk beneath.

Educators are feeling betrayed by their own profession. They are experiencing insufficient mental health support and stress-induced illness, being required to use ineffective behavioral programs and punitive accountability measures with students, and being blamed by parents (and *blaming* parents) for things out of their control. Maybe even worse might be the promising social and emotional learning (SEL) programs meant to prevent or ameliorate such challenges, but that are employed in name only or left on the shelf, without appropriate supports to implement them.

In one video on "Teacher TikTok," a teacher revealed that she was going to the second funeral for a colleague in a month. Of course, the teachers themselves were the ones to organize the remembrance and raise money for the surviving families. And this is saying nothing of the secondary trauma teachers experience when their students are involved in abuse and violence or simply don't have the resources they need to engage in school.

Teaching has always been an extremely challenging profession. It's been said quite a few times that the COVID-19 pandemic didn't cause these problems in the education system but rather laid them bare; much of what was revealed was the fragility of the enterprise itself, even under the best of circumstances. What is more complex and precarious work than humans creating deep, meaningful, and lasting change in other humans? In March 2020, teachers came to us asking questions like, "How can I communicate my facial expressions to children like I did before while wearing a mask?" or "How can I give my students an equal learning experience when I'm talking to a black screen because all their cameras are off?" Teachers and principals believed that they could and should be able to do the impossible. Meanwhile, no one was there affirming for them that they *already were.*

WICKED PROBLEMS IN EDUCATION

In the late 1960s, C. West Churchman (1967) introduced the concept of "wicked problems" in social planning and management. Essentially, wicked problems are complex societal concerns that are social, rather than scientific, in nature, and therefore are ill-defined, have no obvious or immediate right or wrong solutions, and experience vastly different interpretations depending on one's point of view in society (Rittel & Weber, 1973). We can think of no more apt example of this framework than the aspiration that education could possibly become the great equalizer and overcome all the *other* reasons why democracy falls short. Yet, even though educators (including teachers, principals, and district leaders) are those who have agreed to dedicate their lives to grappling with this wicked problem, our society has made a habit of "demonizing teachers as if they were adversaries of their students and treating them as malingerers who required constant evaluation lest they fail to do their duty" (Ravitch, 2020, p. 4).

Multiple scholars and advocates have exposed the harm caused by the education "reform" movement of the last decades (e.g., see Black, 2020; Love, 2019, 2023; Ravitch, 2020), proving once again that wicked problems are wicked by their nature, not because the social planners (in this case, educators) are not smart enough or working hard enough, so this book will not be revisiting that territory. Instead, you might think of this book as part apology, part love letter, and part reparations to educators, for the years of unjustly scapegoating them for the inequities of our society that they have passionately dedicated their lives to disrupting, and the specific ways in which these misguided efforts have siphoned the joy and productivity from their daily lives on the job.

Who Should Read This Book?

This book is neither another self-care directive aimed at teachers (individual level), nor a policy solution for the root causes of problems in education (societal level). Instead, we aim for this book to occupy a "third space" (e.g., Bhabha, 1994; Soja, 1996), in which educators receive a direct infusion of care and repair from *others* that, while not a fix for their wicked problem (which we know now is an oxymoron anyhow), facilitates genuine healing from the harms of their profession and provides tangible means that make a noticeable difference in their ability to do the work they came to do, in ways that nurture their humanity, wellness, productive engagement, and joy. The *others* that we speak of will be referred to as Supporters of Educators (SEs), which include roles such as teacher education faculty, principals, district leaders, union leaders, consultants, professional development facilitators, coaches, mentors, curriculum trainers, etc. At every level of "educator," we wish to reverse the tradition of asking educators to do for others—expertly and with a smile—that which has never been done for them, and instead, shift the burden of healing and repair to "one level up" or whoever in a particular context or set of relationships has a demand or expectation of an educator.

Of course, teachers themselves are also an intended audience for this book, but rather than the pages being filled with instructions on what to do, they are filled with examples of *how they ought to be treated.* We hope that teachers can find in these pages not only validation for the injustices and indecencies they have been enduring, but a new standard for what to expect from others as support for carrying out the tall task before them.

IS THE STATE OF TEACHING REALLY SO BAD?

While the rest of this book is about what the most innovative supporters of educators are doing to humanize, lift up, and reinvigorate teachers, we first need to get up close and personal with *why* such efforts are a dire emergency in this country.

For the purposes of this chapter, we spoke to Jayla[2], a veteran fifth grade teacher who teaches in the Mountain West of the United States, in a school that is in a greater metro area, in a middle- and upper-middle-class neighborhood. Last year, 16 underenrolled schools from mostly lower-income areas of the district closed, and Jayla's school was among the receiver schools. She refers to the circumstance as "the merger." Jayla has been a teacher for over 20 years and had already been teaching at the receiver school—we'll call it Oakwood—for four years at the time of the merger. We were interested in knowing from Jayla what her teaching life was like both before and after the merger.

She describes her school as serving an "average" population (for that region), with a supportive and competent principal, as well as collegial coworkers who regularly rely on each other for emotional and professional support. Jayla's story is an interesting one to tell because of how potentially "average" (but still problematic) the school was before the merger and then how things devolved even *further* when the system was tested:

> *To be a teacher, you are steeped in being a failure every day, by definition. Of course there are successes too, and that's what keeps you going back, but the very nature of the work is a constant struggle against the distractions, to keep the focus on learning. Even before the merger, every year there would be one or two students in my class who would require 50% of my attention, and the school just simply didn't have the resources to help.*

2. All names in this book are pseudonyms.

My school only cares about moving kids to green [grade level]. And the thing is, I do care about test scores! I look really closely at my results. If my kids have a general problem with subtracting fractions, then I assume the problem is with me, and I will consult with my math teacher friends about what I can do to improve. But the way the scores are used is just for public humiliation or praise—you are labeled whatever percent growth, and you are incentivized to focus all your attention on the kids in the yellow, which may only be one or two that year. Students who are at grade level or ahead are ignored and maybe not meeting their own potential because we are told that they are fine and our job performance is not based on them at all.

Another thing is that we have to purchase the next new curriculum from the expensive publishing companies almost every year. It's like, since the school spends the money, we have to go "all the way" each time, being disallowed from using any of our previous materials or methods we liked and being forced to use only the new materials even if they didn't work great for each student.

Our latest literacy curriculum uses 20-page, very boring passages that none of the kids want to read. My kids love *books, and I will see them in the hallway with their nose practically attached to whatever book, like* Wonder *[by R. J. Palacio] or something, and it meets the testing rigor level, but I'm not allowed to use that for my lesson. Not only that, but every member of the teaching team also needed to be on the exact same page of the curriculum at the exact same time. A lot of the veteran teachers worked around the system and did what was best for their students anyway, and the principal pretty much left us alone because he knew we were doing what was right.*

Then when the merger happened, I went from having one or two students who were either behind on grade level or had behavioral challenges, to a third of my class. It was almost like because it was known we had a good principal and were trying to do our best to prepare, the district just "threw us to the wolves" and gave us no support to help the new students and teachers. I heard one story from one of the closing schools, where the movers came and interrupted a lesson on the last day of school and asked the teacher for the books back that she was literally teaching out of at that moment. I can't imagine how awful those experiences must have been, and you can tell that the teachers are traumatized.

We were promised a new program to help with students with emotional and behavioral challenges, and the whole thing has been a nightmare. The therapist was crying every day. The entire staff from that program has turned over multiple times and we're not even one year in. Teachers have had to create triage lists with the principal, and even then, the neediest students will only get 20-30 minutes once or twice a week with a counselor. Almost every one of these 10-year-olds has some kind of diagnosis already of anxiety or depression. We even have kids who hear voices.

Sure, a lot of these issues are just happening in society and it's not the school's fault, but there are so many things that could have been done better to avoid the drastic problems we're seeing now. We could have had real training and support for the kids with intense behavioral needs; they could have done the merger gradually, one grade per year; we could have modified the teacher growth goals so we don't leave so many kids off the radar. So yeah, I'm giving it one more year. I'm holding out hope that we'll get the behavioral program properly staffed by then, and maybe the kids who are new to Oakwood will have adjusted by then too. But if next year is anything like this year, I'm looking at early retirement at a significant financial loss to myself because I just can't keep doing this.

We know that many teachers feel the same way as Jayla does. If you are reading this book, chances are you know many teachers who do, too. The profession that prepares all others is decidedly in crisis, with virtually every indicator showing cause for concern, from job satisfaction, teacher turnover, and teacher stress, to challenges in filling open positions and precipitous drops in students interested in and completing teacher education degree programs.

While some of the most recent changes are attributable to the COVID-19 pandemic—such as 37% of teachers reporting an ability to maintain work–life balance "never or almost never" (Kotowski et al., 2022)—most of the concerning trends started *long before* the pandemic, including a drastic drop in teachers who feel the stress of their job is worth it from 81% to 42% over the last 15 years (Kraft & Lyon, 2022), a 30% drop in those enrolling in teacher preparation programs over the last 12 years, and a stagnation in teacher salaries after accounting for inflation over the last 10 years despite an increase in their educational attainment over the same period (Irwin et al., 2023). So yes, by both subjective and objective measures, the state of teaching today is *that bad*, and very much in need of healing. While the solution to this wicked problem will not come from only one sphere, we felt it was high time to tell the stories of what the innovators and disruptors from within the system are doing in the meantime—to survive, keep going, and every once in a while, to reclaim enough moments of thriving and joy to remember why they chose this line of work in the first place.

WHY THE FRAMING OF SEL?

At least since the 1950s, the American school system has embraced some kind of explicit social, emotional, or moral curriculum, under various names such as Positive Youth Development, Character Education, Civic Engagement, School Turnaround, Service Learning, and most recently and dominantly, Social and Emotional Learning (SEL). The field of SEL has had its own problems and necessary evolution, some of which are taken on by the authors in this volume. But the reason we embrace it despite its ongoing imperfections, even beyond the decades of research that have essentially proven its effectiveness (e.g., Cipriano, Ha et al., 2024; Cipriano, Strambler et al., 2023; Durlak, Mahoney et al., 2022; Durlak, Weissberg et al., 2011; Taylor et al., 2017), is that it is proactive, preventative, and culture-based, as opposed to a problem-based approach such as antibullying or behavior management interventions. SEL programs do not wait for problems to arise; they teach necessary foundational skills for social problem-solving, self-soothing and self-regulation, empathy and kindness, and resilience so that problems are less frequent, less intense, and quicker to resolve when they do happen.

More importantly still, SEL does not "locate" these goals only inside the heads of students. The SEL framework, regardless of the program or approach chosen, acknowledges that social and emotional concerns live throughout the entire system. This latest reawakening has built a consensus across 30 years now around the necessity of proactively embracing a social and emotional education as a legitimate part of the school curriculum. Educators have been clamoring for more SEL in schools, and districts and even unions have now begun to build systems that facilitate comprehensive SEL rollouts, such as the creation of central SEL offices, SEL coordinator positions in schools, and statewide SEL learning standards. In 2013, an SEL bill was introduced to Congress by Tim Ryan and in 2019, as a presidential candidate, he advocated for SEL on national television.

The desire for and aspirations around SEL are no longer in question, but as with any attempt to ameliorate a wicked problem throughout an entire system, implementation challenges are a given. One key challenge was identified with the realization that prominent SEL models and curricula were missing critical elements related to *adults' own SEL skills*. It wasn't long before it became obvious that SEL was somewhat unlike other curricular content in that it is even more dependent on teacher dispositions and "ways of being." Thus, SEL models have now been expanded to include key adult skills and "moves" such as building trusting relationships, creating community, and fostering self-reflection (Markowitz & Bouffard, 2022) that would ideally lead to the SEL outcomes we hope for students.

The 2023 SEL conference held by the field-founding organization Collaboration for Academic, Social, and Emotional Learning (CASEL) had its theme entirely dedicated to the adult leaders of SEL initiatives. The field is actively grappling with the challenge of figuring out the best ways to support educators so they can meet the challenge of supporting students' all-around development and growth. This is the immense challenge of the teaching profession even in the best of times, but in a postpandemic, post George Floyd, late-stage capitalism world, continuing the teacher blame game is beyond absurd—it's becoming catastrophic.

In our years of professional development and research work related to SEL, the editors of the present volume have discovered that the adult skills, actions, moves, and ways of being that will create nurturing learning communities cannot be trained from intellectual or skills-based perspectives alone, and cannot be executed by adults who never had the chance to heal from their own experiences with a lack of such nurturance. In short, we are suggesting that, beyond customary models of adult learning and reflective practice, a space of healing is the critical missing piece in creating a fully realized SEL landscape that can break the cycle of passing harm from one generation to the next.

We have been implementing an approach to healing teaching over the past several years called "SELove" (Moreno et al., 2025), but we wanted to expose readers to more than just our own lens. We assumed—correctly, it turns out—that there are diverse professionals coming from the perspectives of diverse wisdoms, responding dynamically to the wicked problems of our day and, out of necessity, creating healing spaces for the educators they work with. Some of this book's authors would define themselves as coming from within the field of SEL, and some would not, including those who come from traditions that have existed for a lot longer than SEL has, such as critical theories in education, psychodynamic approaches, and Indigenous ways of knowing and learning. This book is an intentional effort to bring these worlds together, to broaden and benefit the dominant paradigm of SEL, in service of the adults we expect to carry its mantle.

WHY ALL THE FOCUS ON EDUCATORS? ISN'T TEACHING SUPPOSED TO BE ABOUT THE STUDENTS?

Does it really need to be said that the ultimate purpose of improving teacher practice is to benefit students' outcomes? Yet, consistent with the punitive accountability and scapegoating of education "reform," this has been taken to mean that if students are failing, then teachers must be the ones responsible. Aside from the enormous number and weight of confounding factors that this fallacious logic ignores, even if teaching *were* responsible for all of student outcomes (actual estimates suggest that teaching quality is responsible for between 8% and 25% of student scores, e.g., see Haertel, 2013), it never works to leapfrog over the process and simply shout the outcomes louder. The authors in this volume are calling upon all of us to slow down and linger with the human beings responsible for the teaching process, to reflect thoughtfully on what *they* need, without rushing, once again, to hasty and ineffective solutions under the guise of "the best interests of the children."

There are plenty of reasons to be skeptical of education initiatives that claim to be student-centered. Often, such claims have been the cornerstone of reform efforts that have created more harm than good. A perfect example of this is the spate of "teacher effectiveness" laws that began to proliferate in the 2010s and still reverberate in teacher evaluation systems throughout the United States today. The premise, which sounded equity-driven and student-centered on its face, was that the most effective teachers were unjustly concentrated among already privileged students, and that all students deserved effective teachers who promoted the highest possible academic outcomes. Sounds good, but after years of effort, billions in consultant contracts, and endless versions of the value-added modeling (VAM) algorithm that was supposed to be able to fairly assess teacher effectiveness above and beyond confounding factors, it turns out that all we really have in the end is the useless and self-evident truth that "some teachers are better than others." Even if we accept the premise for argument's sake that student test score growth is a valid (even if partial) means to assess teacher effectiveness, it is literally a mathematical guarantee that there will always be a top 10% and a bottom 10%; yet, the most "creative" solution that came out of the VAM movement amounted to: "The top 10% of teachers can do it, why can't you?"

While teachers continue to spend their own money on school supplies, our best and brightest economists, researchers, statisticians, and think tank executives were paid countless dollars to come up with this elementary yet somehow impenetrable "formula" that led to not a single new idea about teaching that would be "in the best interests of students." While the number of states requiring student test scores in teacher evaluations has dropped in recent years (Swisher & Saenz-Armstrong, 2022), evaluation efforts that purport to be "about the children" but are really about blaming teachers, continue to reverberate in almost every district. One of our professional development participants—a kindergarten teacher—recently told us that in her district, outside observers are sent in to assess "teaching quality," which involves asking her 5-year-old students directly, "What are the learning objectives for this lesson?" and "How will you know you have met them?" The specter, and the spectacle, of such a methodology for evaluating (i.e., blaming) teachers is shudder-inducing. For the good of the children, indeed.

Even when it comes to social and emotional concerns, it seems that teachers are never allowed to focus on their own wellness, for their own sake. Clichés such as "put on your own oxygen mask first" or "you can't pour from an empty cup" are often repeated in teacher professional development spaces, with the idea being that self-care is necessary only insofar as it *allows teachers to serve students.* It's not that we disagree with the underlying idea, but so much is lost by forcing "productivity" to be the price of admission for teachers' humanity, sanity, and self-preservation.

We have seen how the original intent of mindfulness and contemplative inquiry became co-opted by a corporate "McMindfulness" (Purser, 2019) when the business world learned that allowing time for such wellness activities could increase employees' output. In schools, it is even more the case that the "output" we want to see is irreducibly human. It's not "self-care *in*, student achievement *out*." This is both an unethical and ineffective stance toward improving teaching and learning.

So, if you are earnestly all about the students, we caution you to be skeptical of efforts that parrot that phrase, and instead, we invite you to take the leap of faith with us as we learn about efforts that center the adult educators to envision, not just what whole-hearted teaching can look like, but *how to authentically get there.* We think you'll find that in the end, a book that hardly mentions students is the one that speaks for them most loudly.

BIG DREAMS FOR HEALING TEACHING

Just as the solution to learning challenges is not lowering learning standards, focusing on what teachers need is not "going easy" on teachers, but rather lifting them up as they continue to try to do the impossible. Indeed, the authors in this volume have the biggest and most challenging aspirations for educators including nothing short of actualizing truly liberatory, multicultural, multilingual, equitable, inclusive, nurturing, and stimulating classrooms, buzzing with excitement about learning no matter how wide the range of students' starting skills may be. How do the authors in this book suggest we support educators in meeting these lofty goals?

- By expanding educators' options for meeting student needs, rather than limiting them through standardization
- By supporting their autonomy and self-determination, rather than distrusting, patronizing, and micromanaging
- By acknowledging the perversions and harms embedded in the context, rather than blaming educators for them, or gaslighting educators by pretending the injuries don't exist
- By providing genuine means to cope with, heal from, and if necessary, work around and subvert the harmful practices expected of them
- By centering educators' needs for wellness, wholeness, and belonging, rather than treating them as "achievement producers," or worse, purveying the lie that they don't care about or prioritize student achievement themselves.

The varied approaches to meeting teachers' needs and healing the teaching profession you are about to read about are not offered as a cure-all, either individually or collectively. Rather, each one is a precious behind-the-scenes sneak peek into some of the most progressive, innovative, out-of-the box efforts to help educators survive and thrive despite the ongoing affronts to them and their profession. Each one will include practical, visualizable examples that can be adapted for your own practice or setting, and help you make the case for your constituents for a new way of doing business.

The "bright ideas" of education reform haven't led to any new means of improving teaching, so we're giving a platform to the movers and shakers who've been engaging in the real heart-work to create that needed inspiration, even amidst the complexities and traumas of our time. The radical focus on teachers by the authors in this book is itself an act of resistance, although it shouldn't be considered radical to say that all paths to a better education go through educators. So, let's walk.

REFERENCES

Bhabha, H. K. (1994). *The location of culture.* Routledge.

Black, D. W. (2020). *Schoolhouse burning: Public education and the assault on American democracy.* PublicAffairs.

Churchman, C. W. (1967). Guest editorial: Wicked problems. *Management Science, 14*(4), B141–B142. https://www.jstor.org/stable/2628678

Cipriano, C., Ha, C., Wood, M., Sehgal, K., Ahmad, E., & McCarthy, M. F. (2024). A systematic review and meta-analysis of the effects of universal school-based SEL programs in the United States: Considerations for marginalized students. *Social and Emotional Learning: Research, Practice, and Policy, 3*, 100029. https://doi.org/10.1016/j.sel.2024.100029

Cipriano, C., Strambler, M. J., Naples, L. H., Ha, C., Kirk, M., Wood, M., Sehgal, K., K Zieher, A. K., Eveleigh, A., McCarthy, M., Funaro, M., Ponnock, A., Chow, J. C., & Durlak, J. (2023). The state of evidence for social and emotional learning: A contemporary meta-analysis of universal school-based SEL interventions. *Child Development*, *94*(5), 1181–1204. https://doi.org.10.1111/cdev.13968

Durlak, J. A., Mahoney, J. L., & Boyle, A. E. (2022). What we know, and what we need to find out about universal, school-based social and emotional learning programs for children and adolescents: A review of meta-analyses and directions for future research. *Psychological Bulletin*, *148*(11–12), 765–782. https://doi.org/10.1037/bul0000383

Durlak, J. A., Weissberg, R. P., Dymnicki, A. B., Taylor, R. D., & Schellinger, K. B. (2011). The impact of enhancing students' social and emotional learning: A meta-analysis of school-based universal interventions. *Child Development*, *82*(1), 405–432. https://doi.org/10.1111/j.1467-8624.2010.01564.x

Haertel, E. H. (2013). *Reliability and validity of inferences about teachers based on student scores*. William H. Angoff Memorial Lecture Series. Educational Testing Service.

Irwin, V., Wang, K., Tezil, T., Zhang, J., Filbey, A., Jung, J., AIR, Bullock Mann, F., Dilig, R., & Parker, S. (2023). *Condition of education 2023*. NCES 2023144REV.

Kotowski, S. E., Davis, K. G., & Barratt, C. L. (2022). Teachers feeling the burden of COVID-19: Impact on well-being, stress, and burnout. *Work*, *71*(2), 407–415. https://doi.org/10.3233/WOR-210994

Kraft, M. A., & Lyon, M. A. (2022). *The rise and fall of the teaching profession: Prestige, interest, preparation, and satisfaction over the last half century*. EdWorkingPaper No. 22-679. Annenberg Institute for School Reform at Brown University. https://doi.org/10.26300/7b1a-vk92

Love, B. L. (2019). *We want to do more than survive: Abolitionist teaching and the pursuit of educational freedom*. Beacon Press.

Love, B. L. (2023). *Punished for dreaming: How school reform harms Black children and how we heal*. St. Martin's Press.

Markowitz, N. L., & Bouffard, S. M. (2022). *Teaching with a social, emotional, and cultural lens: A framework for educators and teacher educators*. Harvard Education Press.

Moreno, A., Banashak, J., Kontoudakis, M., Evans, A., Bajet, R., & Laase, A. (2025). Giving to teachers what we ask them to give to others: Supporting adult SEL through reflective insight and healing. *Social and Emotional Learning: Research, Practice, and Policy*, *5*, 100086. https://doi.org/10.1016/j.sel.2025.100086

Purser, R. (2019). *McMindfulness: How mindfulness became the new capitalist spirituality*. Repeater.

Ravitch, D. (2020). *Slaying Goliath: The passionate resistance to privatization and the fight to save America's public schools*. Vintage.

Rittel, H. W., & Webber, M. M. (1973). Dilemmas in a general theory of planning. *Policy Sciences*, *4*(2), 155–169. https://doi.org/10.1007/BF01405730

Soja, E. (1996). *Journeys to Los Angeles and other real-and-imagined places*. Blackwell.

Swisher, A. & Saenz-Armstrong, P. (2022). State of the States 2022: Teacher and Principal Evaluation Policies. National Council on Teacher Quality.

Taylor, R. D., Oberle, E., Durlak, J. A., & Weissberg, R. P. (2017). Promoting positive youth development through school-based social and emotional learning interventions: A meta-analysis of follow-up effects. *Child Development*, *88*(4), 1156–1171. https://doi.org/10.1111/cdev.12864

PART I

COME CLOSER

HEALING TEACHING THROUGH ACTS OF RADICAL PROFESSIONAL INTIMACY

CHAPTER 2

Unconditional Positive Regard

Practicing a Different World

Alex Shevrin Venet

In 2024, the *Wall Street Journal* reported that teacher job satisfaction in the United States had taken a tumble in recent years. The leading cause teachers cited for their stress in a survey conducted by the RAND Corporation (Doan, Steiner, & Pandey, 2024) was managing student behavior. In the political and social chaos of the 2020s, it seems obvious to say that students are struggling and therefore teachers are as well. But looking at this state of affairs through the lens of trauma-informed education, I wonder if the numbers don't tell the whole story. Yes, student behavior is challenging, and schools need more resources to meet this need, not to mention structural changes to address inequities in the education system. But how effective are new resources when dropped into an existing deficit paradigm about students and their behavior? And what if shifting this paradigm was just as important as additional resources when it comes to impacting teacher well-being?

This chapter, like this book overall, is not another superficial self-care directive to just "change your view" to accept the unacceptable. Rather, I will be suggesting how viewing students differently can help us view ourselves and our work differently. In the process, a radically different world can be lived into by recommitting to unconditional positive regard—accepting and valuing a person, including their thoughts, feelings, and behaviors, without any judgment or conditions—each day, in large and small ways.

In trauma-informed education, one of the largest shifts we ask teachers to make is in their perspective. While traditional approaches to student behavior place the blame on student deficiencies, trauma-informed education asks us to see students through a strengths-based lens, recognizing that behavior challenges can be the result of many factors, but that students generally want to do well and are motivated to learn (Venet, 2021). I believe there may be a connection between how we see and understand students and their behavior and *our* well-being as educators. What if seeing our students through a lens of unconditional positive regard transformed our emotional experience of their (and our) behavior? And in that transformation, could we bolster teacher well-being?

In this chapter, I offer a possible connection between a strengths-based view of students and teacher well-being. This commentary is not based on an empirical study (although I hope education researchers will be inspired to investigate these connections); rather, it explores how education philosophy might inform our ideas and practice about teacher wellness. Specifically, I will discuss the link between unconditional positive regard, moral injury, and teacher wellness. My goal is not to instruct teachers to simply think their way out of burnout, but instead to propose that everyone involved in the education community and system—teachers, parents and caregivers, administrators, policy-makers—adopt unconditional positive regard as a school transformation strategy.

UNCONDITIONAL POSITIVE REGARD

Unconditional positive regard was originally developed as a therapeutic tool by psychotherapist Carl Rogers (1957). Rogers wrote, "It means that there are no conditions of acceptance, no feeling of 'I like you only if you are thus and so'" (p. 98). To Rogers, this stance created the possibility for change in the therapy client by providing a nonjudgmental ownership over one's experience and choices, rather than measuring oneself by the values of the therapist. In the decades since its introduction, unconditional positive regard has become a core approach for many mental health practitioners, and more recently, in other fields such as medicine and education.

Education philosopher Alfie Kohn is one champion of unconditional positive regard in teaching. In his essay, "Unconditional Teaching" (Kohn, 2005), he makes the case for educators to practice unconditional acceptance in the classroom by separating a child's value from their behavior and cultivating genuine reciprocal relationships. These conditions allow children to flourish, and they reflect a whole-child approach. Building from Kohn's work, I see unconditional positive regard as a core stance for teachers attempting human-centered approaches like trauma-informed teaching or social and emotional learning (SEL). In my definition of unconditional positive regard, teachers communicate to their students: "I care about you. You have value. You don't have to do anything to prove it to me, and nothing's going to change my mind" (see Venet, 2021).

When teachers effectively demonstrate their unconditional positive regard, students are given the space to take risks, fail, and try again, knowing that their missteps will not result in a withdrawal of care or their removal from the community. Unconditional positive regard is a *humanizing* stance that allows people to be layered and complex, and to expect that caring others won't try to diminish any part of them.

Importantly, Kohn (2005) also names a tension inherent in unconditional teaching: Teachers don't teach in a vacuum. Most teachers are subject to policies that actually *encourage* them to treat children with *conditional* acceptance, such as standardized testing. The culture of testing places value on students through a narrow metric of achievement. The same goes for the culture of letter grades, GPAs, academic ranking, and behavioral approaches such as Positive Behavioral Interventions and Supports (PBIS) that sort students into tiers (Kim & Venet, 2023). While such approaches may not literally label their tiers "good," "bad," and "so-so," even 5-year-olds know exactly what the green, red, and yellow stoplight colors mean. Thus, these systems require teachers to use public humiliation and labeling to get their students to obey. Because of this, teachers may find themselves facing moral injury, torn between a commitment to a humanizing philosophy like unconditional positive regard, and job requirements to enact dehumanizing practices.

MORAL INJURY

Moral injury can happen when teachers experience conflict between their own values and decisions they must make in service to institutional goals, such as following a discipline policy that conflicts with one's own beliefs about student behavior. This sense of injury can also happen when teachers witness others, like coworkers or leaders, making choices they feel are morally wrong, and the feeling of betrayal that is created when we see this behavior on the institutional level (Schwartz, 2019).

Teachers are often asked to make moral choices in the course of their work, such as limiting students' freedom of movement throughout the day or applying a disciplinary policy that may have long-lasting impacts. Yet teachers are not free to make those choices solely in line with their own values because "the nature of the political, economic, and social constraints that shape (and are shaped by) the U.S. education system places educators in situations in which they are obligated to enact moral justice but in which no just action is possible" (Sugrue, 2020, p. 46). Moral injury is not only a response to individual acts, but to a school culture in which social injustices such as racism and classism are normalized and integrated into school policy (Sugrue, 2024).

Moral injury greatly impacts teacher wellness. Teachers experiencing moral injury demonstrated elevated rates of burnout and intent to leave the career (Sugrue, 2020). When teachers witness or commit acts that are not in line with their values and moral injury ensues, their sense of self is impacted to the degree of constituting an injury to the spirit. Guilt and shame often cause teachers to self-isolate as a coping strategy. As Sugrue (2020) wrote, "the resulting isolation leads to a growing belief that not just the act is unforgivable, but that the individual is unforgiveable" (p. 47). In this way, moral injury can break a teacher's sense of their own worthiness of unconditional positive regard, feeling shame not merely for *what they do* but wholly for *who they are*. Healing from moral injury requires meaning-making, and part of that meaning-making can include a recommitment to teaching in a way that is authentic to our values (Posoroff, 2015). When we reconnect with unconditional positive regard, we can begin to heal the harms of moral injury.

PRACTICING NEW WORLDS

Is unconditional positive regard realistic? In his original paper on unconditional positive regard, Carl Rogers (1957) included a footnote saying that "It is probably evident from the description that completely unconditional positive regard would never exist except in theory" (p. 98). Rogers knew, as we do today, that for fallible humans, unconditional positive regard serves as "a matter of degree" (Rogers, 1957, p. 98) in actual practice and an aspirational "North Star." It's something we work toward and strive for, not something we will achieve with perfection. That practice, however, remains a truly essential, and daunting, task.

To practice unconditional positive regard often means swimming against the current not only of school culture, but American culture more broadly. The United States has a legal system that treats human beings as disposable, diminishing a person's humanity when they harm others. In contrast to, "You have value and you don't need to prove it to me," American culture typically says, "You only have value inasmuch as you can prove it to others." These messages filter into schools in many ways. We see it when schools create reward systems for behavior and reserve pizza parties or recognitions only for students who "obey." We hear this when teachers say, "I'll show my students respect when they earn it." We feel it when students hide parts of their identities to gain acceptance from peers and teachers or to feel safe in an environment hostile to those outside the White, Christian, heteropatriarchal norms.

Critics of unconditional positive regard in education have said to me, "This isn't realistic because the world won't treat students with unconditional positive regard. Shouldn't we prepare them for the real world?" To practice unconditional positive regard is to see the harsh realities of the "real world" and say, "I believe things can be different." Carla Shalaby (2017), champion of liberatory teaching, wrote that trying something different is essential: "I am convinced that if we continue to prepare children for the world we have now, we will necessarily reflect and reinforce the everyday harms and assault of punishment, confinement, and exclusion. Instead, we have to begin to prepare children for the world we want" (p. 174).

Practicing new ways of seeing students and their behavior brings us in line with our deepest values about education justice. When we practice unconditional positive regard, we practice a world in which people are not thrown out of community when they harm others. If we value people for being "who they are, not what they do," we refuse to reduce people to their worst days and instead commit to working *through* challenges together. We create classroom- and school-wide celebrations and recognitions where everyone is invited, simply for the joy of being in community together. We actively notice, name, and celebrate students' and teachers' multifaceted identities and work together to keep one another safe from oppression, because we all deserve that safety. When we create these worlds in the classroom, we are preparing students to disrupt and break cycles of inequity and trauma (Venet, 2021).

In a community based on unconditional positive regard and rooted in social justice, our social and emotional learning goes beyond the basics of "responsible decision-making" or "self-management" (Collaborative for Academic, Social, and Emotional Learning [CASEL], n.d.). A liberatory approach to SEL includes the skills needed to develop a love of oneself, a commitment to solidarity, and a sense of self-determination (Camangian & Cariaga, 2021). These skills cultivate a sense of humanization for teachers and students who typically have been dehumanized in the education system. If we dream about a community like this, we might envision schools in which teachers' well-being is inextricably linked to that of students and the broader community. All people in this community continually experience healing, even as they experience harm, because humans are always harmed and always healing simultaneously (Casimir and Baker, 2023). In the trauma-informed world, we see these as cycles of rupture and repair that are needed to establish safe attachment to others (Perry & Winfrey, 2021).

In short, when teachers commit to teaching with unconditional positive regard in the here and now, we are time-traveling to a future where "teacher wellness" as a concept doesn't exist as a separate concern from the overall health of our communities. In our current fragmented system, dreaming and imagining can fuel teachers' work as it reconnects us to the larger purpose of education.

EDUCATION PHILOSOPHY AS WELLNESS PRACTICE: EXAMPLES FROM THE FIELD

There are multiple necessary individual-to-systemic-level entry points for supporting teachers in restoring their wellness in times of stress, but what I have begun to describe in this chapter is a way in which an educational philosophy, especially as it reflects a moral stance, can be a wellness *practice* as well. When we refuse to dehumanize students, we refuse to dehumanize ourselves. This congruence helps to maintain our well-being. In the following examples from the field, I will describe how something as potentially intangible as a philosophy of unconditional positive regard can manifest as concrete behaviors that served to guard against moral injury and allow the educators involved (including me) to recommit to our jobs while feeling well.

I once worked in a therapeutic school in a hybrid teacher–academic case manager role. In this capacity, students had my work phone number to communicate about logistical things like attendance. Once, a student on my caseload was escalated and angry with me for holding a limit with her. To express her anger, she began to text me incredibly offensive insults and hateful images. I was hurt, sad, and angry—human responses to harm. In the context of a school system that meets harm with punishment, it would have been easy for me to demand that this student receive punitive consequences like suspension or similar exclusion from the community. In my best moments, I was (and am) an opponent of these practices. My emotional response to harm might have pushed me to advocate for a more punitive response if I were not called back to my integrity by my community of colleagues holding me to unconditional positive regard.

Because of the consultation opportunities and peer support that was focused on unconditional positive regard available to me, I was able to recenter to my values. Although challenges with my student threatened my well-being, I experienced integration and healing through being reminded that I could still choose unconditional positive regard, even in the most challenging moments. It was healing for me to view this as a choice I could make, rather than being forced into a false binary of "accept harmful behavior" on one hand and "punish the student" on the other. This centering in unconditional positive regard reminds me that I am capable of refusing to participate in cycles of harm. It shows me the boundlessness of my capacity for embracing the complexity of community-building.

At the same therapeutic school, unconditional positive regard was a core philosophy and job expectation. Formally, each teacher participated in regular reflective supervision sessions during which they were supported in developing narratives around our shared values of unconditional positive regard. For example, if a teacher were to come to supervision and say, "I can't work with Kyle because he's unmotivated and lazy," the supervisor used the tools of reflective supervision to help the teacher reframe. They might invite the teacher to question these assumptions or interrogate where they come from. The supervisor might help the teacher recall the students' strengths and past successes and help acknowledge the teacher's own stress, affirming the desire to "vent" while holding them accountable to a school norm that "we always speak about students as though they were in the room."

Through this reframing, a teacher might realign with unconditional positive regard and restate their challenge as: "Kyle is struggling, and I haven't yet figured out how to help him get excited about our class. I also think Kyle might need some support around building momentum with new academic tasks." This reframe doesn't diminish the fact that the teacher is struggling with a student, but restores Kyle's humanity through seeing the challenges as something Kyle is *experiencing,* not something he just *is.* In that reframing, the teacher reclaims their own humanity, as well.

When I came to supervision venting about a student, I didn't feel good about it. I knew that disliking and judging a student in my care wasn't "who I was." I didn't need to hide my own human frustration, but judgment toward a student having a hard time actively harmed my wellness because it conflicted with my view of myself as an empathetic, supportive teacher. When my supervisor helped me return to my core values, it decreased the internal tensions and helped restore my well-being. This dynamic was even more present when my frustration or stress led me not simply to a deficit-based narrative about students, but toward the impulse to exclude or punish students for their behavior, as in my previous example with the student who had texted me. In that situation, support also meant connecting reflection to action: When it was clear that I should not handle the follow-up with that student on my own, colleagues and supervisors stepped in to walk the student through a process of accountability while also supporting me to work through my response and get my own emotional needs met. With this support, the student and I were eventually able to have a reparative conversation and work together again.

Outside of reflective supervision, school leaders at this school cultivated a culture where peers informally supported one another in this narrative meaning-making. Our schedule allowed for peer conversation and consultation after the end of the day, allowing teachers to authentically connect with one another. We would hear one another's frustrations or successes and support one another to return to a strengths-based perspective of students. This created a shared sense of the importance of unconditional positive regard, and a regular container to grapple with its complexities.

As Rogers himself acknowledged, unconditional positive regard is nearly impossible to continuously maintain in all situations. Teachers are people. It is natural for us to find ourselves judging or wanting to reject our students when we find their behavior or beliefs objectionable. But a teacher's job has a component of emotional labor (Kaplan, 2019), requiring us to cultivate a specific emotional presence for the benefit of our students. Peer support was a key component in allowing us to do that emotional labor, and that support again benefited our well-being.

SUPPORTING TEACHERS TO LIVE IN THEIR INTEGRITY

Perhaps the most important thing that we can do to support teachers in their practice of unconditional positive regard is to treat *them* with unconditional positive regard. We can provide teachers with an embodied experience of how it feels to be held in the care of others who believe that your value is in who you are, not what you produce. In a political environment where teachers and their human-centered work are under attack, this work of care is even more important. Teacher supporters can express their unconditional positive regard in big and small ways.

Teacher educators can support identity development in preservice teachers to foster a strong sense of self, both as a teacher and as a human being whose current role is teaching (creating a distinction between "who we are" and "what we do"). Shamari Reid's book, *Humans Who Teach* (2024), provides a helpful framework and reflection tools for developing this sense of self. As Reid wrote, "we must engage with our own hearts and humanity, especially if our goal is to engage with the hearts and humanity of our students" (p. xii).

In service of this humanization, principals and other building administrators can work to build authentic relationships with teachers and keep that relationship central even when having hard conversations or holding teachers accountable to professional goals (reflective supervision is a helpful structure for this). Teachers should not feel like replaceable cogs in the learning machine but instead feel seen and celebrated for their unique contributions. Feeling this sense of being valued can help teachers to cultivate the same in their students.

Unconditional positive regard for teachers should go past the interpersonal and be woven into policy. In addition to securing fair working conditions, building-level administrators can put humanity into the daily policies of running a school. A guiding question here is "How does my policy communicate that I trust and respect my teachers as professionals?" Administrators who seek detailed documentation of learning plans for their review are not communicating this trust. Neither are those who limit how teachers may use their time off (such as requiring doctor's notes to use sick time). If we value teachers and do not require that they prove this value to us, we trust them in our policy-making.

Finally, families and community members can approach teachers with a sense of curiosity and collaboration when seeking to problem-solve school challenges. Teachers own their part of this dynamic, of course, and often hold greater power in these interactions (such as a tense conversation with a parent about their child's behavior). But families and caregivers who seek to support teachers can contribute to teacher well-being by coming to these conversations with a spirit of collaboration and joining with the teacher in the pursuit of student learning and well-being. Families and community members can also support teacher well-being via political advocacy at the local and national levels for human-centered and equitable school policy.

Once teachers feel an embodied sense of unconditional positive regard, we can support them to pass the feeling on to their students. On social media, teachers joke about the inanity of professional development that asks them to "remember their 'why.'" Teachers roll their eyes at this because in times of stress, trauma, and political attempts to dismantle public education, they need more than a reminder about the importance of "we're doing it for the kids." They need fair working conditions and true support, both within schools and from the broader public. Helping teachers practice unconditional positive regard needs to be more robust than "inspirational" content. To that end, those who support teachers can consider: "What are the material conditions teachers need in order to practice unconditional positive regard?" Those material conditions might be appropriate working hours and compensation, time to authentically consult with colleagues, and clearly articulated school-wide values consistent with unconditional positive regard.

While we actively fight for these necessary conditions, we can simultaneously engage teachers in developing the philosophical and moral practices that lead to healing and wellness for all. We can support their understanding of unconditional positive regard and how it looks and feels in the classroom. We can help reflect and make meaning when conflict and harm challenge our ability to uphold unconditional positive regard. And we can support teachers in their ongoing values development and aligning their teaching practices to those values.

CONCLUSION

In an era of fascistic leadership in the United States, it may be impossible to avoid moral injury in the teaching profession. Teachers are in a position to witness injustice and make hard choices about their own complicity in it. When we can stand in our values of equity and justice, we find the inner well-being of integrity. Committing to unconditional positive regard is an act of well-being because it allows us to stay whole in a profession that sometimes seems as though it would rather we compartmentalize our humanity. When teachers have systemic support, fair working conditions, and the lived experience of unconditional positive regard, they are positioned to engage in this transformative mindset in all parts of their work. Teaching from this integrity, we elevate our interconnected well-being and practice the world we want to see.

REFERENCES

Camangian, P., & Cariaga, S. (2021). Social and emotional learning is hegemonic miseducation: Students deserve humanization instead. *Race Ethnicity and Education*, *25*(7), 901–921. https://doi.org/10.1080/13613324.2020.1798374

Casimir, A. E., & Baker, C. N. (2023). *Trauma-responsive pedagogy: Teaching for healing and transformation*. Heinemann.

Doan, S., Steiner, E. D., & Pandey, R. (2024). *Teacher well-being and intentions to leave in 2024: Findings from the 2024 state of the American Teacher Survey*. RAND Corporation. https://www.rand.org/pubs/research_reports/RRA1108-12.html

Kaplan, E. (2019, July 19). *Teaching your heart out: Emotional labor and the need for systemic change*. Edutopia. https://www.edutopia.org/article/teaching-your-heart-out-emotional-labor-and-need-systemic-change/

Kim, R. M., & Venet, A. S. (2023). Unsnarling PBIS and trauma-informed education. *Urban Education*, *60*(3), 700–728. https://doi.org/10.1177/00420859231175670

Kohn, A. (2005). Unconditional teaching. *Educational Leadership*, *63*(1), 20.

Perry, B. D., & Winfrey, O. (2021). *What happened to you? Conversations on trauma, resilience, and healing*. Flatiron.

Posoroff, L. (2015, August 25). *Healing from moral injury | Learning for Justice*. https://www.learningforjustice.org/magazine/fall-2015/healing-from-moral-injury

Reid, S. (2024). *Humans who teach: A guide for centering love, justice, and liberation in schools*. Heinemann.

Rogers, C. R. (1957). The necessary and sufficient conditions of therapeutic personality change. *Journal of Consulting Psychology*, *21*(2), 95–103. https://doi.org/10.1037/h0045357

Schwartz, S. (2019, May 23). Teachers often experience "moral injury" on the job, study finds. *Education Week*. https://www.edweek.org/teaching-learning/teachers-often-experience-moral-injury-on-the-job-study-finds/2019/05

Shalaby, C. (2017). *Troublemakers: Lessons in freedom from young children at school*. The New Press.

Sugrue, E. (2024). Moral injury in K-12 education: A phenomenological inquiry at the intersection of race and class. *Journal of Trauma Studies in Education*, *3*(1), Article 1.

Sugrue, E. P. (2020). Moral injury among professionals in K–12 education. *American Educational Research Journal*, *57*(1), 43–68. https://doi.org/10.3102/0002831219848690

Venet, A. S. (2021). *Equity-centered trauma-informed education*. W.W. Norton & Company.

CHAPTER 3

Unlocking HEART Potential

Nurturing Educators for a Joyful and Purposeful Life

Lorea Martínez

> "HEART in Mind gave me the reminder that we are all human, the freedom to own my own actions and interactions, and to know that I alone have the power to decide what kind of person I want to be. We can only control our own actions, and we can only heal ourselves. By choosing to use the HEART skills, we offer ourselves a gentle opportunity to be the very best version of ourselves and to see others through eyes of kindness and empathy rather than judgement and aggression. We truly can change the world, one HEART at a time."
>
> —Alicia D., HEART in Mind participant

Picture this. During a staff meeting, a principal facilitates a check-in activity asking educators to report their stress level on a scale from 0 to 10. Given that student reports are due very soon, most teachers report high levels of stress and feeling overwhelmed by the upcoming deadline. The principal acknowledges the challenge and encourages staff to check the "self-care tips" that she had previously shared with them, so they can finish their work on time without having to take it home. When self-care is used superficially and transiently like this, devoid of a systemic lens and employed merely as a tool to maintain "efficiency," it can be counterproductive, leading to resentment and further stress, rather than being a source of relaxation and renewal.

This has been my experience when supporting schools, districts, and educators with implementation of Social Emotional Learning (SEL) programs and practices. Over more than two decades, I have worked with PK–12 teachers and administrators across the globe. There is a pattern that repeats time and time again: The immense impact of teaching upon educators' well-being, the lack of wellness support received, and the insufficient consideration given to the untenable working conditions that create such an urgent need for self-care in the first place. However, there is a growing recognition that educator well-being is not dependent solely on the individual educator; rather, it is a dynamic experience between what an individual experiences and the context and conditions in which the individual exists (Yoder et al., 2024). Recognizing the limitations of early approaches and the need for a more systemic solution, many organizations have started shifting their focus away from isolated and, frankly, victim-blaming activities toward more holistic (and effective) approaches to educator well-being.

For me, this journey is not just theoretical; it's deeply personal. As a White Hispanic, first-generation college graduate, immigrant educator in the United States, my foray into the world of SEL was one of self-discovery. When I moved to the United States 20 years ago, I did not speak much English and knew very little about the educational system. Trying to fit in, I changed my ways to adapt to a new context, but through that process I forgot who I *really* was.

While the SEL field itself is not perfect, I am grateful for the permission it has given the education community to attend not just to academics, but to our whole, true selves. The skills of emotional intelligence gave me a path back to myself—the courage to honor my story and realize my potential, and the ability to take on life's challenges with optimism. This personal experience is one of the main reasons I became so passionate about helping adults build these skills and led me to develop a framework called the HEART in Mind® Model, as well as write a book called *Teaching with the HEART in Mind: A Complete Educator's Guide to Social Emotional Learning* (Martínez Pérez, 2021).

My purpose is to help educators unlock their HEART potential by developing essential social and emotional skills and reclaiming more peace and joy in their careers given the current challenging context and who they are as humans. Developing these skills doesn't eliminate teachers' challenges, but it does provide powerful tools for facing them with confidence, purpose, and a healthy dose of hope. Growing Your HEART Skills was born from a deep desire to create an intentional space for educators to reflect on their own emotional intelligence and learn new tools and strategies that would support their personal and professional growth. Most importantly, HEART Skills free us from the "self-care trap" by turning away from temporary and superficial relief of "symptoms," and toward deep, skills-based development that "gets under the skin," and can be called upon regardless of the setting or the chaotic fluctuations of the times.

THE PHILOSOPHY BEHIND HEART SKILLS: WE TEACH WHO WE ARE

Parker J. Palmer's famous quote, "We teach who we are," (1998, p. 2) reminds us that teaching is a deeply personal and interconnected process—we cannot separate who we are from the labor of teaching. Students observe their teachers closely, not just for academic knowledge, but also for how they interact with others, manage emotions, and navigate challenges. Teachers become role models for their students as they demonstrate values, attitudes, and behaviors (Jones et al., 2013). We all know intuitively that when teachers are calm, positive, and content, students learn better and overcome challenges more easily. When educators practice their own SEL skills regularly, they are better equipped to help students with emotional challenges (Jennings, 2018), and guide students' growth of SEL skills by offering authentic experiences and explaining concepts in ways that are genuine to students (McMahon et al., 2024). Despite these findings, many SEL initiatives continue to operate on the assumption that teachers are prepared to effectively act as a competent social–emotional role model just by following the student SEL program manual "with fidelity" (Oliveira et al., 2021).

Therefore, while organizations address crucial systemic issues that contribute to educator stress such as workload, resources, pay, and support systems, we cannot forget the importance of supporting educators to strengthen their own social and emotional competencies as a vital step toward enhancing educator well-being. I am not talking about asking teachers to use a calm corner when stressed or track their moods using an app, although such tools can be helpful. I am referring to authentically and respectfully supporting educators to be "humans in a job" by creating healing spaces where teachers can be heard, and their experiences and struggles are welcomed and validated. When these supportive spaces are created, educators can engage in developing self-awareness, practicing self-compassion, cultivating positive relationships, and rekindling their purpose, ultimately incorporating comprehensive tools to better navigate the challenges they face in the classroom and beyond.

Like so many others, my SEL journey began with a focus on curriculum implementation, but I soon realized that a sustainable approach requires centering the well-being of the educators themselves. "We cannot teach what we don't practice" has been a guiding message in my work, but I would take it a step further: *Asking teachers to focus on implementation fidelity while dismissing their well-being is unreasonable and contrary to the healing spirit of this work.* I believe educators are better positioned to advocate for systemic change and create a more supportive and sustainable working environment for themselves and their colleagues when they are well, physically, socially, emotionally, and spiritually. To achieve this new reality, educational leaders and administrators have a responsibility and opportunity to engage teachers in coconstructing school environments that forefront the well-being of the adults.

GROWING HEART SKILLS: THE PROGRAM

Growing Your HEART Skills (GHS) is a hybrid synchronous and asynchronous professional development experience I developed and then enhanced in partnership with Suzanne Denham and Robyn McKeen, SEL Leaders from the Santa Cruz County Office of Education. This program centers adult SEL to embody the philosophies just discussed, namely, moving beyond the "self-care trap" and surface-level fidelity checklists to do deep "heartwork" and "skillwork" with educators that will transverse changes in context, settings, and time. At every step, it has been vital to us to validate the challenges that have been prevalent in teachers' experiences in recent decades, so they understand that for every "ask" we may make of them, we also present something of value *to* them, that will make their work more possible to do, while feeling well at the same time.

Asynchronous Component—Online Modules

The GHS program's online modules comprise an adult SEL curriculum designed to enhance educators' social and emotional competencies through the HEART in Mind Model, a CASEL-aligned integrated framework that encompasses five essential skills represented by the acronym HEART: Honoring Your Emotions, Electing Your Responses, Applying Empathy, Reigniting Your Relationships, and Transforming with Purpose (see Table 3.1 for definitions). The model intentionally uses *verbs* to indicate specific actions to put each skill into practice. Grounded in principles of emotional intelligence, affective neuroscience, and positive psychology, the program delivers its content online, enabling individuals to learn independently and at their own pace, while organizations can foster collaboration through community of practice models and integration into school-wide initiatives.

The online instructional model employs a structured, cyclical approach—learn, practice, reflect—to facilitate adult learning and skill development. Each module begins with engaging video-based content, followed by practical application through downloadable tools designed for real-world implementation. Participants are encouraged to reflect on their experiences by completing reflection activities in the online program and sharing their insights with their community of practice peers (described further as follows) and begin planning how they may use some of these new skills and tools in their life. This iterative process, combined with pre- and post-assessments, supports continuous skill refinement and integration into daily practice. In total, the asynchronous aspect of the GHS program includes seven content modules, 14 downloadable practice tools (e.g., emotion iceberg, 5 steps to manage emotions, self-compassion pause, conflict reflection tool), and pre- and post-assessments.

Practicing HEART skills doesn't always entail making big changes that would be obvious to an external observer, but shifts can occur just from new *awareness*. Embracing this journey takes courage to acknowledge our imperfections and recognize areas for growth. As Brené Brown (2012) eloquently stated, "Courage starts with showing up and letting ourselves be seen" (p. 30). Showing up can take many forms, varying greatly based on our individual identities, cultural backgrounds, religious beliefs, and life experiences. Each of us navigates our HEART skills differently, often creating protective barriers to shield our authentic selves from judgment. The tools provided in the online modules provide a "101" course for educators to begin exploring emotions and triggers on their own as well as with colleagues in their own settings; then unpacking these layers can reveal a deeper, more joyful and purposeful path forward in the supportive company of others within the broader Community of Practice (CoP) groups.

Table 3.1. HEART Skills With Definitions.

Intrapersonal Skills	H	Honor Your Emotions	Naming, interpreting, and appropriately communicating feelings
	E	Elect Your Responses	Creating space to make constructive and safe decisions
Interpersonal Skills	A	Apply Empathy	Recognizing and valuing the emotions and perspectives of others and taking action to support them. Nurturing self-compassion
	R	Reignite Your Relationships	Nurturing a positive and supporting network by actively using communication and conflict-resolution skills and working cooperatively with diverse individuals and groups
Cognitive Skills	T	Transform with Purpose	Using personal assets and interests to positively contribute to self and others

Synchronous Component—The Community of Practice

We designed the CoP to intentionally foster a sense of community among educators, recognizing that a collaborative learning experience would be more impactful and sustainable, and ultimately more effective. Through eight virtual 90-minute after-school sessions, participants came together to learn and practice new tools, share their successes, and receive support from one another. Hosted by County Offices of Education, these CoPs were open to all educators in the county, attracting classroom teachers, school leaders, counselors, parent educators, and even central office business staff. Facilitators created a space where participants could experience meaningful connections and build trusting relationships with colleagues across the region. The sessions were designed and facilitated to ensure that group members were able to "come as you are," and have authentic and courageous conversations about what they were learning and the challenges they encountered.

The CoPs were also an opportunity for participants to share with one another how they made use of the HEART skills tools from the online modules. One of the CoP participants had a particularly moving experience with her use of the Self-Compassion Pause tool that she shared with us in the sessions. She was a second-generation Latina who had been told growing up "do not cry"—a common message emphasizing stoicism and emotional suppression. She realized how difficult it was to show herself kindness when she was struggling with a work conflict or something going sideways at home. She had learned to push forward no matter how challenging the situation and swallow her feelings, so her emotions would not pull her down.

She found that self-compassion was a particularly challenging practice for her, since it involves "treating themselves like they would treat a friend." With the self-compassion exercise, participants are asked to identify a mistake they had recently made and write down what they told themselves, noting their feelings and actions. Then educators journal what they would tell a friend in the same situation. The final part of the tool asks participants to compare the two and reflect on what would happen if they treated themselves like they would treat a friend. With practice, this teacher started noticing instances when she was having a difficult time, and a voice of criticism would emerge. Instead of following that unhelpful voice, she started offering herself encouraging messages and taking action to meet her suffering with kindness. At the end of the CoP, she felt relieved to have found a more compassionate and caring way to treat herself, and to have gained emotional distance from difficult situations that were out of her control.

Lastly, to ensure engagement and make the program accessible, facilitators prioritized practicality. They minimized the amount of independent work outside of the sessions, focusing on intimate discussions and collaborative activities during the meetings. To further incentivize participation, a modest monetary reward was offered for completing specific requirements, such as consistent attendance and the creation of a capstone project that shared their learning with others. Participants were surprised by how deeply they had absorbed the skills taught in the course and found it empowering to share their journey with their colleagues and supervisors. In their capstone presentations, they realized that many adults in their school community also struggle to engage in self-care. One participant shared, "My colleagues were all surprised at how adults can engage in self-care skills. This was important because we often encourage students to practice their self-care, but we forget our own. Seeing it click for my colleagues was a special moment because they were reminded of how they can take care of themselves." You can see some of these capstone projects by going to the Santa Cruz County Office of Education website.

Witnessing educators cultivate self-awareness, identify behavior patterns, practice self-compassion, and foster deeper connections within their communities has been incredibly rewarding. I *know* that when adult SEL is intentionally focused on creating a healing space for educators, it can become a transformative journey. Alicia D. was a veteran educator who enrolled in the program expecting to learn strategies to support students with concerning behaviors, but what she found was something different. She shared, "I came into this course not expecting what I have experienced. I thought I would walk away with new skills to help students, and I walked away with an entire toolkit to heal my own heart, so I could be present and better able to help other people. It was a life-altering experience." Consequently, this work has solidified *my* belief in the power of collective learning and the transformative potential of supporting educators' social and emotional growth.

Program Impact

Quantitative and qualitative data collected during the CoPs suggests that the program was valuable in helping participants develop their SEL skills. Pre- and post-assessment results show 96% of participants increased their use of HEART skills. At the completion of the CoP, participants reported that the space had helped them with self-awareness, emotional regulation, empathy, and self-compassion. As illustrated by the following quotes, participants valued the practical tools included in the program and the opportunity to connect in community with other educators. Overall, participants shared a commitment to continue growing and practicing these skills in their daily lives.

Self-Awareness and Emotional Regulation

> Participants gained valuable insights into their own emotions, triggers, and patterns, recognizing the importance of self-awareness for emotional regulation. One participant shared: "*Being more aware of my emotions and the skill to elect my responses—total game changer!*" Several participants mentioned the importance of honoring emotions, with one noting: "*The importance of honoring our emotions and that finding purpose in life is a process.*" Another participant expressed: "*Learning to be more gentle and forgiving with myself and others. This applies to allowing myself to identify and sit in my emotions.*"

Empathy and Self-Compassion

> Developing empathy, particularly self-empathy, was a significant takeaway, such as: "*How to apply empathy, including self-empathy, was my biggest takeaway. Taking time to pause and give myself grace is something I intend to be more intentional about.*" The connection between inner work and outward impact was also noted: "*We must look inward before we can help outward. Healing or at the very least identifying our inner issues is the first step before we are even available to listen or help others.*" One educator connected the impact to her students: "*The main takeaway is the opportunity to be mindful of the need to be introspective and evaluate my holistic mental health. Doing so has led me to also connect to the mental, social, and emotional well-being of my students.*"

Practical Tools and Community Support

> The program's tools and the CoP were highly valued. "*The tools and practices for reflection and communication were particularly helpful to me,*" one participant noted. Another added, "*The worksheet on identifying triggers to better understand our patterns was really helpful and I look forward to using that tool with students and in my future work.*" Another highlighted: "*For me, it was the community of practice together*

and being able to talk about the HEART Skills and how it goes and getting feedback and encouragement from each other."

Commitment to Continued Growth

One participant shared her commitment to ongoing practice: *"I will refer back to the modules and the sessions and look at my purpose by having it pinned on my daily planner and phone."* Another participant shared a concrete plan to continue: "*The area I need to improve the most is being gentle and kind in my self-talk when I'm struggling with something. I will greatly reduce the amount of time I spend ruminating . . . or negative self-talk . . . and instead practice my HEART skills . . . to notice, name, and communicate.*" A therapist participant noted the importance of intentionality: "*With any work, it can become 'automatic,' which takes away from the intentionality—directly affecting the progress. I need to remain in my purpose and/or intention.*" This highlights the ongoing effort required to maintain SEL skills, even for those already working in related fields.

UNLOCKING HEART POTENTIAL FOR EDUCATORS EVERYWHERE

The impact of Growing Your HEART Skills, as shared by participating educators, highlights a clear opportunity: by prioritizing the well-being and social–emotional growth of our educators, we can create lasting positive change in education. As stated in the introduction to this book, "all paths to a better education go through educators." When educators feel supported, empowered, and equipped to navigate the daily challenges of their profession, the positive ripple effects extend far beyond individual well-being, transforming classrooms and school communities. For school and district leaders, the time is now to take up the mantle of authentic wellness and SEL skills for teachers, with the urgency it clearly needs. Yes, this effort will require compromises and difficult decisions, but this investment is worth the transformation it can create in our educational communities:

- **Carve Out the Time for Stronger Peer Communities:** School leaders know better than anyone that teacher recruitment and retention are possibly the most urgent education challenges of our time. If there is one lesson we learned from our experiences with the GHS CoPs it is the criticality of time spent in facilitated peer support. These sessions create a stronger sense of community, combat feelings of isolation, promote trust, and cultivate a culture where every educator feels seen and valued. Leaders at the district and city levels clearly have the power to support principals in creating a wider culture of peer support across local geographies, where educators can receive emotional support and also exchange fresh, practical ideas. A growing body of research suggests that structured peer support is not simply a "nice to have" but is a "must have" within the set of teacher needs, and that school leaders who adopt this understanding are likely to reduce the challenge of turnover in their contexts.

- **Skills and Meaning "Make Perfect"**: While the growing appreciation of SEL in education across the world is heartening, many schools still want a quick fix and believe if they adopt a student-facing program that includes a "teacher training," that this is equivalent to supporting adult SEL. It is not. Very few programs adequately address both student and adult needs comprehensively. The message of this book is that educators have their own unique needs, especially in the current educational landscape. The good news is that there are programs such as Growing Your HEART Skills that are cost- and time-effective, although of course some meaningful commitment is required—*meaning* being the key word. When the content is meaningful to adults and adds genuine value to their teaching practice and their lives in general, it can be transformative in a relatively short period of time. This can apply to any new content, not just SEL. School leaders should give teachers time and space to absorb new content meaningfully and find ways to connect skills to their own lives, rather than force rigid adherence to superficial fidelity checklists or timelines. The bold school leaders of the future will allow teachers the autonomy they need to grow their skills in ways that are authentic to them, and therefore sustainable.
- ***Lead* with the HEART in Mind**: As discussed in my book *Teaching with the HEART in Mind*, directed at teachers for implementing authentic SEL with students, my message to conclude this chapter is for supporters of educators at all levels to *lead* with the heart in mind. Simply put, this means that the humanity of the teachers and other educators in your charge must be prioritized at every turn. My book supported teachers in how to be a buffer for their students; now those of us who support teachers must be that buffer for *them*. Whether it is the lingering effects of the pandemic, the youth mental health crisis, or top-down education directives, teachers will quickly determine whether we have their backs or are just passing the burden to them. It's that simple. When leaders and supporters of educators also make the commitment to follow the principles of HEART: Honoring Emotions, Electing Responses, Applying Empathy, Reigniting Relationships, and Transforming with Purpose—while not easy, the path to healing teaching becomes imminently clear.

CONCLUSION

In short, even as various SEL initiatives aim to improve social, emotional and academic outcomes for students, prioritizing the well-being of educators remains paramount. Educators deserve access to resources that nurture their well-being, a strong sense of community within their schools, and a healthy work culture that promotes their flourishing. Let's make this a reality for all educators.

REFERENCES

Brown, B. (2012). *Daring greatly: How the courage to be vulnerable transforms the way we live, love, parent, and lead.* Gotham Books.

Doan, S., Steiner, E. D., & Pandey, R. (2024). *Teacher well-being and intentions to leave in 2024: Findings from the 2024 State of the American Teacher Survey.* RAND Corporation. https://www.rand.org/pubs/research_reports/RRA1108-12.html

Jennings, P. A. (2018). *The trauma-sensitive classroom: Building resilience with compassionate teaching.* W. W. Norton & Company.

Jones, S. M., Bouffard, S. M., & Weissbourd, R. (2013). Educators' social and emotional skills vital to learning. *Phi Delta Kappan, 94*(8), 62–65.

Martínez Pérez, L. (2021). *Teaching with the heart in mind: A complete educator's guide to social emotional learning.* Brisca Publishing.

McMahon, M., Hegenauer, C., & Zheng, L. R. (2024). Translating research into action: Leveraging educator expertise to adapt and improve SEL programming. *Social and Emotional Learning: Research, Practice, and Policy, 3*, 100039. https://doi.org/10.1016/j.sel.2024.100039

Oliveira, S., Roberto, M. S., Pereira, N. S., Marques-Pinto, A., & Veiga-Simão, A. M. (2021). Impacts of social and emotional learning interventions for teachers on teachers' outcomes: A systematic review with meta-analysis. *Frontiers in Psychology, 12*, 677217. https://doi.org/10.3389/fpsyg.2021.677217

Palmer, P. J. (1998). *The courage to teach: Exploring the inner landscape of a teacher's life.* Jossey-Bass.

Yoder, N., Hollingsworth, C., & Krohn, C. (2024, July). *Moving beyond self-care: Practice and policy conditions to support educator well-being.* American Institutes for Research & The Council of Chief State School Officers.

CHAPTER 4

Good Grief

A Case for Queering Teachers' Gender- and Sexual Diversity-Focused Professional Learning

Sara Staley

This chapter is dedicated to Andrea "Ankle" Gibson (August 13, 1975—July 14, 2025), who taught me that it hurts to become. May we all endeavor to live a life that stretches our hearts beyond what we imagined was possible.

"Good Grief"

Let your
heart break

so your spirit
doesn't.

—Andrea Gibson

Lately, I've been wearing this poem across my heart. (It's on a T-shirt.) The author is Andrea Gibson (they/them), a queer, nonbinary spoken-word poet and activist whose writing about love, mental health, queerness, and justice has been healing me for more than a decade. Their words provide a gentle reminder to stay tender, present, and open to the heartbreak of living, because feeling—not evading—that "good grief" sustains the spirit and soul.

As a White, cisgender, queer femme and teacher educator seeking collective liberation, I understand, deeply and viscerally, that in this historical moment, Gibson's guidance is not easily followed. Since 2021, hundreds of bills restricting the rights of lesbian, gay, bisexual, transgender, and queer (LGBTQ+) people have been proposed and passed in the United States. Today, transgender and nonbinary youth are uniquely targeted. An executive order has been signed by the 47th president eliminating protections for trans students, including their rights to be recognized as trans, to be called by their names and pronouns, and to have access to bathrooms and locker rooms consistent with their gender identities (Exec. Order No. 14190, 2025). State-level legislatures have attacked trans youths' rights to gender-affirming health care (among other things) and teachers' rights to include LGBTQ+ identities in curricula. For queer and trans youth, and youth of color especially, these attacks are distressing (Nath et al., 2024).

Certainly, this shifting policy environment exacerbates a need, long heralded by teacher education scholars (e.g., Airton & Koecher, 2019; Brant & Willox, 2021; Gorski, Davis, & Reiter, 2013) for teachers to have greater access to gender and sexual diversity (GSD)-focused professional learning that attends to the unique demands of their state and local contexts. But that need raises an important question: What kind of professional learning do teachers of LGBTQ+ youth *deserve* in this politically fraught moment?

Too often, GSD-focused learning opportunities are designed to target presumed gaps in teachers' knowledge and, as such, they approach learning as an endeavor in acquiring new knowledge about gender and sexuality, inclusive pedagogical strategies, and LGBTQ+ youths' experiences in schools. Developing such knowledge is necessary, in part, because of a persistent silence that has surrounded LGBTQ+ topics in teacher education (Clark & Kosciw, 2022). To be sure, there is much learning to do. But limiting our efforts to correcting teachers' knowledge deficits about GSD is shortsighted. Not only does this practice privilege cisgender, heterosexual ways of (not) knowing about LGBTQ+ lives, but it also fails to account for the emotional, sometimes heartbreaking dynamics of engaging with "difficult knowledge" (Britzman, 1998) surrounding a history of institutional refusal by schools to affirm LGBTQ+ identities (Staley & Leonardi, 2021). I suggest that the current sociopolitical context has intensified that emotional landscape, sharpening the contours of hesitation, uncertainty, and fear that often surround teachers' efforts to learn and enact queer- and trans-affirming practices.

For these reasons, I argue that teachers deserve access to queered GSD-focused professional learning opportunities that care for our hearts as much as our minds. I will develop the case in this chapter that queering professional learning means carefully attending to the emotionality that surfaces for teachers as we grapple with the cis-heteronormative context of schools and what we *all* do to reinforce norms that affect the lived experiences of students—sometimes in harmful ways.

A queer approach animates a promising pathway toward healing, as it welcomes complex emotions like heartbreak into the learning process. In fact, queering, as I conceptualize it, frames the vulnerability involved in feeling such complex emotions, rather than resisting them, as a "good grief" (Gibson, 2021)—one that, as Gibson suggests, is paradoxically heartbreaking and spirit sustaining. In this way, queering enables possibilities for moving through rather than getting "stuck" (Staley, 2018) in the limitations of our present conditions, including restrictive policies that squeeze educators' capacities to show up as supportive adults not just for queer and trans youth but also youth who are immigrants, youth of color, and youth who are multiply marginalized in schools.

In this chapter, I make the case for queering teachers' GSD-focused professional learning by leveraging queer theory and perspectives on healing. To do this, I draw on my experience facilitating educators' GSD-focused professional learning. Ultimately, consistent with the aims of this book, I hope to help envision a future of teacher education that prepares teachers—lovingly and unapologetically—to organize learning environments in which LGBTQ+ youth can thrive.

LOCATING MYSELF IN THE CASE FOR QUEERING

My argument is profoundly shaped by my role as cofounder/codirector of A Queer Endeavor, a nationally recognized center for educational research and outreach aimed at developing educators' GSD-focused professional learning. Our mission is to break the historical silence that surrounds GSD in P–12 schools and teacher education and, through deep partnerships with educators and district and school leadership, to create safer, more humanizing school communities for LGBTQ+ youth, families, and staff. Since cofounding the organization in 2013, my collaborator, Bethy Leonardi, and I have facilitated GSD-focused professional learning for tens of thousands of prospective and practicing teachers, counselors, and school and district leaders. At its core, that work involves supporting participants to critically investigate the intersections of normativity, identity, power, and schooling as they map onto our own lived experiences. My research has documented how these learning opportunities are generative, but also vulnerable for participants no matter where they are in their professional learning journeys, that is, as novice teachers or teachers who have been in classrooms for decades (Staley & Leonardi, 2016, 2019). I have found that learning to think differently about one's teaching practice respective to relations of power, privilege, normativity, and oppression does not follow linearly from acquiring information in one context to applying it in another. Rather, educators often experience a messier, disorienting learning process (Staley & Leonardi, 2021).

These findings have provoked me to think queerly about teacher learning and my own praxis as both a university-based teacher educator and facilitator of in-service teacher learning. "Thinking queerly" has meant bringing queer perspectives (Britzman, 1995; Kumashiro, 2000; Luhmann, 1998; Waite, 2017) to bear on how I design invitations for teachers to contend with difficult knowledge surrounding GSD in schools.

WHAT IS QUEERING?

Drawing on queer theoretical and pedagogical perspectives, I conceptualize queering as involving three interrelated strands: questioning, feeling discomfort, and implicating the self. I develop each below and then consider how braiding those strands together can facilitate productive spaces for teachers' learning and healing.[3]

3. For a fuller exploration of my conceptualization of *queering*, I point readers to Staley and Blackburn (2023).

Questioning

Queer theory (Jagose, 1996; Sedgwick, 1990) is interested in how knowledge, power, and normativity function to regulate bodies and lives. As a mode of critical inquiry, queering questions what counts as normal, how ideas of normal/different are constructed, and how self-identifications are enabled and constrained by those constructions (Britzman, 1995). In educational settings, queering encourages teachers to engage in questioning of ourselves, one another, and society more broadly. At the heart of such questioning is the refusal to accept what is understood as normal (Luhmann, 1998). The goal is not to be assimilated into normalcy but to interrogate and even subvert the very notion of normal. Subverting normativity requires not just learning but also *un*learning; it demands an "unscripting" (Keenan, 2017).

Feeling Emotional Discomfort

In theorizing queer pedagogy, Luhmann (1998) argued that teachers should pose questions not about what is taught and how but "how we come to know" (p. 100). This is because queer pedagogy presumes that under typical circumstances, we desire teaching and learning that reproduce "common sense" (Kumashiro, 2024) or that feel familiar. For that reason, a queer pedagogical lens focuses on teachers' unconscious desires to teach and learn in ways that affirm what we already know about ourselves, for example, that we are "good people," and to resist learning about our complicity with oppression (Kumashiro, 2000, p.43). In this way, queering teachers' professional learning involves "put[ting] into crisis what is known" (Luhmann, 1998, p. 147). This approach requires teachers to unlearn comforting narratives and feel emotional discomfort that comes from changing how we see and do things, including how we see ourselves. This is vulnerable and uncomfortable work. To create the conditions for "leaning in" to that discomfort (Staley & Leonardi, 2016), teachers must be invited to explore the emotionality of teaching and learning about oppression.

Implicating the Self

Queering involves posing "questions of implication" (Luhmann, 1998, p. 150) about the self and what is being learned: What does this information do to my sense of self? What does this knowledge ask me to reconsider about myself? Where are my resistances to this knowledge? Such questions provoke reflections on what difference teaching and learning are making, and where they are failing to make a difference, to consider why. As Kumashiro (2004) suggests, teachers might ask,

> What assumptions did I make about who the students are, what they feel, and what they are open to discussing? How did different groups of students feel forced to respond . . . ?

> Whom did this discussion privilege, and how? What issues did this discussion ignore, and what hidden messages did those gaps convey? (pp. 114–115)

This complicated work of reflecting, looking beyond what is taught and learned, and implicating the self in difficult knowledge, is essential to queering.

QUEERING AS A HEALING PRACTICE

As discussed so far, queer pedagogy presumes that learning is "messy" (Luhmann, 1998, p. 151) and invites teachers to confront that messiness by feeling uncomfortable emotions, including grief and heartbreak, and implicating ourselves in the systems we wish to change. So, how might that also cultivate healing?

Drawing on Indigenous spiritual knowledges and Chicana feminisms, Mendoza et al. (2024) defined healing as a "journey back to ourselves" (p. 213) and toward wholeness. As Pyles (2018) observed, oppressive social, cultural, and political norms and practices can engender a profound sense of "fracturedness" (p. xix) that separates us from ourselves and one another. To heal that disconnection, Pyles advocates for healing justice—a humanizing practice of attending to the body, heart, and emotions as practitioners "change the way they relate to each other and themselves and continually interrogate their tactics and interventions" (2018, p. xix). This can be challenging to square for teachers in U.S. culture because practices of "being called out and in" with respect to interrogating one's own complicity in oppression are commonly overly individualistic and inconsiderate of systemic issues, "mechanistic" as opposed to emotion-based or embodied, or too prone to "confessionals," surveillance, and control. No wonder we have trouble embracing self-interrogation, and need support in imagining how, when engaged in differently, it can result in healing and liberation.

Bringing this perspective into alignment with my conceptualization of queering reveals exciting potentiality for queering as a healing practice. This is because, in principle, a queer approach attends deeply to the heart and emotionality. Moreover, the queer pedagogical practices support teachers to reconsider normative beliefs and practices that divide us into categories of normal/different, self/other, us/them. Guided by Mendoza et al. (2024), I suggest that for teachers, the journey back to ourselves and our wholeness is charted by interrogating and subverting those divisions, questioning our resistances to difficult knowledge, and feeling the "good grief" of learning and teaching against oppression.

CASE IN POINT: SNAPSHOTS OF QUEERING TEACHERS' GSD-FOCUSED LEARNING

To illustrate what it looks, sounds, and feels like to enact this conceptual vision of queering, I share two praxis-based snapshots below. Each is rooted in my facilitation work with A Queer Endeavor. I have implemented each with thousands of educators and across contexts of university-based teacher education and in-service professional development.

Snapshot 1: Vulnerabilities and Strengths

Given the different ways that we are implicated in conversations about gender and sexuality, I often ask folks to reflect on how they are showing up and to consider how their colleagues are showing up. Digging in here is crucial. Sometimes educators want to jump straight to action steps—e.g., "What can I do to make my practices more affirming?" I like to remind folks that the work begins with ourselves, which this quote from Gloria Anzaldúa captures beautifully: "The struggle is inner. . . . The struggle has always been inner and is played out in outer terrains. Awareness of our situation must come before inner changes, which in turn come before changes in society. Nothing happens in the 'real' world unless it first happens in the images in our heads" (Anzaldúa, 1987, p. 109).

Conversations about identity, equity, and diversity are rarely easy to have, and avoiding them can arise from our fears of being vulnerable. So, before we begin, I invite participants in our sessions to take a moment to silently consider this question: *What will a discussion about GSD and organizing more LGBTQ+-affirming spaces bring up for me? Check in with what you're feeling in your body in this moment.* (Pause for reflection.) *Now, take a moment to think about a vulnerability you're holding—something that could limit your willingness to participate wholeheartedly in this conversation.* (Pause.) *Now, think about a strength you bring that will help you to engage openly and honestly.* (Pause.) *Finally, think about vulnerabilities and strengths that others in this room might be holding.*

This exercise, inspired by a tool created by Learning for Justice (Teaching Tolerance, 2015), invites participants to notice and name the emotions they feel in relation to the learning in which they are about to engage. Indeed, for some, sitting silently through this reflective exercise is itself a vulnerable act. Silent reflection is followed by pair-sharing their vulnerabilities and strengths, and then voluntary whole-group sharing. Almost certainly, teachers voice their deep care for students, fears of unintentionally causing harm, vulnerability around what they do not yet know, and, for queer and trans educators, the strength and vulnerability of their embodied knowledge. In a recent session, for example:

Lily shared, "One vulnerability I have is that I don't want to slip and say the wrong thing and offend anyone unintentionally. Sometimes that causes me to not want to speak up all the time in conversations as big as these."

Alejandro shared, "A vulnerability I have is not being informed about some of the struggles surrounding other groups. I feel like I have focused on my identity, but neglected understanding other groups."

Jax shared, "Sometimes, just showing up to work every day is my vulnerability. It can feel exhausting to be the only visibly queer teacher at my school and to feel like I have to carry this work. If I don't, who will?"

Carly shared, "I grew up in an area where gender and sexual diversity was not openly discussed, so it's something I don't know a lot about. And I feel like I should be taking more time than I have been to learn about it. But I want to be the best teacher I can for my students and that means learning and showing up for them in ways they need me to, including the willingness to learn the best ways to be there for them."

Organizing this opportunity for teachers to name and to listen to what makes us feel vulnerable and resourced in GSD-focused professional learning, is one way that I attempt to create the conditions for participants to feel a sense of community, an openness to emotional discomfort, and a willingness to engage with difficult knowledge.

Snapshot 2: Questioning What Counts as Normal in "Your Life"

Another consistent and crucial feature of the GSD-focused professional learning sessions I facilitate involves explaining what queer means as an adjective (i.e., a signifier of identities that are not cisgender and/or heterosexual) and a verb (i.e., to question what counts as normal). In elaborating on the verb form, I explain that GSD-affirming education involves "moving beyond inclusion" (Blackburn & Smith, 2010) of LGBTQ+ identities in the curriculum. Representation matters. However, merely including more identities that are otherwise marked as "different" or "other" does very little—if anything at all—to subvert the norm. Toward that end, questioning is key. Snapshot 2 invites teachers into the queer practice of questioning normativity as it operates in the context of their own lives.

Figure 4.1 provides a snapshot of the slide I project to extend that invitation. It includes a photo of Gibson, their pronouns, and the title "Your Life," a powerful spoken-word poem (which can be found on YouTube) that Gibson wrote as a love letter to queer, transgender, and nonbinary youth who might be struggling to embrace the full range of what gender and queerness can be. To invite teachers to implicate themselves in oppressive norms that Gibson's poem animates, I prompt them to "locate" themselves in the text by noticing "what feels normal" and "what feels strange." Then, I play the video. Afterwards, it is not uncommon to see folks wiping away tears.

From there, I invite participants to practice questioning normativity by reflecting on and discussing these questions: *Growing up, when did you feel like you were a "normal" kid in school? What made you feel that way? Thinking about your identities and their intersections, how did you see yourself reflected in the curriculum? How did that feel? When did you learn there was such a thing as diversity? What were the messages you received about what counts as "different"?*

I pose these questions because they position our multiple identities and lived experiences as central to learning to question and subvert normativity. Crafted in this way, my hope is that these questions will challenge teachers *not* to circumvent implicating themselves in their learning by intellectualizing normativity as an abstract system that operates outside of us. Because queering aims to orient learners to potentially

Figure 4.1. Questioning Normativity Slide

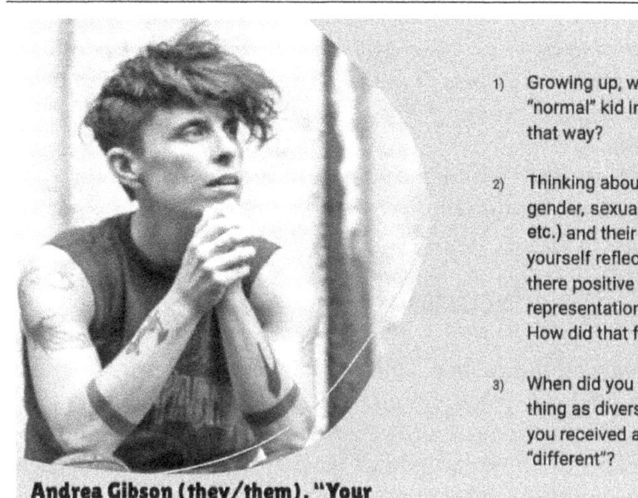

uncomfortable dimensions of implicating ourselves in oppressive systems, I frequently ask participants to notice what they are feeling as they ask and answer these questions.

Before moving into paired discussion, I point to the ways in which Gibson's video captures the diversity of the LGBTQ+ community. Guided by my understanding that queering involves bringing explicit attention to race and racism, I encourage participants to keep intersectionality at the center of their discussions. During in-person facilitations, I can walk around the room to listen to teachers' conversations. Generally, teachers take up my challenge to question normativity and to adopt a reflexive gaze. In turn, I have listened to teachers implicate their White, straight, cisgender identities in what has made them feel "pretty normal" in school. Katy, for example, put it this way: "Someone once described me as having won 'the birth lottery.' I understood what they meant. When it comes to privileges, it seems like I have just about all of them. I am White, able-bodied, cisgender, heterosexual. I am a U.S. citizen. I speak English. I am financially stable. These privileges have allowed me to seamlessly fit into the American dominant culture."

I have also listened to teachers recall how traditional scripts of masculinity and femininity were reinforced at school, and I have listened to queer and trans teachers recall having a single space (or no space at all) where they could explore and express their identities. For Gemini, that space was gym:

> *I wore a skirt at school every day until I was 12. I remember gym class and being delighted when I would shed my uniform of a plaid jumper skirt to don my school-issued navy and white gym shorts underneath. I wasn't allowed boys' clothes as a kid, but I did have an attachment to a camouflage hat. It was like a trucker cap before trucker caps were a thing.*

> *I don't remember where or how I got it, but I loved it and wore it everywhere I could until my dad hid it in a drawer in the utility room. I went to private school and wasn't allowed to wear it anywhere but gym class. So, in gym class, wearing shorts and my camo hat, doing pull-ups and wall sits and the shuttle run, that might have been the first time I experienced gender euphoria at the expense of fitting in and being seen as normal.*

The ways that teachers like Katy and Gemini participate in these conversations consistently strike me as honest and emotionally connected.

CONCLUSION

External attacks on public education, teachers, and teacher preparation are not new. But in the present moment, they are constructing justice-oriented teaching as particularly vulnerable, risky work for novices and veteran teachers alike. I argue that the present moment implicates the broader field of teacher education in a critical need for action. Posed as a question, then, I ask, how will teacher educators respond in this moment?

Following Kumashiro (2024), I suggest that naming the moment on our own terms creates opportunities to reframe dominant narratives and to pursue new directions for teacher education practice. Rather than being immobilized by the toxic and, in some cases, overwhelmingly restrictive policy contexts that challenge teachers' efforts to organize more humanizing classrooms for all young people, I challenge my colleagues in university-based teacher education to ask and answer these questions: How will you reframe the narrative in your context and community? What meaningful action will you take to prepare teachers to advance justice for LGBTQ+ youth, youth of color, and multiply marginalized youth? How might you hold healing, wholeness, and good grief as principles for guiding the learning opportunities that you design and extend to teachers?

What counts as meaningful action will shift according to context and circumstance, and even small shifts in practice matter. So, where to begin? To open conversations about GSD, normativity, and schooling, teacher educators can draw on the activities described in the aforementioned snapshots. They can invite teachers to practice questioning (and subverting) normativity by asking these questions of a syllabus, textbook, lesson, or unit: What counts as normal here? How do ideas of normal/different show up? What about stereotypes? When and where do learners encounter them? Whose voices are amplified, silenced, and/or missing? What might happen if new voices are added? How might that change the story that gets told? Teacher educators can also support teachers to understand state- and district-level laws and policies that enable and constrain queer- and trans-affirming education and practice responding, together, to imaginary, purposefully sticky scenarios that afford multiple ways of responding. These are, of course, just a few entry points. I encourage my colleagues to imagine and enact others.

Queer of color theorist José Esteban Muñoz (2009) argued that queerness is a "longing . . . that thing that lets us feel that this world is not enough, that indeed something is missing" (p. 1). Put differently, queerness insists on hope and imagining new worlds of possibility. Framed this way, I offer queering as a pathway toward possibility, as it honors teachers' full humanity, creates space to feel the emotionality of teaching toward justice in these times, and holds us all accountable to subverting normativity in the service of transformation and change. Imagine what new worlds we might forge by collectively reframing, reimagining, and reinvigorating what has counted as normal in teacher education. That is the dreamscape I want to occupy. Don't you?

REFERENCES

Airton, L., & Koecher, A. (2019). How to hit a moving target: 35 years of gender and sexual diversity in teacher education. *Teaching and Teacher Education, 80*, 190–204. https://doi.org/10.1016/j.tate.2018.11.004

Anzaldúa, G. (1987). *Borderlands/la frontera: The new mestiza.* Aunt Lute Books.

Blackburn, M. V., & Smith, J. M. (2010). Moving beyond the inclusion of LGBT-themed literature in English language arts classrooms: Interrogating hetero-normativity and exploring intersectionality. *Journal of Adolescent & Adult Literacy, 53*, 625–634. https://doi.org/10.1598/JAAL.53.8.1

Brant, C., & Willox, L. (2021). Queering teacher education: Teacher educators' self-efficacy in addressing LGBTQ issues. *Action in Teacher Education, 43*(2), 128–143. EJ1293713.

Britzman, D. P. (1995). Is there a queer pedagogy? Or, stop reading straight. *Educational Theory, 45*(2), 151–165. https://doi.org/10.1111/j.1741-5446.1995.00151.x

Clark, C. M., & Kosciw, J. G. (2022). *Educating educators: Knowledge, beliefs, and practice of teacher educators on LGBTQ issues.* GLSEN.

Exec. Order No. 14,190 (2025). https://www.whitehouse.gov/presidential-actions/2025/01/ending-radical-indoctrination-in-k-12-schooling/

Gibson, A. (2021). *You better be lightning*. SCB Distributors.

Gorski, P., Davis, S. N., & Reiter, A. (2013). An examination of the (in)visibility of sexual orientation, heterosexism, homophobia, and other LGBTQ+ concerns in U.S. multicultural teacher education coursework. *Journal of LGBT Youth, 10*(3), 224–248. https://doi.org/10.1080/19361653.2013.798986

Jagose, A. (1996). *Queer theory*. University of Otago Press.

Keenan, H. B. (2017). Unscripting curriculum: Toward a critical trans pedagogy. *Harvard Educational Review, 87*(4), 538–556. https://doi.org/10.17763/1943-5045-87.4.538

Kumashiro, K. K. (2000). Toward a theory of anti-oppressive education. *Review of Educational Research, 70*, 25–53. https://doi.org/10.3102/00346543070001025

Kumashiro, K. K. (2004). Uncertain beginnings: Learning to teach paradoxically. *Theory Into Practice, 43*(2), 111–115. https://doi.org/10.1207/s15430421tip4302_3

Kumashiro, K. K. (2024). *Against common sense: Teaching and learning toward social justice* (4th ed.). Routledge.

Luhmann, S. (1998). Queering/querying pedagogy? Or, pedagogy is a pretty queer thing. In W. Pinar (Ed.), *Queer theory in education* (pp. 141–155). Lawrence Erlbaum.

Mendoza, E., Padilla-Chavez, A., Salazar, B., & Jurow, A. S. (2024). Integrating learning and hummingbird medicine to heal academic harm. *Journal of Ethnic and Cultural Studies*, *11*(5), 211–229. https://doi.org/10.29333/ejecs/2305

Muñoz, J. E. (2009). *Cruising utopia: The then and there of queer futurity*. New York University Press.

Nath, R., Matthews, D. D., DeChants, J. P., Hobaica, S., Clark, C. M., Taylor, A. B., & Muñoz, G. (2024). *2024 U.S. national survey on the mental health of LGBTQ+ young people*. The Trevor Project. www.thetrevorproject.org/survey-2024

Pyles, L. (2018). *Healing justice: Holistic self-care for change makers*. Oxford University Press.

Sedgwick, E. (1990). *Epistemology of the closet*. University of California Press.

Staley, S. (2018). On getting stuck: Moving through stuck places in and beyond gender and sexual diversity-focused educational research. *Harvard Educational Review*, *88*(3), 287–307. EJ1193540

Staley S., & Blackburn M. V. (2023). Troubling emotional discomfort: Teaching and learning queerly in teacher education. *Teaching and Teacher Education*, *124*, 1–9. https://doi.org/10.1016/j.tate.2023.104030

Staley, S., & Leonardi, B. (2016). Leaning in to discomfort: Preparing preservice teachers for gender and sexual diversity. *Research in the Teaching of English, 51*(2), 209–229. https://doi.org/10.58680/rte201628875

Staley, S., & Leonardi, B. (2019). Complicating what we know: Focusing on educators' processes of becoming gender and sexual diversity inclusive. *Theory Into Practice*, *58*(1), 29–38. https://doi.org/10.1080/00405841.2018.1536916

Staley, S., & Leonardi, B. (2021). A pretty queer thing: Thinking queerly about teachers' gender and sexual diversity-focused professional learning. *Journal of Teacher Education, 72*(5), 511–522. https://doi.org/10.1177/002248712097158

Teaching Tolerance. (2015) *Let's talk: Discussing race, racism and other difficult topics with students*. http://www.tolerance.org/sites/default/files/general/Difficult_Conversations_Self_Assessment.pdf

Waite, S. (2017). *Teaching queer: Radical possibilities for writing and knowing*. University of Pittsburgh Press.

CHAPTER 5

Dialogic Inquiry as Care

Healing Early Years Educators With Professional Learning About Multicultural Education

Eseta Tualaulelei

Jemma is an early learning educator who, after arriving in the morning at her center each day, has around 20 minutes to prepare equipment and activities for her class before her first child arrives. The next several hours pass by in a blur of play, singing, dancing, story time, arts and crafts, children's meals, restroom breaks, chatting with families, communicating with colleagues, documentation and reporting of children's learning, and administration. By the end of the day, Jemma has not had time for lunch (again) and still must complete an online professional reflection on her day's teaching. She logs a functional reflection, enough to satisfy her supervisor, then leaves for the day to return to her busy home life.

"WHY DO MY TEACHERS KEEP LEAVING, MOMMY?"

Considering the above, very average day in the life of an early childhood educator, to say nothing of what truly hectic days are like, perhaps it is not so surprising the level of turnover we have in our field (Hamel et al., 2025). I find myself in frequent conversations with parents who struggle to explain to their young children why they must meet a new teacher so many times during the same school year. One parent of a 3-year-old boy told me that he had five different preschool educators in the same year, one of whom stayed only for 2 weeks. "Why do they keep changing?" she asks me. "It's really hard for my son every time they leave because he gets close to them." I tell her that yes, having five teachers in a year is extreme, but I add that early childhood education and care has a higher turnover rate compared with other educational sectors. We then chat about how her son copes each time these significant adults in his life leave.

What I don't tell her (and what I don't tell my preservice teacher students) is that all around the world, educators are leaving the teaching profession and in the early childhood sector, the situation is especially dire. International research cites annual staff turnover figures of between 26% and 62% in early childhood education and care, and those who have not yet left the profession are thinking about it (Carson et al., 2016; Heilala et al., 2021). There are myriad reasons why early years educators leave. Among them is the persistently low pay (far lower than K–12 education), a lack of job satisfaction, feeling undervalued, increasing job stress, and limited opportunities for career progression (Kwon et al., 2020; McDonald et al., 2018). The demand for higher qualifications also places pressure on educators as they pursue further education while simultaneously managing their existing workloads (Heilala et al., 2021). It seems urgent that we find ways to ensure that early years educators, who care for our most precious and vulnerable members of society, are supported to maintain the passion for early years education that motivated them to enter the field in the first place.

ELEVATING PROFESSIONAL LEARNING WITH DIALOGIC INQUIRY

One retention strategy highlighted in the literature is ongoing professional development (PD). While teachers at all levels engage in professional development, for early learning teachers, PD often serves a compensatory and therefore more urgent role, since their preservice training is lesser in both amount and quality than what is accessible for K–12 educators. Early years educators feel more engaged and competent in their work when they are given opportunities for quality professional learning (Hur et al., 2022; Sims & Waniganayake, 2015). For effective professional learning, resources must be flexible and accessible, and educators also prefer practical, hands-on experiences that are contextually relevant (Tualaulelei & Green, 2022).

Professional learning is linked to teacher quality, which in turn is strongly linked to children's care and education quality (Sims & Hui, 2017). Knowledgeable educators can better engage with and care for children, use a wider range of teaching strategies, and provide leadership for others (Sims & Waniganayake, 2015). However, not all professional learning experiences are of high-enough quality to produce changes in teachers' professional wellness and, therefore, have the potential to help stem the tide of teacher turnover.

This chapter offers dialogic inquiry—an educational approach that emphasizes collaborative knowledge building through dialogue and interaction—as a tool for humanizing and deepening professional learning for early years educators, rejuvenating their professional knowledge and well-being, and helping to heal the profession. Teachers regularly dialogue with their students and their colleagues, but there is great untapped potential in capitalizing on its benefits for social and emotional connection within the context of professional learning. Too often, the burden lies with individual teachers to develop professional knowledge and maintain their own well-being, but dialogic inquiry offers a means to share these burdens with others.

In the remainder of this chapter, I present dialogic inquiry as a powerful tool for professional development through which educators can heal from the forces that have drained the joy from their profession. Drawing upon Freire's (2000) notion of dialogue as a transformational and humanizing act, the chapter explores how early years educators can be supported, and yes, perhaps even healed, through dialogic inquiry within a professional development setting.

THE CONTEXT FOR THIS JOURNEY

I teach a course about intercultural communication at a midsized regional university in the state of Queensland in Australia. Queensland has many vibrant Indigenous and multicultural communities, so a key part of the course is to guide preservice teachers teaching culturally and linguistically diverse children and enhance their knowledge of reconciliation with and for Australia's Indigenous peoples. What drew me to this work initially were my own educational experiences being raised Samoan but attending schools and universities in English, which highlighted for me dissonances between my cultural and linguistic community and the broader community. Many children experience these dissonances when they move from home into various educational settings, so my research focuses on this area.

Multicultural education is focused on developing people's cultural knowledge and critical consciousness in an effort toward educational equity for all learners (Banks & Banks, 2004; Gay, 2004; Kennedy & Aman, 2024). We found in an earlier study that quality professional development in this area was sorely lacking (Tualaulelei & Halse, 2021). Given the range of experiences educators have with these topics and the sensitivity of some of the issues, professional learning in this space offered a rich context for using dialogic inquiry as an authentic and deep lens through which to explore teachers' vulnerability, assumptions, and experiences around issues of "difference."

The present chapter reflects experiences from one project I ran between 2019 and 2023 that brought together in-service early years educators and preservice teachers from my multicultural education course. We held a series of dialogic inquiries to develop multicultural educational materials. By locating multicultural ideas within early years educators' situated realities, dialogic inquiry encouraged them toward critical thinking, not as an end in itself, but as part of a process of care—care for each other, care for the profession, and care for children.

FREIRE'S FRAMEWORK FOR DIALOGUE AS LOVE

Dialogic inquiry arises from the work of Paulo Freire (2000), and it centers dialogue in any search for knowledge or understanding. Dialogue or "dialogics" as he called it, helps to realize education as a practice of freedom. It is a theory of cultural action in direct opposition to the transactional "banking" model of education that sought to "deposit" information into people's heads. Freire's dialogics is part of a liberatory education because first and foremost "dialogue is an encounter among women and men who name the world, it must not be a situation where some name on behalf of others" (Freire, 2000, p. 89). When people dialogue, they come to the dialogue as equals, prepared to engage and learn with and from each other. Second, dialogue requires love for both people and the world we live in. In Freire's words, "If I do not love the world—if I do not love life—if I do not love people—I cannot enter into dialogue" (p. 90). Third, "dialogue cannot exist without humility" (p. 90). One cannot dialogue with another if they do not acknowledge their own limitations in knowledge and understanding.

Fourth, dialogue "requires an intense faith in humankind, faith in their power to make and remake, to create and re-create, faith in their vocation to be more fully human (which is not the privilege of an elite, but the birthright of all)" (Freire, 2000, p. 90). Fifth, dialogue requires hope: "Hope is rooted in men's [*sic*] incompletion, from which they move out in constant search—a search which can be carried out only in communion with others." Sixth, dialogue requires critical thinking and in turn generates critical thinking. This goes beyond thinking about the "normalized 'today'" (p. 92) and moving toward transformative actions that can arise out of the dialogue. These six foundations—equality, love, humility, faith, hope, and critical thinking—form the basis upon which inquiry proceeds. There is no prescribed process for dialogic inquiry. In fact, a strict method is discouraged because every context is different (Freire, 2000), but there are ways that the principles of dialogic inquiry can be upheld. These are outlined in the next few sections.

Create the Conditions for Dialogic Inquiry: Equality and Humility

In dialogic inquiry, there are facilitators and participants rather than teachers and students or any other dyadic description that places one person in the position of giver and the other as receiver. Everyone comes to the interaction as "knowers" with different types of knowing, but everyone is also positioned to learn from others. The role of the facilitator is to prompt, encourage, and participate rather than to lead the discussion with ideas that others must consume. Facilitating dialogic inquiry therefore requires an understanding of the nature of verbal interactions. There are ebbs and flows to dialogue that can be managed with the use of conversational devices. For instance, small talk can ease people into conversing, particularly when participants are not familiar with each other. Facilitators can assist with pacing people's interactions as the conversation warms up, particularly if the discussion gets heated. Silence, too, has a function in dialogue, perhaps as an opportunity for reflection and wondering. In the modern context of online dialogues, facilitators need to be aware of the way in which conversational devices may operate differently (e.g., chat function, lack of eye contact, cameras on or off).

To help create the conditions for dialogic inquiry:

- *Use greetings, acknowledgments, and introductions*: Greetings, while commonplace, are an important social convention that respects participants' presence and sets the tone for the dialogue. Here on traditional Yuggera lands, I generally start with "Gurumba bigi" which is Hello or "G'day" in the local Indigenous language, before moving to English greetings, although any contextually appropriate greeting can be used.

  Acknowledgements of the Indigenous custodians of lands, where appropriate, suggests mindfulness of the larger contexts of time, space, and knowledge. I typically acknowledge country and Indigenous elders, which is customary for formal gatherings in Australia. Introductions serve a similar purpose by sharing aspects of identity, experience, or understanding that can help others relate to other participants. Consider the humility shown in the introduction of one of our participants who had 20 years of teaching experience and 10 years of Indigenous community experience: "[I'm] quite new to refugee children and things that arise with that kind of child, so yes, looking for more learning."
- *Check in with intentionality to build trust:* An important practice is to check in with participants on their well-being or their current state of mind with a question such as, "How do you come to us today?" Checking in allows participants to articulate their affective state without judgement and welcomes humility. Check-ins help educators heal by drawing attention to our humanity. We are not always fine, ready to learn, and eager to dive into professional learning; sometimes we are a little sad or tired or still thinking about an incident from yesterday. Aim to keep check-ins inclusive of everyone attending but brief to allow more time for dialogic inquiry.
- *Support participants to keep dialogue inclusive and relevant*: All participants come to dialogues holding knowledge, but conversations sometimes require redirection. Our facilitators interjected in situations when there was too much crosstalk. When one dialogue devolved into a complaint session about the Queensland Department of Education, the facilitator acknowledged how the educators felt and then pivoted the dialogue by asking for actionable ideas educators used to cope with the pressures they felt. Similarly, to rein in a rather chatty educator who was dominating the dialogue, I interjected occasionally to redirect toward other participants. Inexperienced facilitators may feel it is disrespectful to ever "interrupt" but with experience, it becomes clear that the larger group dynamic experiences a healing containment from skillful reframing and redirecting.

Promoting Praxis: Critical Thinking for Action

Dialogic inquiry generates critical thinking as participants think through ideas and as they work together to reach a fuller understanding of the topics at hand. Moreover, in dialogics, critical thinking is not just an intellectual exercise, but a process that should lead to or be tied to action, or in Freire's words, "praxis" (2000, p. 100). Both reflection and action are needed because either one without the other does not create the conditions for transforming realities. For educators coming together to evolve their professional development, the point is not to just reflect and discuss issues. Dialogic inquiry should be connected to the transformation of professional practices and the world in which these practices occur.

An example of dialogics moving from reflection to action was the case of a center director who attended one of our sessions run by the head librarian of the local Indigenous library. The center director learned of a children's picture book about how Aboriginal people care for their children across extended families, and she described the impact of sharing this book with her staff:

> One of my educators, she had read that story to the children, and then . . . the little girls went outside and played with their babies. One of them was like, "Oh, you can go to Auntie Lenora and you can stay with her now, and she'll look after you, and then you can come back to me later." She [the educator] couldn't figure out where that came from until she reread the book again. It was from the book that she was teaching, which was really interesting.

The director's anecdote was a powerful example of how critical thinking leads to action that was transmitted all the way from librarian, to center director, to teacher, to children. What started with a simple children's book became a lesson in multicultural understanding that radiated healing across people, settings, and ages, as multifamily care arrangements were no longer "otherized." In another session, an educator described teaching her students how to acknowledge the lands of Australia's First Nations people, after which one of the children taught her mother about this when they were out playing at a park, saying, "You're thanking the people who were here first, Mom." In early years education and care, these ripple effects help heal educators as evidenced by their sharing of these "wins" in their practice.

To promote critical thinking for action:

- *Ask open questions*: Using open questions or prompts can get a dialogue going and move it forward. Questions like "What does ___ mean to you?," "What's your experience with ____?," and the sentence starter "Tell me (more) about _____" encouraged participants to engage with the dialogue.
- *Emphasize praxis*: Ask for examples that bring reflective ideas to life with questions such as, "What could [value, idea, framework, technique, etc.] look like in your classroom?" or more directly, "How can we make this happen?" A risk with peer groups is that they become navel-gazing or complaint sessions. The emphasis on praxis helps keep forward

momentum and, as shown in the example of the girls playing with their babies, it can transform children's lives as well. Such positive outcomes lift teachers' morale, healing them with reminders of the value of their work.

Humanize Dialogue: Exemplifying Love, Faith, and Hope

While capitalist and neoliberal forces distort the nature of early years education as an "industry," those who work in the sector do so for the purpose of nurturing children, instilling in them values that serve communities and preparing them for a future of abundant living and learning. Damage caused by market-based perspectives of early childcare can be healed through dialogic inquiry that values teachers' views and recognizes their contributions to education. In our dialogues, the Freirean principles of love, faith, and hope could be seen in the way educators spoke with passion about their vocations, and in the aspirations they expressed for themselves and the children they cared for.

These foundational principles became especially important when discussing difficult topics, for instance, when speaking about incidents of racism. An educator shared how she had suggested to a colleague to embed First Nations perspectives into her teaching and the colleague's response was, "What am I going to do? Teach them how to steal cars?" Confronted with this blatant racism, the educator was at a loss.

Another participant described how four family daycare educators from culturally diverse backgrounds she worked with "tend to refuse to have Aboriginal things" in their settings. She reminded them that it was part of the early years' curriculum and national quality standards. At this point, two other participants agreed:

Jesse: Trying to educate educators. That is so much a big part of the [curriculum] framework now that they need to be aware of. And that's the thing where that's not part of their culture, but then to be multicultural, they have to invite all those cultures into their environment. When you've got those language issues or communication issues, trying to explain [multicultural inclusion to diverse educators] can be really tricky sometimes.

As the participants inquired more into the challenges of racism and cultural diversity, they shared strategies and resources for helping reluctant or racist educators, those with monocultural centers, and those who did not understand the value of First Nations education or cultural diversity. Dialogic inquiry does not just dwell on what is—it visualizes what could be and how that vision can be achieved.

To humanize dialogue:

- *Meet challenges head-on*: When challenging topics arise in dialogic inquiry, let them be aired, and do not allow discomfort to serve as a justification for avoidance. See where the dialogue goes because the goal of inquiry is to come to an understanding alongside the participants about their challenges, and this cannot be achieved if difficult topics are off the table. These are instances where the facilitator should refrain from prematurely providing containment and allow the space for educators' inner wisdom to explore and take hold, even if uncomfortable.

- *Allow emotions and values to be shared*: Dialogic inquiry is not a methodical, emotionless problem-solving process. Dialogic inquiry recognizes humans as fallible, working toward holistic being but understanding our incompleteness. Teachers might therefore wonder aloud, correct themselves or others, laugh or cry, or use strong language. Uncertainty and mistakes, emotions and values are all part of the process toward plenitude.

Across all the professional learning dialogues we have had with early years educators, both within this project and outside it, they consistently raised their appreciation for the opportunity to come together. As one educator put it, "We feel connection. We feel intertwined. That's why moments like this are really important, coming together." Some, particularly those who were the sole educator in their context, wanted more opportunities to connect with others for professional learning. Dialogic inquiry responds to this need for human connection by recognizing the social nature of learning. Important too is the emotional support that educators gained. They felt "supported," "safe," "comforted," and "respected"; one educator described her cup as being full. These feelings can help counter the pervasive lack of job satisfaction and feelings of being undervalued that are driving many early years educators from the profession. Dialogic inquiry also offers an alternative to individual professional learning that can often feel isolating and performative.

WEAVING DIALOGIC INQUIRY INTO THE FABRIC OF TEACHER TRAINING

Ultimately, what is healing about dialogic inquiry are the Freirean principles that underpin it. When professional learning is approached with an emphasis on equality, love, humility, faith, hope, and critical thinking, these ideas are also likely to flow through to practice. This is especially important in multicultural education where the practice and action for equity is as important as learning about it (Tualaulelei & Halse, 2023). By participating in dialogic inquiry, early years educators reaffirmed their commitments to education, and their shared values for educating and caring for children and communities. They also shared some of the burden of professional learning, helping to heal others and identifying healing opportunities within the early years education and care system. Professional learning was not an exercise in compliance, but a genuine, restorative educational experience that had positive flow-on effects for children and families.

Embedding dialogic inquiry will look different across the teacher education pipeline. During preservice, dialogic inquiry and its affirming principles can be used by teacher educators to familiarize teachers-in-training with the nature of professional dialogue, critical thinking, and reflection for action. Dialogic inquiry may be particularly effective around topics such as responding to racism, collaborating with diverse children and their families, and supporting bi/multilingualism. With in-service professional development, facilitators can use dialogic inquiry as an exploratory activity to gauge educators' concerns of professional practice and, based on these reflections, create future actions that are contextually relevant, practical, and achievable.

School and center directors and leaders can schedule dialogic inquiry for professional development within busy early years educators' workdays as an alternative to individualized pursuits. They can further promote communities of inquiry and allocate the time and resources needed for all staff to participate in these communities. Whether preservice or in-service, it seems clear that dialogic inquiry can be a helpful lens through which to embrace, rather than avoid, the complexity and discomfort that often arise in the messy world of education. It creates further harm—never healing—to pretend these complexities such as teacher turnover, racism toward Indigenous families, and lack of time for teachers to eat, don't really exist. The suggestions discussed here aim to heal early childhood educators who feel undervalued and overworked by helping them enact the changes they voice they need for themselves and the children in their care.

Returning to our story from the field, here's how dialogic inquiry might help heal the early years sector:

> Jemma is an early childcare educator who, after arriving in the morning at her Center each day, has around 20 minutes to prepare equipment and activities for her class before her first child arrives. The next several hours pass by in a blur but her director has blocked out a lunch hour for Jemma to re-energize personally and professionally. She eats lunch and relaxes for half an hour and then in the remaining half hour, she logs online to participate in a professional dialogue with virtual colleagues. By the end of the day, Jemma leaves feeling satisfied with the day's activities and motivated to try out some of the ideas she learned about in the dialogue. She leaves for the day to return to her busy home life.

CONCLUSION

To conclude, there are two overarching actions we can take today to make this second story the norm rather than the exception. First, we should acknowledge that paying attention to adult SEL supports early years educators to sustain their practice. When educators find nourishment and fulfilment in their work, they may stay longer in the profession. Second, organizations or leaders are encouraged to create opportunities and the conditions for educators to engage in dialogic inquiry.

Professional development is often a source of new ideas and inspiration; dialogic inquiry can elevate it into a source of healing and well-being.

REFERENCES

Banks, J. A., & Banks, C. A. M. (2004). *Handbook of research on multicultural education* (2nd ed.). Jossey-Bass.

Carson, R. L., Baumgartner, J. J., Ota, C. L., Kuhn, A. P., & Durr, A. (2016). An ecological momentary assessment of burnout, rejuvenation strategies, job satisfaction, and quitting intentions in childcare teachers. *Early Childhood Education Journal*, *45*(6), 801–808. https://doi.org/10.1007/s10643-016-0831-9

Freire, P. (2000). *Pedagogy of the oppressed* (M. B. Ramos, Trans.). Continuum.

Gay, G. (2004). The importance of multicultural education. In D. J. Flinders, S. J. Thornton (Eds.), *The curriculum studies reader* (pp. 315–322). Routledge.

Hamel, E. E., Avari, P., Hatton-Bowers, H., & Schachter, R. E. (2025). "The Kids. That's my number one motivator": Understanding teachers' motivators and challenges to working in early childhood education. *Early Childhood Education Journal*, *53*(2), 563–574. https://doi.org/10.1007/s10643-023-01612-6

Heilala, C., Kalland, M., Lundkvist, M., Forsius, M., Vincze, L., & Santavirta, N. (2021). Work demands and work resources: Testing a model of factors predicting turnover intentions in early childhood education. *Early Childhood Education Journal*, *50*(3), 399–409. https://doi.org/10.1007/s10643-021-01166-5

Hur, E. H., Ardeleanu, K., Satchell, T. W., & Jeon, L. (2022). Why are they leaving? Understanding associations between early childhood program policies and teacher turnover rates. *Child & Youth Care Forum*, *52*(2), 417–440. https://doi.org/10.1007/s10566-022-09693-x

Kennedy, K. J., & Aman, N. (2024). Multiculturalism in "troubled" times: Meeting diversity's challenges with care. *Multicultural Education Review, 16*(2), 94–108. https://doi.org/10.1080/2005615x.2024.2389024

Kwon, K.-A., Malek, A., Horm, D., & Castle, S. (2020). Turnover and retention of infant-toddler teachers: Reasons, consequences, and implications for practice and policy. *Children and Youth Services Review*, *115*(105061). https://doi.org/10.1016/j.childyouth.2020.105061

McDonald, P., Thorpe, K., & Irvine, S. (2018). Low pay but still we stay: Retention in early childhood education and care. *Journal of Industrial Relations*, *60*(5), 647–668. https://doi.org/10.1177/0022185618800351

Sims, M., & Hui, S. K. F. (2017). Neoliberalism and early childhood. *Cogent Education*, *4*(1), 1365411. https://doi.org/10.1080/2331186x.2017.1365411

Sims, M., & Waniganayake, M. (2015). The role of staff in quality improvement in early childhood. *Journal of Education and Training Studies*, *3*(5), 187–194. https://doi.org/10.11114/jets.v3i5.942

Tualaulelei, E., & Green, N. C. (2022). Supporting educators' professional learning for equity pedagogy: The promise of open educational practices. *Journal for Multicultural Education*, *49*(1), 99–122. https://doi.org/10.1108/JME-12-2021-0225

Tualaulelei, E., & Halse, C. (2021). A scoping study of in-service teacher professional development for inter/multicultural education and teaching culturally and linguistically diverse students. *Professional Development in Education, 20*(5), 847–861. https://doi.org/10.1080/19415257.2021.1973074

Tualaulelei, E., & Halse, C. (2023). Why interculturalism does not always translate into action: Insights from teachers in an Australian primary school. *The Australian Educational Researcher*, *50*(3), 747–762. https://doi.org/10.1007/s13384-022-00523-6

PART II

BEYOND CULTURAL AFFINITY

HEALING TEACHING BY AND FOR TEACHERS OF COLOR

CHAPTER 6

Community Cultural Healing in Teaching and Teacher Education

Rooted in Plática, Growing in Justice

Mariana Souto-Manning, Jessica Martell, and Benelly Álvarez

As educators from systemically excluded communities, we have each navigated professional spaces shaped by dominant norms that privilege Whiteness, Eurocentrism, monolingualism, and institutional conformity. These environments often demand that we silence aspects of who we are—our languages, cultural practices, pedagogies, and epistemologies—to be seen as "professional." The cost of this assimilation is steep: the erasure of community-rooted and culturally situated knowledges, the denial of our full humanity, and the ongoing struggle for recognition, validation, and well-being.

This chapter emerges from our shared journey—one marked by resistance, reimagining, and reclaiming. We write as Latina women of color, mothers, educators, and justice-seeking scholar-practitioners. Mariana is a first-generation immigrant from Brazil; Jessica and Benelly are daughters of Puerto Rican and Dominican im/migrants. We write from lives that are not separate from our scholarship but deeply intertwined with the stories of our children, our students, and our communities. We are oldest daughters and mothers to children whose names and knowledges are too often mispronounced, misunderstood, or made invisible in U.S. schools. Our personal and professional paths have been shaped by the very injustices we seek to dismantle—and by the joy, resistance, and brilliance we have inherited and witnessed. We are coauthors, colleagues, *hermanas y compañeras*. We walk alongside each other in community, in humor, in humility, and in hope.

We reject deficit-based framings and resist narrow definitions of what it means to know, to teach, and to learn. We are committed to pedagogies that are expansive, relational, and rooted in the cultural wealth of the global majority (Souto-Manning & Rabadi-Raol, 2018). We anchor our work in *platicando en comunidad*—a deliberate practice of coming together in dialogue. These are not casual conversations; they are sacred spaces where we speak truth, ask hard questions, listen deeply, and imagine otherwise. Through pláticas (Fierros & Bernal, 2016), we honored our lived experiences, theorized in the flesh, nurtured our cultural identities and linguistic practices, and cultivated conditions for collective transformation (Delgado Bernal et al., 2023). Pláticas are informal and relational, yet deeply intellectual and affective—spaces of story-sharing, meaning-making, and solidarity-building.

In doing this work, we stand on the shoulders of those who have come before us—Indigenous, Black, Latinx, and other knowledge keepers who have long engaged in communal forms of learning as acts of survival, resistance, and regeneration—whether written or oral, published in journals or spoken at kitchen tables. We draw from this lineage as we offer a framework for shared reflection and transformative teacher education. Our vision is not simply to make room within existing structures, but to fundamentally reshape those structures.

We are not interested in reform that accommodates—we seek transformation that liberates. We propose a reimagining of teacher education rooted in justice, cultural integrity, and relational answerability, one that makes space for educators from historically excluded communities not just to be present, but to lead, to create, and to reauthor the field itself. In reclaiming knowledge for cultural healing, we affirm that teacher learning must be a site of radical possibility, communal care, and systemic change—spaces that reflect the fullness, complexity, and humanity of all who belong there.

HEALING, LEARNING, AND BUILDING TOWARD COLLECTIVE TRANSFORMATION

As educators and scholar-practitioners whose identities have long been excluded from the center of teacher education, we know what it means to carry the weight of cultural taxation (Padilla, 1994), isolation, and unspoken expectations to endure. We have moved through institutions not built with us in mind—spaces that often overlook our languages, histories, pedagogies, and ways of knowing. Within these systems, the burden is frequently placed on us to adapt, persist, and survive, rather than to be supported, seen, and sustained. In response to these realities, we have turned to each other and to our communities. Together, we cultivated *community cultural healing spaces*—spaces that nourish us emotionally, intellectually, and spiritually. These are not simply places of refuge; they are sites of collective resistance, relational learning, and professional renewal. They remind us that healing is not separate from transformation—that tending to our well-being is essential to reimagining education.

These *counterspaces* (Solórzano & Villalpando, 1998) are intentionally created environments that affirm our epistemologies, honor our lived experiences, and offer the kind of solidarity rarely found in traditional professional development settings. For us, these are not optional or extracurricular—they are necessary. In them, we process harm, build coalitions, and reclaim our power as educators who live and work at the intersections of systems of exclusion rooted in race, language, culture, and more.

The toll of being systemically othered in educational institutions is real and deep. We have felt racial battle fatigue (Smith, 2004) in our bodies and witnessed it in our colleagues—the emotional exhaustion, the quiet departures of brilliant educators who could no longer carry the weight alone. Without intentional spaces for renewal and connection, the result is often burnout, disillusionment, and loss—not just of individuals, but of collective wisdom and possibility (Kohli et al., 2017).

Community cultural healing spaces disrupt the harmful myth of individual resilience—the idea that we must push through in silence. Instead, they allow us to breathe, to grieve, to laugh, to question, and to imagine otherwise. They are built on radical collective care, not compliance. Within them, we:

- Engage in communal processing of the emotional and professional burdens we carry
- Refuse isolation by creating spaces of relational belonging and answerability
- Reframe resilience as a shared, sustained act of resistance and renewal
- Cultivate agency by equipping ourselves and one another with tools to navigate, challenge, and transform institutional structures.

What we offer here is not a blueprint to replicate, but an invitation to reflect. We hope to shed light onto possibilities—ways of being, knowing, and learning that center healing, affirmation, and liberation in teaching and teacher education.

COMMUNITY CULTURAL HEALING THROUGH STORYTELLING: CONFRONTING COLORISM

We situate our work in *community cultural healing spaces*—affirming circles where educators come together to share stories, confront pain, and foster collective growth. In one such plática, we turned our focus to the often-taboo topic of colorism. To spark dialogue, we began by sharing a *reel*—a short-form video (like those on Instagram, TikTok, or YouTube)—that directly tackled colorism in communities of color. The reel we chose was a brief YouTube clip featuring people of diverse backgrounds speaking candidly about how skin-tone bias shaped their lives (from family preferences for lighter skin to experiences of being treated as "less than" for having darker complexions). This digital storytelling medium immediately grabbed everyone's attention: as the video voices described painful childhood memories and hard-earned self-acceptance, we witnessed knowing nods and deep sighs around the room. The reel became our mirror and provocation, prompting us to reflect on our own experiences.

After it ended, we posed the very questions it raised: **Do you see your experiences reflected in the experiences shared in this video? In what ways?** These questions hung in the air as we settled into a circle. What followed was an outpouring of **storytelling, reflection, and dialogue** that exemplified the healing potential of community cultural spaces.

Defining Colorism in Our Context

Before delving into our stories, we collectively defined *colorism* to ground our discussion. We affirmed that colorism is a form of **internalized racism** that privileges people with lighter skin over those with darker skin, operating both across and *within* communities of color (Webb, 2016). Unlike overt racism between different racial groups, colorism's insidious harm often occurs among people of the *same* community—for example, when a Black child is teased for having the darkest skin in the family, or when a Latina is told she'd be "prettier" if she were lighter. We acknowledged that this bias stems from the legacy of colonialism and White supremacy, yet it's reproduced in our own homes, schools, and media to this day. Naming this truth was important because too often colorism is **unspoken**—a source of pain carried in silence or shame. By putting a name to it, we set the stage for honest dialogue.

STORYTELLING AS HEALING

In our pláticas we embraced a first-person, relational approach: speaking *with* each other rather than at each other, and allowing vulnerability to guide us and storytelling to cultivate healing. What follows is a *composite* conversation (reconstructed here from our collective memories and notes).

A Composite Dialogue

We began tentatively, but soon the stories flowed with an urgency and trust built over years of solidarity. One of our colleagues, Rosie, a veteran early childhood teacher, broke the ice. "*Growing up,*" she said, "*I was always told by my mamá to stay out of the sun so I wouldn't get* ***más morena*** *(darker). At five years old, I already felt my brown skin was undesirable, problematic.*" Rosie's voice trembled as she described how, even now in her classroom, that past lingers: "*Just last month, a Latina mom at my school asked me if her daughter could wear a hat during recess 'so she doesn't get too dark.'*" A few of us gasped softly—the familiarity of that request hit home. Rosie shared how she gently educated that parent about embracing all skin tones, even as the exchange reopened her own childhood wounds. Her experience reverberated with each of us; this was not an isolated issue, but a situated representation of a broader phenomenon.

In **community healing space**, this kind of storytelling is not a mere recounting of events; it is an act of **bearing witness** to one another's truths, creating what Sara Lawrence-Lightfoot (1995) calls an "ancestral wisdom" circle across generations. In Rosie's story, we heard the echo of her mother's voice—itself shaped by elders before her—warning about skin tone as if it were fate. Such ancestral messages, passed down through generations, can harm or heal. By surfacing them, we start to **break their tacit hold**, transforming them into lessons for change.

Next, Amara, a kindergarten teacher, spoke up. "*In my family*," she said, "*I'm the darkest of three siblings. And it always felt like I had to prove I was 'good enough' because of it. My light-skinned brother . . . he was the one everyone called handsome.*" Amara paused, her eyes welling. "*I internalized that. For years, I avoided pictures and stayed quiet in class, thinking I should take up less space.*" A silence fell as we absorbed this. Many of us nodded—We knew that ache. Amara continued: "*Now here I am, making sure none of my students ever feel that way.*"

She described how in her classroom she intentionally celebrates each child's skin tone. Amara intentionally read aloud books like *Sulwe* (written by Lupita Nyong'o and illustrated by Vashti Harrison), talking about how it feels to have "skin the color of midnight" or "being darker than everyone in your family." As they read and discussed *Sulwe*, Amara shared how she felt when she was dubbed "Black Coal" when she was cast in the school play *Snow White* at age seven. "*It's still something I hide. It hurts. I don't want any of you to feel the hurt I felt and to question your beauty like I did.*" In sharing this, Amara illustrated how **storytelling and reflection translate into pedagogical action**. Her lived experience of colorism's pain fuels her commitment to an actively anticolorist practice in the classroom. We recognized this as part of our collective journey—turning **suffering into healing and action**. Indeed, educators of color often create "healing spaces within harmful institutions" (Farinde-Wu et al., 2025, p. 765), working to **transform suffering into healing** at personal and collective levels Amara's classroom had become one such space, and our plática was becoming another.

Elena, a teacher of Afro-Latinx heritage, chimed in next, offering a different vantage point. "*For me, colorism has two sides*," she said. "*I'm lighter-skinned—what my Dominican abuela would prize as* ***'trigueñita'****—and I know I've been given unearned advantage for it. But that came with its own confusion.*" She described how as a child she witnessed her darker cousins being scolded to "ponte crema" (put on skin-lightening cream) and how family members fawned over Elena's **"pelo bueno"** (good hair) because it was wavy, not "coily" like her sister's. "*It messed with my head*," Elena confessed. "*I loved my family, but I hated how they treated my sister. I started speaking up as a teenager—I'd tell my tía, 'Stop saying that! Her hair is good hair, just different.'*" In the circle, Elena admitted she still carries guilt that her lighter skin afforded her kindness that her loved ones were denied. "*As a teacher*," she continued, "*I'm super conscious not to play favorites with the lighter-skinned Latine kids in my class. And I teach my students words like colorism and prejudice early on—even at 8 years old, they get it.*" We felt the passion in her voice.

Elena's story underscored that **healing** is not only for those directly hurt by colorism's sting, but also for those who have benefited from its unjust hierarchy and seek to **interrupt it**. Her openness about unlearning bias modeled the kind of reflective practice we all strive for. It reminded us of Delgado Bernal's concept of *cultural intuition* (1998)—the idea that as people of color, we draw knowledge from deep wells of personal, familial, and communal experience. Elena was tapping into that intuition, using her *conciencia* (critical consciousness) to notice subtle biases in herself and her teaching, and to challenge them. In doing so, she was embracing what Delgado Bernal (1998) describes as an epistemology that is **experiential, collective, and dynamic,** informed by both the pain and the wisdom passed down to us.

As each story unfolded, a **pedagogy of storytelling** took shape. We weren't just talking *about* colorism in theory; we were laying bare how it lives within us and our practice. This process was deeply reflective and scholarly in its own right—we were, in essence, analyzing social conditioning and educational contexts through lived narratives. Yet it was also accessible and relational: We spoke in active, first-person voices, affirmed each other with "mm-hm" and "I feel you," and translanguaged without needing to translate for one another. Our plática was a living example of what it means to center *comunidad* in teacher education. It embodied *cultural intuition* because we saw how our collective stories generated insights no lecture or textbook could provide.

In sharing **testimonios**, we validated our experiential knowledge and spiritual/emotional truths in scholarly discourse. We drew on our *ancestral wisdom*, as Lawrence-Lightfoot (1995) described, that "powerful piece of our legacy" handed down through generations. Each of us, whether quoting a grandmother's saying or recounting a family ritual, was invoking the ancestors—sometimes to critique their colorist beliefs, sometimes to reclaim their strength. In this way, **storytelling became a form of healing:** We were, as a collective, reweaving the broken threads of identity that colorism had frayed in each of us.

Throughout, emotions ran high—tears, laughter, moments of silence where only breathing and the hum of the overhead lights could be heard. Yet, the vulnerability did not weaken us; it bound us closer. We experienced *truth-telling as healing* as we engaged in collective storytelling to confront the "epistemic violence" of a system that historically silenced us (Teacher of Color Collective & Souto-Manning, 2022). By **centering our voices** and listening deeply to each other, we were "naming our own realities" through counter-storytelling. We felt a sense of validation—*I am not alone in this; my pain is real, and it matters.* This relational affirmation and its connection to our current personal and professional lives is what made our healing space powerful. It transformed what we might have perceived as individual trauma into **collective catharsis**, and eventually, into collective **action**.

From Story to Pedagogical Transformation

Importantly, our conversation did not end with storytelling for its own sake. Story alone can heal, but story coupled with critical reflection can also inform practice. As we talked, we naturally began to **pivot to action**—asking: *So, what does this mean for us as educators, and what will we do differently?* The insights gleaned from our plática started to crystallize into pedagogical commitments. For example, one teacher planned a new lesson for her first graders using multicultural crayons and picture books like *Shades of Black* (written by Sandra L. Pinkney and photographed by Myles C. Pinkney) and *Skin Like Mine* (written by Latashia M. Perry and illustrated by Bea Jackson). *"I realized I've never directly addressed skin-tone diversity with my kids,"* she admitted. *"That changes now."*

A pre-K teacher decided she would invite families to a workshop on positive racial identity development, hoping to gently educate parents who might unintentionally pass on colorist beliefs. We discussed strategies for responding to colorist remarks in real time: one colleague shared a simple phrase she now uses when she hears a child say someone is "too dark" or "too light": *"There's no such thing. All our skin is just right!"* We laughed at the simplicity of it, but recognized that for a young child, such clear affirmation from a teacher can be powerful, and what children would likely not notice is how teachers would be healing themselves at the same time with such practices.

FROM STORY TO SYSTEMIC CHANGE: REIMAGINING TEACHER EDUCATION VIA COLLECTIVE HEALING

Our plática on colorism did not end when the stories did. As the dialogue deepened, we found ourselves reflecting not only on our lived experiences, but also on the systems that failed to name, address, or disrupt the intra-community oppressions we'd long carried in silence. In particular, we turned our attention to teacher education—our own preparation, the programs we now lead and teach in, and the structural gaps we continue to witness. The absence of critical conversations about colorism in our formal training became glaring. As one of us asked aloud, *"If we hadn't created this space for ourselves, would we ever have had these conversations?"* That question lingered—both as a lament and as a call to action.

In response, we coconstructed a set of commitments—recommendations not born from policy mandates or institutional checklists, but from our shared knowing, cultural intuition, and yearning for justice. We agreed: **Teacher education must make room for community cultural knowledge and healing practices.** That means integrating pláticas—relational, reciprocal dialogue spaces—into preservice and in-service professional learning, moving beyond superficial conversations about "diversity" and addressing intra-community dynamics like colorism and internalized oppression as core curriculum, and using multimodal tools—like the reel that launched our discussion—as meaningful resources that speak to the lived realities of communities of color.

We envisioned more expansive teacher learning ecologies (Teacher of Color Collective & Souto-Manning, 2022) where healing and justice are treated not as competing priorities but as intertwined necessities. In short, we argued for a reorientation of teacher education—one that centers humanity, not just compliance. This vision resonates in relational, coconstructed environments where educators and scholars of color come together across roles and institutions to disrupt hierarchical, top-down knowledge structures (Souto-Manning & Martell, 2019). Our plática lived outside the constraints of formal PD (professional development) and deliberately flattened power so that each voice carried wisdom. The result was more than emotional restoration—it was the emergence of a **blueprint for systemic change** grounded in the real, everyday truths of educators of color.

By the end of our session, we felt a shift in the air. A sense of gravity remained—after all, these were not easy stories to tell—but it was mingled with clarity and resolve. We closed with the question, *¿Qué vamos a hacer?*—What are we going to do? This return to the collective "we" was not rhetorical. It was an affirmation of agency. Together, we committed to continue these pláticas as an ongoing practice. Healing from racism and colorism is not a one-time event; it is an ongoing, relational, and transformative process.

We also made concrete plans. Some of us began coplanning lessons to engage children in early grades around skin tone, fairness, and self-love. Others developed materials for parent workshops, offering caregivers gentle and culturally grounded ways to talk with children about identity. A few committed to leading faculty discussions at their schools and universities, ensuring that these conversations ripple outward. In doing so, we were connecting the micro-level (our classrooms, our teams) to the macro-level (our institutions, our field), practicing what we believe: that **healing and justice must grow in tandem.**

Transformation in teacher education must begin by centering the voices and lived knowledge of those historically marginalized by the field (Teacher of Color Collective & Souto-Manning, 2022). In our plática, we centered those voices—our voices—and found within them the seeds of a more just educational future. We know that colorism is not just personal; it is structural. And so, our stories were not just catharsis—they were theory, resistance, and strategy.

A PATHWAY TO HEALING TEACHER EDUCATION

From this experience, we offer a simple but radical truth: Community cultural healing spaces are not ancillary to teacher development—they are essential and indeed provide the very model for the fabric of a system that is to heal and sustain the humans inside of it. As Paulo Freire taught us, a mechanistic education is no education at all. For us, the creation of a community cultural healing space was an act of **fugitivity** (Stovall & Mosely, 2022), born from the knowledge that existing systems were not built for our thriving. But for the next generation of educators, this need not be the case. Healing is not only needed, it is also possible. And imagining a nonhierarchical model of teacher education does not mean eliminating guidance or structure. It means reimagining the *praxis* of teaching and learning as reciprocal, relational, and rooted in shared humanity.

We dream of teacher education spaces where reciprocal learning and intergenerational knowledge-sharing are the norm. Where experienced educators and emerging scholars uplift one another, validate struggle, and coconstruct meaningful responses to injustice. Where courses, field experiences, and everyday pedagogical choices are not shaped by hierarchy but by the collective wisdom of communities in motion. We envision a teacher education that affirms that every participant—regardless of title or experience—has something vital to contribute. We call on teacher education leaders to consider the following starting ideas, not as a recipe or checklist, but as initial signals of their acceptance of our challenge to grow in justice.

Storytelling, Collective Meaning-Making, and Lived Experiences as Scholarship

Storytelling is foundational to learning within counter-spaces. Through counter-narratives and testimonios, educators validate their lived experiences, dismantle deficit-based narratives, and reframe their challenges as systemic rather than personal. Research affirms that educators who engage in storytelling within affinity spaces experience greater professional self-efficacy, solidarity, and healing.

Wellness Practices and Emotional Renewal

Teaching has always been deeply emotional work, especially so for those with racialized or otherwise marginalized identities. Leaders must make generous, non-negotiable space for ongoing wellness practices such as:

- Mindfulness and restorative practices that foster self-preservation in emotionally taxing environments
- Rituals of care, such as affirmations, meditation, and embodied practices, to sustain emotional well-being and prevent burnout
- Critical emotional literacy to help educators recognize and navigate the racialized emotional landscapes of teaching.

Community-Building and Collective Care

Teacher education modeled on cultural counter-spaces should cultivate cross-institutional and intergenerational professional networks and promote practices such as:

- Mentorship structures that extend beyond traditional hierarchies, fostering sustained professional development and leadership opportunities
- Accountability partnerships to reinforce career advancement, pedagogical innovation, and institutional advocacy
- Opportunities for joy, reminding educators that their work is not solely defined by struggle but also by celebration, creativity, and affirmation.

Action-Oriented Reflection and Professional Agency

Based on the model of pláticas, the discourses we create within teacher education are not just places to process emotions—they become linked to strategic action, including:

- Advocacy and policy engagements to disrupt inequitable structures
- Reclaiming pedagogical autonomy, enabling educators to center culturally sustaining teaching practices
- Developing tools and strategies that challenge systemic barriers and promote long-term change.

This is not a utopian vision—it is a reclaiming. Honoring the knowledge of our ancestors, communities, and selves, we recognize the journey of becoming an educator as one of cultural healing, intellectual sovereignty, and intergenerational continuity. We teach these values in our progressive education courses, weaving them into syllabi and classroom conversations. But this work must move beyond the syllabus. It is time to live what we teach—not just for the benefit of our students, but for our teachers. We must begin the path of healing the split between what we say and what we do, between what we know and what we honor.

CONCLUSION

In naming colorism, engaging in plática, and building from story to strategy, we are not simply reflecting—we are reimagining. And in doing so, we affirm what we have long known: That collective healing is not just personal restoration, it is professional transformation. That love, truth-telling, and solidarity are not "soft skills"—they are essential tools of justice. And that, together, we are not just surviving educational spaces—we are reshaping them.

REFERENCES

Delgado Bernal, D. (1998). Using a Chicana feminist epistemology in educational research. *Harvard Educational Review, 68*(4), 555–582.

Delgado Bernal, D., Flores, A., Gaxiola Serrano, T., & Morales, S. (2023). An introduction: Chicana/Latina feminista pláticas in educational research. *International Journal of Qualitative Studies in Education, 36*(9), 1627–1630. https://doi.org/10.1080/09518398.2023.2203113

Farinde-Wu, A., Alvarez, A., & Kunimoto, N. (2025). Teach like a Black woman: A trauma-informed Black feminist praxis. *Urban Education, 60*(3), 761–791. https://doi.org/10.1177/0042085923117566

Fierros, C., & Delgado Bernal, D. (2016). Vamos a platicar: The contours of pláticas as Chicana/Latina feminist methodology. *Chicana/Latina Studies, 15*(2), 98–121. http://www.jstor.org/stable/43941617

Kohli, R., Pizarro, M., & Nevárez, A. (2017). The "new racism" of K–12 schools: Centering critical research on racism. *Review of Research in Education, 41*(1), 182–202. https://doi.org/10.3102/0091732X16686949

Lawrence-Lightfoot, S. (1995). *I've known rivers: Lives of loss and liberation.* Penguin.

Padilla, A. (1994). Ethnic minority scholars. research, and mentoring: Current and future issues. *Educational Researcher, 23*(4), 24–27. https://www.jstor.org/stable/1176259

Smith, W. (2004). Black faculty coping with racial battle fatigue: The campus racial climate and the academic experience. In D. Cleveland (Ed.), *A long way to go: Conversations about race by African American faculty and graduate students* (pp.171–190). Peter Lang Publishers.

Solórzano, D., & Villalpando, O. (1998). Critical race theory, marginality, and the experience of students of color in higher education. In C. A. Torres & T. R. Mitchell (Eds.), *Sociology of education: Emerging perpectives* (pp. 211–222). State University of New York Press.

Souto-Manning, M., & Martell, J. (2019). Toward critically transformative possibilities: Considering tensions and undoing inequities in the spatialization of teacher education. *Teachers College Record*, *121*(6), 1–42. https://doi.org/10.1177/01614681191 2100603

Souto-Manning, M., & Rabadi-Raol, A. (2018). (Re)Centering quality in early childhood education: Toward intersectional justice for minoritized children. *Review of Research in Education*, *42*, 203–225. https://doi.org/10.3102/0091732X18759550

Stovall, J., & Mosely, M. (2023). "We just do us": How Black teachers co-construct Black teacher fugitive space in the face of anti-Blackness. *Race Ethnicity and Education*, *26*(3), 298–317. https://doi.org/10.1080/13613324.2022.2122424

Teacher of Color Collective, & Souto-Manning, M. (2022). On the mis-education of teachers of color: A letter to teacher educators. *Journal of Teacher Education*, *73*(1), 66–80. https://doi.org/10.1177/00224871211057487

Webb, S. (2016, January 25). Recognizing and addressing colorism in schools. *Learning for Justice*. https://www.learningforjustice.org/magazine/recognizing-and-addressing-colo rism-in-schools

CHAPTER 7

Black Educators Healing Together

The Power of Homeplace

Micia Mosely

WHAT DO BLACK TEACHERS NEED HEALING FROM?

Education in this country was founded to support capitalism by separating people into owners, managers, and workers. Thus, the very nature of public education is dehumanizing, creating harm for all of us that requires healing. Black people specifically have been harmed in this country since its inception, and this intergenerational pain doesn't go away with temporary legislation or promotions up the ladder in systems built on the same principles that created this harm in the first place.

Black people have been taught that our history begins with enslavement. As Black folks who chose to reenter institutions that were designed to rob us of our history, culture, and humanity, Black educators can expect to be harmed as part of our professional experience. For example, many programs that prepare teachers to work in urban (read Black) schools don't teach about the legacy of Black education (King, 2019; Logan et al., 2018). The first universities were in Africa, but timelines often begin with the United States and Horace Mann. Schools often don't acknowledge the reading and writing of African languages, including hieroglyphics, that preceded enslavement. When our ancestors were enslaved, they were not allowed to learn to read and write English, leading to generations of illiteracy and providing spurious "evidence" to the eugenics movement that continues to affect education policy today.

Once we were "allowed" to have our own schools, they were under-resourced and policed to ensure that pro-White, anti-Black propaganda was being taught. Even under these conditions many Black people were able to learn and work toward liberation. As educated Black leaders fought for resources, they found themselves still working within a harmful paradigm. Black people are often seen as the only people responsible for the education of Black children even if people of other races are the paid teachers. At the same time, we are seen as being perpetually in service of non-Black people, including serving their desire to avoid dealing with "those Black kids." In short, it is always the Black adults who are treated as "the help" but not the professionals, regardless of the identities of those being served.

While there are pockets of powerful work happening in terms of culturally responsive teaching, overall, our education and teacher preparation systems are still mired in the same problematic mindsets. On the one hand, colleges of education are recognizing that they are not adequately preparing teachers to work beneficially in our diverse and changing society, but on the other hand, they continue to situate their reform efforts inside of a deficit model where Black and Brown children are underperforming and are not seen as having the skills of their White and Asian counterparts (Gardner-Neblett et al., 2023).

Teacher preparation programs largely also reflect the racial demographics of the U.S. teaching force; that is, many White people preparing many White women to teach increasing numbers of Black and Brown children. As a result, the critical lens of examining anti-Blackness of White dominant culture is often unattended to. This leaves many educators of color and Black educators in particular feeling unseen and without their needs met. Many Black preservice teachers experience anti-Blackness in their preparation and will find in the future that they experience it in their time in the classroom too. By not addressing anti-Blackness as early as possible in the teacher pipeline, we do a disservice to all teachers such that they are not able to critically evaluate the root causes of systemic inequities.

Another harm that needs healing for Black teachers manifests in the interpersonal relationships between adults across race. Too often Black teacher preparation candidates find themselves in programs that emphasize the importance of diversity while experiencing racist behaviors by students and professors alike. Professors are typically ill-equipped to address these actions and thus often do nothing in response. This does not allow teacher candidates to learn how to identify and interrupt anti-Blackness in themselves, their colleagues, and their students. This is the responsibility of all educators who are working within an inherently anti-Black system. As we consider what needs to be healed, we must understand the harm of anti-Blackness for all.

THE BLACK TEACHER PROJECT

The Black Teacher Project was born out of my desire to address anti-Blackness in my own life and in educational communities. I was bussed to predominately White schools in the 1970s and 1980s where I felt the sting of anti-Blackness when teachers questioned my intelligence even as I sat in gifted and talented classes. While high school offered the relief of a large Black academically excellent community, I found myself back in the throes of anti-Blackness in college when an education professor questioned whether I would make a good teacher in the Boston area given the number of White students. I often wondered if that professor would have had the same questions had *he* been taught by a Black teacher.

I founded the Black Teacher Project (BTP) to address the factors that push Black teachers out of the classroom including internalized, interpersonal, and systemic racism. I reconnected with a former student/current Black teacher who was considering leaving the field due to anti-Blackness. BTP supports Black teachers by providing racial affinity-based professional development, addressing the policies and practices in their environments that lead to pushout, and shifting the narrative about Black teachers. In the remainder of this chapter, I will describe practices that can be implemented in your own settings to support Black teachers and address anti-Blackness in schools. This work is about healing teachers and creating an experience of "homeplace" (Love, 2019) where they and their students can thrive.

Pathways to Healing: Tenets of Our Model

My colleagues and I at the BTP believe that healing is part of our professional practice. Our work in PK–12 systems is not limited to a mechanical transmission of information from adults to young people. We aspire to provide a model for the full education pipeline in which the subject matter is teaching people how to live in community, be fully human, and cocreate a world that works for everyone. We speak about self and community care to move away from the individualism of western culture and toward kinship and responsibility to the village. We uphold that self and community care are not only reasonable to include in the curriculum but further, that the entire educational enterprise is illegitimate without them.

The following are some of the key principles we employ for authentic implementation of healing-centered education that starts with the adults. They have been inspired by several theoretical frameworks including Liberatory Design (National Equity Project, 2024), the Bridge to Thriving Framework (Darling-Hammond & Evans-Santiago, 2024), and Healing-Centered Engagement (Ginwright, 2015; 2022).

- **Centering Black history and education for liberation.** Black teachers across the country are still being threatened with dismissal if they share the truth of how Black people have been harmed and have worked to heal from it. But we root ourselves in the histories of Black educators who have tied knowledge, critical thinking, and skill-building to the upliftment and progress of Black people, and as a result, of this country overall. This foundation reclaims and reveals our empowered legacy of education as liberation and undercuts false narratives being told about the "achievement gap." In turn, Black educators can focus more on pride and building upon their ancestral legacy versus the typical messages of having to work "around" or "despite" it.

- **Love is the curriculum.** Countless Black Educators have discussed the importance of love being at the center of teaching and learning. While Black educators have always known that love is an essential component of learning, it is not part of most if any state standards. While this is gradually changing, even the zeitgeist of social and emotional learning (SEL) is well-known to be rooted more in "behavior" and "responsible decision-making" than nurturance and love. As such, Black teachers are forced to weave their love- and healing-centered work into their practice "on the down-low," without drawing attention that would bring critique. In the BTP model, we seek to bring this work out of the shadows and help build the understanding that learning and love are inseparable domains.
- **Fugitivity as healing.** Just because Black educators understand the centrality of love in learning does not mean that we accept mistreatment without a response. *Fugitivity*, far different from the dictionary definition of "escape," instead reflects active practices of resistance and refusal (Gross-Wyrtzen & Moulton, 2023), which have been a necessary tool in the toolbox of Black educators since time immemorial. State control is nothing new to us, and part of healing Black teachers is to affirm and support their ability to resist. In his book, *Fugitive Pedagogy* (2021), Jarvis Givens describes this process in terms of how Black teachers create "an interior world within their veiled existence . . . even as they engage[d] in various practices of acquiescing to the mainstream social order" (pg.14). In other words, we have always balanced surviving and thriving, managing what is while fighting for what should be, and the BTP model honors and builds on this tradition.
- **Bringing our full selves.** Another one of the Black Teacher Project's pillars is what we call "Leadership for Black Liberation." Leadership is about taking responsibility for what matters to you (Weissglass, 1998). Being whole human beings, not just bodies producing labor, matters to Black teachers. So many Black teachers are dancers, yoga instructors, poets, musicians, etc., and these gifts too should not be forced into the shadows or thought of as separate from education. We want people to be fully self-expressed and have an opportunity to bring their knowledge, talents, and passions to their colleagues. Thus, all of our offerings involve Black classroom teachers leading wellness and creativity practices.
- **Hospitality and tangible resources.** Helping teachers to feel physically nourished and comfortable, thought about and planned for, and compensated for their labor is not optional; it creates the necessary container for Black teachers to shine. As an organization, we take the curation of these spaces very seriously and depending on modality (e.g., online or in person), we provide various types of tangible resources to make the work we are asking for more possible including compensation/stipends, hot meals, and child care. In addition, many of our events include services and enjoyable activities that are not necessarily a direct

"exchange" for their work, such as wellness services (e.g., chair massage, African drumming, dancing); presentations or panels from speakers, elder teachers, and storytellers; homebuying workshops; nature retreats, etc. Through this thoughtful, hospitable experience curation, we aim to send a message of valuing Black teachers' humanity and creating a model for education systems to follow. In the next section, I describe some example practices the Black Teacher Project has offered to embody these principles, at a more concrete level, including how we structure the flow of activities.

"I See You": A Word on Virtual Healing Spaces

The copandemics of 2020—COVID-19 and the live capturing of state violence against Black people—caused global reckonings around both mental health and the ongoing impact of racism. It also affirmed teaching and learning to be about physical, social, and mental health just as much as academic subjects. This confluence of events facilitated making the case for why the social–emotional health of Black teachers and their students was a matter of concern for everyone. At BTP we asked members who led in-person wellness programs to develop online offerings using the techniques they were already employing with their students. This allowed Black teachers across the globe to access healing in the form of our offerings.

At BTP, our experiences with online learning with Black teachers led to several lessons learned. For example, hospitality can still be exemplified during online learning. We played music during participants' arrival into the digital room, which reduces awkwardness and sets the tone. The chat function allows everyone, rather than just a few, to share their intention-setting for the day, and undoubtedly opens up new ways of participating for folks who don't like to speak in groups. Similarly, the physical practices we shared such as Kemetic yoga, Zumba, and African dance could be practiced with the option of turning cameras off or out of the screen's range, allowing folks more options to deal with potential shyness or reticence than in person. While small group breakouts are possible both in person and virtually, online they are more private from others and are often not attended or visited by the facilitators, allowing for a different sort of intimacy with peers. Finally, the convenience and lack of travel expenses meant that we could cast a much wider net not only for participants, but also guest speakers and facilitators. For example, in our online "Liberation Labs," former educational leaders in the Black Panther Party shared their experiences and lessons for current Black teachers. In our "Black Teacher Design Lab," a multi-session, virtual course for teams of two to four Black educators, participants codesigned healing-centered engagements specific to students' needs and also received coaching in between sessions. Coaching is also a more attainable enhancement in an online environment. In short, we encourage others on a healing journey with teachers to focus on the unique advantages and new options provided by online learning settings.

"I Feel You": In Person Wellness Convenings

Black Teacher Wellness Sessions and Convenings immerse Black teachers in a cocoon of Black love where participants connect to ancestral wisdom and their humanity as Black educators and leaders. At BTP we primarily offer short-term experiences, typically 1–4 hours on a single day, or 1–2 day-long intensives. By trying on mindsets and practices that cultivate and enrich their thriving inside and outside of schools, participants build capacity for continuing Black educators' legacy of taking action toward a liberated future. Aspirationally, these experiences should ultimately reflect what their whole teaching career is like, but until that time, we have seen that these salient "tastes" can ignite (or reignite) their energy and pride in their profession and ancestry, reconnect them with their passions for education, find community with like-minded individuals, and continue to inject thriving into their surviving.

Examples of Half-Day Experiences

- **Black Teacher Love Day.** At this event we created an all-Black affinity space where folks got to know a community of Black educators and engage in healing of the mind and body. The agenda for our time together included a visualization exercise that combined mindfulness and visual arts, meditation, energy healing that involved working with chakras, movement, and trap yoga, a form of yoga that combines asana practice with trap-style hip-hop.
- **Partner Event with Outdoor Afro.** This gentle hike was designed as an opportunity to integrate mindfulness, yoga, and nature. Participants took some time to restore, set intentions, and connect with nature. The whole hike and yoga session took about 2 hours. There were parts of the hike where we honored the silence and engaged deeply with ourselves and our natural surroundings. The yoga portion was led by a yoga teacher who made connections to Black history, teaching, and learning from nature. She also ensured the class was accessible to all levels of physical ability.
- **Self-Care in the Age of Assault on Black People.** Teaching while Black can be challenging, especially with increased attention on the murders of Black people in the United States. This experience was designed in 2017 to meet the sociopolitical moment where the murders of Black people were overwhelming the news and impacting teaching and learning. Sadly, this theme remains relevant today. Teachers walked away with practical tools they could use to sustain themselves during those intense times including identifying what burns them out and how they can care for themselves.
- **Elder Wisdom.** What do our Black teacher elders have to say about these times? BTP hosted conversations with veteran Black teachers who have stories and wisdom to share. This was an all-Black, multigenerational

space. We offered fellowship, dinner, a short discussion panel, and small group engagement to wrap it all up.

- **Drop It Like It's Hot.** Making time for lesson planning and grading, and completing graduate work can be one of the hardest parts of being a new teacher. Folks joined us for "open house" sessions on Saturdays to get things done! The Drop It Like It's Hot Center was a peer support space with plenty of electrical outlets, pens, and quiet spaces so folks could focus and find help if they needed it. We also had a local Black educator offer a homebuying workshop for those who were interested. This event sought to deeply connect to wellness by offering: time and material support to complete "invisible" work they would be doing anyway; free childcare from licensed and skilled educators; and free chair massages from local massage school students needing to complete practice hours. Finally, I made waffles to order using my grandmother's recipe. They were delicious if I do say so myself! This led to swapping stories about recipes that were passed down, including measurements like a "lil' bit" and "tinse." Rather than spending money in a cafe or isolating oneself at home, this "workspace" turned "homeplace" allowed teachers to be well while doing that often invisible weekend labor with other educators.

A Typical 1–2 Day Intensive Schedule. The intensives allow us a bit of breathing room to be able to combine more conventional professional development content (e.g., inclusion of theoretical models, introduction to the scholarship and evidence behind the wellness practices we focus on) along with the embodied and creative engagements that form the core of our identity as a program.

- ***Morning and/or Day One.*** The day begins with a nourishing breakfast (hot food). After greeting and registration, we begin with a libation ceremony (a ritual of pouring water to honor ancestors), acknowledging that we are part of a legacy of Black educators. Next, we create intentional opportunities for participants to connect with one another such as table conversations.

  We then explore one of the core frameworks mentioned above to ground us in the "why and how" of healing-centered education. A local guest speaker will root the frameworks in scholarship as well as real-life stories about Black wellness. Storytelling is a long-standing practice in Black culture. The *griot* bases the delivery of information in the telling of tales, personalization, drama, or comedy. In short, our speakers know they must "bring it" when they come to be in front of our all-Black audience. Participants engage in writing, talking, and embodied practices to make connections to their personal and professional lives. At times we require practices to calm the nervous system when a speaker has talked about the harms we are healing from. At other times, we focus on joy and thriving.

- *Afternoon and/or Day Two.* After a healthy and tasty lunch or a restful night we return with regrounding in the space and with each other. These activities often involve stretching, affirmations, and fun and light warm-ups. We then create spaces for teacher leaders to facilitate practices. This is organized into smaller breakouts with one to three rounds of 60–90-minute sessions that participants rotate through. Examples of teacher-led wellness sessions have included writing, African dance, drumming, self-love, and yoga. We then come back together to end the day as a whole group. We create space for participants to reflect and consider how they will take what they experienced back to their professional spaces. We often take a picture and provide folks with something physical to remind them of our time together (pens, affirmation cards, etc.)

Examples of Impact

We have seen the power of homeplace that teachers find within BTP both in real time inside the sessions, as well as often hearing about lasting impact on practice. For example, a fifth-grade teacher and her students codesigned a daily practice of affirmations including both behavioral language such as "you are kind" and academic language such as "you are a good reader." Over the course of the year, reading scores increased for this class. One day the teacher was having a bad morning and forgot to lead the practice, but the students reminded her, showering her with affirmations of being a good teacher who cares about them. She was able to create a homeplace for herself and her students where everyone was held accountable to the goal of wellness and healing.

Another teacher codesigned a wellness center with her students, starting small with the repurposing of an existing room and drop-in sessions during lunch. Due to the popularity of the center, the school received a grant to refurbish a larger space and hire a part-time staff member to provide services (counseling, meditation, yoga, etc.). This is just one example of many demonstrating how even a brief experience reconnecting Black teachers with their own humanity can have reverberation effects, creating healing homeplace experiences through spaces and generations.

Our shorter-term experiences have demonstrated impact as well. For example, one of the teachers who attended our yoga classes was inspired to learn more and decided to get her certification. She now incorporates yoga in her classes with formerly incarcerated youth. She notes the importance of including movement as a form of releasing trauma to help her students focus. Another teacher who attended our drop-in space was able to learn more about which administrative credentialing programs were more welcoming to Black teachers. He is currently an assistant principal and has used many of the BTP practices to lead healing groups with students. He said that he didn't want to be the stereotypical Black male "enforcer" dean who ran around punishing young people. It is clear that BTP attracts educators who want to conduct business differently, and it is also clear that from BTP, these educators receive ample inspiration and the soul-nourishment they need to enact the next steps their communities require.

WHERE DO WE GO FROM HERE?

When Black teachers are engaged in healing it pushes against oppressive structures in schools, forces liberatory spaces to be created, and demonstrates that learning and love are inextricably linked. Black teachers on a healing journey make schools safer for students and allow them to learn in ways they can be free. BTP members understand that their work is necessary even in environments that are not hospitable to this work, so that when inevitable misalignments occur, they can look past the moment to a greater context. We support this by helping them learn the history of Black education and Black teachers. While the work of creating healed education systems does not rest solely on the shoulders of teachers, staying rooted in the history reminds teachers that they are the owners of their personal wellness, and that they deserve to be fortified in their profession to be able to flow with changes in the times, institutions, and leadership.

What could it look like if the education system learned these lessons from BTP, and removed some of the burden from Black teachers to create healed people and spaces? A healed system would encourage rather than punish any historical truths being told. It would create learning environments that demand rigor not only in mastery of academics, but in human-centered skills (e.g., How are you taking care of yourself and each other? How are you taking action for everyone to succeed?). The system would demand alignment between what is expected from the graduates of it and what is happening while they are *in* it.

As of now, we expect teachers to engage in pedagogical practices they do not see or experience in their preparation. We must prepare teachers to engage in wellness as part of their professional practice. When administrators are assessing teachers, academic and cultural priorities should be given equal weight and support. While teacher evaluation systems do include relational aspects, teachers, especially Black teachers, know that when it comes to the real world, these issues are often tokenized, moved to the back burner, cordoned off to the "SEL block," or pushed to the school social worker. The entire school culture must be a homeplace, otherwise education rings hollow. Bonding, celebration, joy, and nourishment create healing by connecting people back to their own humanity—their literal "aliveness."

CONCLUSION

Much of today's focus on teacher diversity is limited to hiring and retaining Black teachers. We must move beyond the utilization of Black bodies and tend to the *experience*. For example, a key retention practice includes providing Black teachers with leadership opportunities. In one district a number of Black teachers were included on the hiring committee. Unfortunately, their recommendations were rarely listened to. Healing is not just about a seat at the table, it's about power. These kinds of performative "inclusion" initiatives for Black educators are more the rule than the exception. Systems must learn how to listen to Black teachers and embed responsive supports in schools. Providing spaces for teachers to reflect on how their identity is connected to their practice can help. Moving beyond affinity to create spaces of homeplace involves a deeper understanding of how you take what is gained from an affinity space and shift the larger environment. Black teachers come with so many gifts and talents that go beyond their technical expertise as teachers. System leaders should seek to engage the fullness of what they have to offer, not from an extractive lens, but from an integrative perspective, bringing their authentic selves, creating true belonging, and engendering an altogether more humane culture.

A homeplace education system vision, like the one we offer at BTP, creates an opportunity to experience joy and connection while teaching and learning. As we consider how to create educational ecosystems where everyone can thrive, we must tell the truth about anti-Blackness and engage in structures and practices that promote healing so that we can get to our best version of teaching and learning. As Toni Morrison states, "The function, the very serious function of racism is distraction. It keeps you from doing your work. It keeps you explaining, over and over again, your reason for being." Black teachers are caught in this loop of explanation. As Kia Darling Hammond's Thriving Framework emphasizes, our goal is to just be.

REFERENCES

Darling-Hammond, K. & Evans-Santiago, B. (Eds.). (2024). *T* is for thriving: Blueprints for affirming trans* and gender creative lives and learning in schools.* Stylus Publishing, LLC.

Gardner-Neblett, N., Iruka, I. U., & Humphries, M. (2023). Dismantling the Black–White achievement gap paradigm: Why and how we need to focus instead on systemic change. *Journal of Education, 203*(2), 433–441. https://doi.org/10.1177/00220574211031958

Ginwright, S. (2015). *Hope and healing in urban education: How urban activists and teachers are reclaiming matters of the heart.* Routledge.

Ginwright, S. A. (2022). *The four pivots: Reimagining justice, reimagining ourselves.* North Atlantic Books.

Givens, J. R. (2021). *Fugitive pedagogy: Carter G. Woodson and the art of Black teaching.* Harvard University Press.

Gross-Wyrtzen, L., & Moulton, A. A. (2023). Toward "fugitivity as method": An introduction to the special issue. *ACME, 22*(5), 1258–1272. https://doi.org/10.14288/acme.v22i5.2337

King, L. J. (2019). Interpreting Black history: Toward a Black history framework for teacher education. *Urban Education, 54*(3), 368–396. https://doi.org/10.1177/0042085918756716

Logan, S. R., Hilton, A. A., Watson, D. C., & Kirkland-Holmes, G. (2018). African American history and culture: What White teachers should know. *Educational Foundations*, *31*, 7–26. EJ1211883

Love, B. L. (2019). *We want to do more than survive: Abolitionist teaching and the pursuit of educational freedom*. Beacon Press.

National Equity Project (2024). *Introduction to liberatory design*. https://www.nationalequityproject.org/frameworks/liberatory-design

Weissglass, J. (1998). *Ripples of hope: Building relationships for educational change*. University of California Center for Educational Change in Mathematics and Science.

CHAPTER 8

Who Cares for the Carers?

A Holistic Approach to Teacher Well-Being in a Tribal Head Start Context

Hilary Gourneau, Teresa N. Brockie, and Deborah H. Wilson

> "We are a silent voice sometimes, and it's not too healthy. You know? Kind of like we're on the frontlines. In order to be a fruitful person, in order to be on the frontline with other people, you got to take care of your own self."
>
> —Head Start teacher from Fort Peck Native American Reservation, Montana, USA

Often, our focus when investigating the stress and well-being of teachers is how it affects the students they teach. A teacher's levels of stress, depression, and well-being affect the socioemotional and academic development of the children they teach (Herman et al., 2017), not to mention that students can carry physical, mental, social, or learning challenges that teachers are ill-supported in handling (Sun et al., 2024). Nevertheless, as pointed out in this book as well as our prior work, far less time and fewer resources have been spent on valuing teachers as individuals who themselves need psychological support and resources to optimize their health and well-being (Dreer, 2023; Wilson et al., 2022). When working as researchers with a Tribal Head Start program, we became interested in the well-being of teachers as their human right rather than as a means to an end.

POSITIONALITY OF THE AUTHORS

Research at the Fort Peck Tribal Head Start program began with Dr. Teresa N. Brockie, an Indigenous nurse researcher and professor whose work focuses on community-based prevention and intervention around suicide, trauma, and adverse childhood experiences among Indigenous communities. Dr. Brockie is a member of the A'aninin Nation from the Fort Belknap Reservation, Montana, and has developed strong research-practice partnerships with the Fort Belknap and Fort Peck Reservation communities. In collaboration with Tribal members on the Fort Peck Reservation she codesigned an intervention called Wakȟáŋyeža (Little Holy One; Brockie et al., 2021). Little Holy One aims to instill traditional values in children to prevent adolescent suicide and substance use and teach parents and caregivers positive parenting practices and methods for coping with trauma and stress.

Hilary Gourneau is a member of the Fort Peck Assiniboine and Sioux Tribes and is the Head Start Director. Her expertise is in counselor education and trauma-informed services. Ms. Gourneau started her position in July 2020, finding herself in uncharted waters during a global pandemic. This only intensified her drive to advocate and provide services to Tribal Head Start students, families, and teachers.

Dr. Debbie Wilson is a White European nurse who worked with Dr. Brockie while completing her doctoral work. Dr. Wilson noticed unmet needs regarding the health and well-being of the Tribal Head Start teachers. This began discussions that resulted in the decision to adapt the Little Holy One program for the well-being of the Fort Peck Head Start teachers.

THE PILOT RESEARCH STUDY

All phases of the research study were completed with ethics approval from the university, Tribal council ethics boards, and Head Start administration, with community involvement and feedback throughout the entire project development and implementation process.

The Need

"When we'd go into our meetings every week, you could see teachers struggling because we lost a lot of people [during COVID]. And how we deal with it—well—you could just see that we need more support now." —Tribal Head Start teacher

"The school counselors were White and did not live in the area, and so they weren't familiar and accustomed to our culture. And just like the spirituality of the culture but also the poverty and the violence that happened and the traumas that took place. And so . . . you just didn't really visit the school counselor." —Tribal Head Start Supervisor

The first quote underscores that these Tribal Head Start teachers were interested in and in need of support even more after COVID-19, while the second quote illustrates how the pre-existing model of school counseling was not culturally sustaining, and thus the community simply couldn't make use of it. This fits the growing awareness that the western paradigm of treating mental illness is not the worldview of Native American or Indigenous peoples. Interventions need to consider Native American worldviews and the damages done due to colonization if they are to foster healing and well-being (Blume, 2020; Gone, 2023).

Consistent with the Head Start model, having teachers and students from the same cultural background comes with enormous advantages, but it also means that both community strengths *and* challenges will be shared. Our interviews identified that these teachers were living with immense stress and trauma within themselves, their family, and community, and that these needs become neglected as their attention is focused on the children they teach or their family. This potentially compounds existing historical traumas stemming from the systematic colonization practices of the U.S. government (e.g., genocide, boarding schools, forced relocation to reservations) that have been documented extensively elsewhere (Brave Heart & DeBruyn, 1998; Brockie et al., 2015). On the other hand, interviews also revealed a people and community steeped in rich cultural and community strengths.

The Choice to Highlight Native Culture

"I think being a strong, resilient teacher is, living in the community that we live in, that through [our native] language and culture, that it saves families. Living the cultural way of life protects from the negative world, the drugs and alcohol or a toxic spouse. I think it helps them. It changes them into a better person. Of course, I don't want to push that onto a teacher that maybe isn't familiar with our cultural and traditional ways and language learning. But I think that, if we were able to incorporate that somehow in a teacher's life and show them that there is something better. You are worthy. You are worth it." —Head Start volunteer and mother

In this quote, a Head Start volunteer, mother, and cultural advisor was asked what a strong, resilient teacher looks like. Her recognition that reconnecting Indigenous peoples to their tradition and culture may be deeply healing, strengthening, and empowering comports with data showing Native peoples prefer culturally informed care that respects Native perspectives on health and well-being (Gone, 2023). Further, she was cognizant that many of her people have embraced the Christian faith taught by missionaries and thus it is a delicate process in which traditional practices are not to be imposed. This highlighted the context in which we would be working. We would need to gently work with the teachers since our choice to implement cultural lessons may trigger adults who potentially struggle with shame or resistance at not being so familiar with their Native cultural practices and beliefs.

The Findings

We engaged with our Tribal Advisory Board to adapt five lessons (see Table 8.1) from the Little Holy One curriculum to suit the teacher context using the findings obtained during the interviews and focus groups. Further details of the adaptation and implementation process are published elsewhere (Wilson, German et al., 2023; Wilson, Nelson et al., 2023). One lesson was delivered per week, during working hours with teaching staff who signed up to participate, at each center.

Table 8.1 Description of the Five Lessons Included in this Intervention.

Cultural Sessions	Description of Sessions
Promoting Tribal Identity	Connects one to the Creator, responsibility to live a good life by walking spiritual path
Smudging to Reduce Stress	Therapeutic healing practice to resolve unsettling feelings and thoughts
Understanding your Emotions	Understand association among thoughts, feelings, and behavior
Healing Historical & Contemporary Trauma	Identify imbalances in physical, emotional, mental, and spiritual domains created by historical trauma.
Strengthening Family and Community	Therapeutic value of connectedness to relatives and community

The adapted intervention for teachers was a brief, 5-week program and therefore not expected to create sustainable change, but the intent was to create a framework for healing and teacher well-being that, if shown to be promising, could be expanded into a new way of doing business center-wide. Results overall from the quantitative and qualitative evaluation were positive. There was a decrease in depression, increases in Tribal identity, communal mastery, and resilience, while life satisfaction remained unchanged and stress worsened. It is not unusual for posttests in school-based research to decline (e.g., end-of-year stress such as testing). Additionally, in short-term interventions, increasing people's awareness often results in higher "standards" at posttest. In the focus groups, teachers expressed appreciation for the time spent and the time focused on them. They expressed appreciation to their administration for allowing them to do this during work hours. Food was provided and a safe space that the teachers were familiar with, avoiding the need to travel. One teacher expressed: "*Thank you. All these traumas I just thought they were part of my life. But [during the intervention] I got to know myself and how they still affect me. I haven't looked at it like that before.*"

LESSONS OF HEALING FROM THE FIVE SESSIONS

In the following section, we expand on each of the five program sessions, with quotes, anecdotal healing experiences, and lessons learned to deepen our interpretation of study findings and target them for an educator, rather than researcher audience. We hope to paint a richer picture of *what healing can look like* among a Tribal community of teachers. A community member who identifies as Assiniboine and Sioux was trained to deliver the cultural sessions. It was essential to us that the teacher program would be delivered by a Native person familiar with the community.

Lesson One: Tribal Identity

"I think there's a little piece in everyone, in the Native community here, that want to learn their cultural ways, language, and traditions." —Participant

In this lesson, participants were asked to reflect on what values they have, think of somebody they look up to, and identify what values they display. They were also asked how they identify culturally and what Tribal identity means. The importance of relatives, greeting relatives in the community, and learning how to greet relatives/community members in the Nakota or Dakota languages were all highlighted. The topic of traditional names and naming ceremonies was discussed with the interventionist, who allowed for the expression of other religious ceremonies of importance. This helped highlight that the values discussed in the session were universal to all participants regardless of spiritual orientation. With this inclusive atmosphere, the interventionist skillfully worked to enhance Tribal identity and re-engage participants with Tribal culture. It was interesting to note that teachers who identified as Christian were still describing the importance of some traditional ceremonies. For example, they discussed preparing their children for powwows, and sewing special outfits for the occasion. With the positive shifts in Tribal identity in the posttest survey, it may be that by bringing consciousness to the value of tradition and describing their experiences, participants had begun to heal connections that had been damaged through colonization practices.

Lesson Two: Smudging to Reduce Stress

"We know about it [smudging] and what it's for, but it should be done more often." —Teacher focus group

This session focuses on smudging—a traditional activity to remove negative thoughts, feelings, and promote positive energy by burning sweetgrass, cedar, or sage (Charleyboy, 2012). The session involved finding out what people knew about the practice and performing the activity of smudging. This practice was then used before and after each subsequent session to pave the way for good work and thoughts. Since these traditional practices were banned in the USA until the 1970s, some people have never seen smudging practiced, but the facilitator emphasized that it can be practiced by any religion and by the whole family. In subsequent sessions, teachers shared their favorite spots on the reservation to collect sweet grass or sage, and the facilitator asked willing participants to lead the smudging. The skill of the facilitator, her familiarity with traditional cultural practices, and knowledge of the community was evident in this session as she worked to bring everyone together.

"It's really important when teaching these lessons to affirm why our families may or may not have continued these traditions and that it's ok to not know certain things or do certain things. It's about normalizing our cultural practices, beliefs, and understandings." —Interventionist

Lesson Three: Managing Your Emotions

"I don't even think teachers have been asked about it [stress and coping], so I don't even think it's on their radar. . . . As Natives we are just taught to zip it up." —Head Start administrator

"With this pandemic, mental health has really come under the spotlight. So those needs I think are becoming greater and it's hard to turn a blind eye when people are struggling with depression, some form of trauma, grief." —Tribal Head Start supervisor

These two quotes illustrate that Native Americans in this community don't talk about stress, but COVID-19 had pushed stressors to the forefront. In this session, participants were encouraged to describe if they could recognize how stress affected them physically and identify one-time and long-term stressors. The same was done for recognizing and managing depression and anger. Some stress-relieving activities were practiced. The session was finished with a visualization activity that everyone enjoyed. This session was quieter than the others, perhaps because it was led by Dr. Wilson, who is White (because it was not a cultural lesson per se), or maybe learning to speak about and identifying emotions takes practice. However, there were requests to continue learning more about stress and emotion regulation.

Lesson Four: Healing Historical and Contemporary Trauma

"I feel that for my people, it's just like we have been trying to be wiped out for generations, genocide and everything." —Teacher

This teacher spoke clearly about historical traumatic events such as forced attendance at boarding schools, starvation, and being made to relocate to reservations away from traditional homelands and hunting grounds. Session four acknowledges these traumatic events but highlights that this history of colonization does not define Native Americans as a people; they are strong, resilient. However, the effects of historical trauma are profound and can have effects such as depression, suicidal ideation, and lack of self-worth (Gone, 2013). We focused on engaging and showing the teachers that their life has value and that there are healthy ways to cope with the effects of these traumas.

Teachers shared contemporary traumatic experiences that they had not had a safe forum in which to discuss before. There were community traumas that the group was still actively struggling with, that "spilled out" when this opportunity was provided. For example, a community member and his family were killed in a car crash that occurred outside one teacher's home. Each participant clearly recalled that event and discussed its effect on them and the community. This was the first time they had discussed the trauma collectively and therefore understood now that they were not the only ones who were still impacted by it. Teachers spoke of other traumas or crimes for which they couldn't forgive the perpetrators, and how this lingering pain had shaped their lives. The session then moved on to managing the effects of trauma, describing healthy ways to release the feelings and take control. This session provided a much-needed space for teachers to center their own experiences, as opposed to the typical demands on them to always center the children or their teaching methods.

Lesson Five: Strengthening Family and Community

"*What really stresses me out is when I see our young Native Americans homeless, on drugs and not just dealing but stealing and breaking things. When I see that, I just go home and I pray and ask God to put a cover over our reservation, and that he could help our young people get off drugs or, you know, show us the light or something.*" —Teacher

This quote was one of many that highlighted participants' experiences with family members struggling with substance use and criminal behavior. Intergenerational trauma results in high levels of psychological distress that manifests in unhealthy behaviors, depression, shame, and suicidality (Brave Heart & DeBruyn, 1998; Brockie et al., 2015). In this session, the focus was on what it means to be a good relative. The facilitator and teachers agreed that this generally means mutual nurturing among individuals, the community, and the land. Exercises included a discussion of ways to be a good relative and drawing and sharing their family trees. The discussions of relatives past and present, and connections through marriage, adoption, and to other Tribes nearby were discussed with great animation. Even ancestral connections among teachers that some didn't know about before were revealed. The power of community connections and kinship in the room was palpable. While the theme of trauma and struggles remained, a number of teachers said there was no place else they would want to live. This session shifted attention to the power, strength, and beauty of both their Native American and Head Start communities, and how they must hold both strengths and troubles as they move toward healing.

MOVING BEYOND THE INTERVENTION

Results from our study provided support for community level interventions as culturally safe psychological care. As a brief pilot program, it would require additional components, a multilevel approach, and sustaining efforts for the teachers' continued well-being to be effective and comprehensive. Given how Native American communities have been harmed by past research, it was critically important to involve the Tribal Council and Head Start Administration to begin the process of constructing next steps. All data from the research was shared with and is owned by the Tribe and Tribal Head Start, and has been used to present at conferences and obtain funding. The following sections describe some ideas we discussed that could possibly apply to other Tribal communities, Head Start contexts, and early childhood education centers looking to repair the longstanding neglect of their teachers' well-being.

Structural Change

A complaint that teachers had was a lack of ergonomically sound equipment, such as diaper changing tables, forcing them to change diapers on the floor. Given this was an aging workforce with 87% of the teachers being over 50, the Head Start director quickly ordered new furniture including changing tables. Furthermore, each of the Head Start communities were using prefab classrooms that were separated by a great distance. Plans were established with the Tribal Council to design and build classrooms and administration buildings that represented the dignity, importance, and safety of Head Start to the Tribal community. In addition, the new design is reflective of the community culture such as a teepee at the center and murals painted on the walls depicting the buffalo and star people narratives.

Talking Circles

Plans were discussed to create in-service days focused on teacher well-being and healing. These days, called Talking Circles, came out of teachers' appreciation for time spent together during the sessions. The study revealed that these teachers have not had the opportunity before to acknowledge or start to process the fallout from COVID-19 or the historical traumas and loss that Native American Tribes have endured. Having a facilitator who was from the community, who knew the reservation and Tribal history, thereby enabling them to receive culturally appropriate support, indicated clearly that having such an individual on staff full-time would be a critical piece of ongoing well-being for teachers.

Improving Physical Health

While physical health was not the specific focus of the intervention, it is well known that Native Americans disproportionally struggle with diabetes, hypertension, arthritis, and depression (Lewis et al., 2021), and many teachers expressed these concerns. This was further compounded by this reservation being very rural, which leads to lack of access to healthy foods, and the reservation water supply being contaminated with mining extracts. Weights, resistance bands, and ellipticals have been purchased for the Head Start community in the new building. The Tribal Council has also approved 3.5 hours per week of employee paid time to help encourage staff to take care of their physical health, e.g., a weekly routine that gets teachers outside to walk for 30 minutes. A further support from school leadership that would help sustain this plan would be an incentive, as by their own admission teachers do not have the time or energy to maintain a regular exercise regime.

Other Activities

Teachers spoke of wanting a spa day, a Head Start retreat, or a weekend away with other reservation-based Head Start teachers. Currently, Head Start administration is working with Tribal Council to facilitate an event to celebrate Fort Peck teachers and recognize their contribution to the community. This is one part of an ongoing conversation to focus on partnership and boost morale. Further, in response to teachers expressing concerns about children with depression or struggling with behavior issues, the Head Start director is putting in place Safe Talk training (livingWorks, 2025). This will provide teachers with critical support in facing ongoing tragic issues for the Tribe including youth trauma and suicide.

CONCLUSION

This chapter outlines a pilot intervention for Native American Head Start teachers focused solely on them, to support their well-being. There was no expectation that these sessions would make them "better teachers" or improve the socioemotional learning of the children. Therefore, it not only focused on the teaching context but on the life experiences of the teachers, the richness of their culture and heritage, and the historical traumas that have occurred as a result of colonization practices. The success of this project rested on time spent developing a respectful and trusting relationship between the researchers, the Tribe, and Tribal Head Start, centering the teachers and community throughout and using a Native American interventionist who is from the community.

While additional funding and sustainability efforts will be required, the stories from the sessions clearly indicate that the path to healing had begun, and that these teachers had sorely needed the opportunity to commune with one another around their collective traumas, aspirations, and strengths. Supporters of teachers in Tribal communities and other contexts suffering from multiple copandemics (historical and ongoing) would do well to savor the wisdom shared by the stakeholders in this chapter. Teachers in such communities have been holding too much—all the burdens and hopes of generations past, present, and future, quite literally. It is time for their supporters to see teachers as their own revered group, with unique needs for advocacy and well-being, not merely the "conduit" for other people's needs. When we learn the sacred lessons from the Fort Peck Tribal Head Start teachers, we may begin to see an education system more aligned with elder wisdom, where "school" and "community" function as interconnected parts of a living whole, healing becomes more shared, and thus more possible.

REFERENCES

Blume, A. (2020). *A new psychology based on community, equality, and care of the earth: An Indigenous American perspective* (1st ed.). ABC-CLIO, LLC. https://doi.org/10.5040/9798400691201

Brave Heart, M. Y., & DeBruyn, L. M. (1998). The American Indian holocaust: Healing historical unresolved grief. *American Indian and Alaska Native Mental Health Research*, *8*(2), 60–78. https://doi.org/10.5820/aian.0802.1998.60

Brockie, T., Dana-Sacco, G., Wallen, G., Wilcox, H., & Campbell, J. (2015). The relationship of Adverse Childhood Experiences to PTSD, depression, poly-drug use and suicide attempt in reservation-based Native American adolescents and young adults. *American Journal of Community Psychology*, *55*(3), 411–421. https://doi.org/10.1007/s10464-015-9721-3

Brockie, T., Haroz, E. E., Nelson, K. E., Cwik, M., Decker, E., Ricker, A., Littlepage, S., Mayhew, J., Wilson, D., Wetsit, L., & Barlow, A. (2021). Wakȟáŋyeža (Little Holy One) - an intergenerational intervention for Native American parents and children: A protocol for a randomized controlled trial with embedded single-case experimental design. *BMC Public Health*, *21*(1), 2298. https://doi.org/10.1186/s12889-021-12272-9

Charleyboy, L. (2012). The ancient art of smudging: purify yourself and your home with a traditional Native American practice. (INNER + OUTER WORLDS: Inner life). *Spirituality & Health*, *15*(6), 24.

Dreer, B. (2023). On the outcomes of teacher well-being: A systematic review of research. *Frontiers in Psychology*, *14*, 1205179. https://doi.org/10.3389/fpsyg.2023.1205179

Gone, J. P. (2013). Reconsidering American Indian historical trauma: lessons from an early Gros Ventre war narrative. *Transcultural Psychiatry*, *51*(3), 387–406. https://doi.org/10.1177/1363461513489722

Gone, J. P. (2023). Community mental health services for American Indians and Alaska Natives: Reconciling evidence-based practice and alter-native psy-ence. *Annual Review of Clinical Psychology*, *19*(1), 23–49. https://doi.org/https://doi.org/10.1146/annurev-clinpsy-080921-072950

Herman, K. C., Hickmon-Rosa, J., & Reinke, W. M. (2017). Empirically derived profiles of teacher stress, burnout, self-efficacy, and coping and associated student outcomes. *Journal of Positive Behavior Interventions*, *20*(2), 90–100. https://doi.org/10.1177/1098300717732066

Lewis, M. E., Volpert-Esmond, H. I., Deen, J. F., Modde, E., & Warne, D. (2021). Stress and cardiometabolic disease risk for indigenous populations throughout the lifespan. *International Journal of Environmental Research and Public Health*, *18*(4), 1821. https://doi.org/10.3390/ijerph18041821

livingWorks. (2025). *Safe Talk*. https://livingworks.net/training/livingworks-safetalk/

Sun, Y., Tamblyn, A., Morris, H., Boothby, C., Skouteris, H., & Blewitt, C. (2024). Early childhood and primary school teachers' experiences and needs in working with trauma-impacted children: A systematic review and thematic synthesis. *Children and Youth Services Review*, *156*, 107344. https://doi.org/https://doi.org/10.1016/j.childyouth.2023.107344

Wilson, D. H., German, D., Ricker, A., Gourneau, H., Hanson, G. C., Mayhew, J., Brockie, T. N., & Sarche, M. (2023). Feasibility, acceptability and effectiveness of a culturally informed intervention to decrease stress and promote well-being in reservation-based

Native American Head Start teachers. *BMC Public Health*, *23*(1), 2088. https://doi.org/10.1186/s12889-023-16913-z

Wilson, D. H., Nelson, K. E., Gresh, A., Ricker, A., Littlepage, S., Krienke, L. K., & Brockie, T. N. (2023). The pre-implementation process of adapting a culturally informed stress reduction intervention for Native American head start teachers. *Global Implementation Research Applications, 3*, 16–30. https://doi.org/10.1007/s43477-022-00070-3

Wilson, D., Plesko, C., Brockie, T. N., & Glass, N. (2022). The well-being of Head Start teachers: a scoping literature review. *Journal of Early Childhood Teacher Education*, 1–26. https://doi.org/10.1080/10901027.2022.2147880

CHAPTER 9

Healing Teaching With the Power of Language and Cultural Connection

Alzando Mi Voz, Cultivando Identidad

Ivette Marlenne Alvarez and Rebeca Itzkowich

Language is more than a means of communication. It is the heartbeat of cultural identity, and it carries the wisdom, beliefs, and values of those who speak it. The vocabulary, grammar, and expressions used in a particular language often reflect the cultural nuances and experiences of its speakers. The use of specific words, idioms, or metaphors can reveal cultural values and practices. Language is a powerful force that influences our identity, sense of belonging, and perception of the world in profound ways. The way we speak, including our accent, dialect, and use of language varieties, can influence how we perceive ourselves, how we are perceived by others, and how we perceive them. Linguistic stereotypes can also lead to assumptions about a person's background, education, or social status. Bilingual educators constantly navigate language and identity within a normative monolingual English context. Especially when participating in professional development (PD) offered in English—even regarding teaching they are doing in both Spanish and English—native Spanish-speaking teachers face cultural dissonance, linguistic stereotypes, and the challenge of adapting content so it is culturally and linguistically relevant for their students.

Our immersive Spanish-language PD initiative entitled Project Connect provided a transformative space where Spanish-speaking bilingual educators could connect, heal, and thrive professionally through the centering of their language, identities, and expertise. Project Connect was a 3-year program that reached more than 250 teachers across Illinois and aimed to support kindergarten teachers' ability to observe, document, and interpret children's behavior and thinking. The professional learning communities (PLCs) were offered synchronously online during the school day, allowing teachers protected time to try out the literacy and math routines they learned in each session, in their own classrooms. These PLCs occurred in small cohorts of fewer than 20 teachers each from across Illinois, including one or two cohorts that we conducted in Spanish each year. Project Connect Spanish-language cohorts were designed for kindergarten teachers who use Spanish as a language of instruction in their classrooms. The program promoted bilingualism and biliteracy by immersing bilingual educators in a Spanish learning experience just like their students.

Our hope in creating this cohort was for teachers to be genuinely seen, with their needs as teachers of bilingual students front and center, and their contributions and expertise in the field welcomed and valued. To accomplish this, we took the radical step of assigning teachers to the Spanish language cohorts if they identified Spanish as a language of instruction in their classroom on the intake form. By not requiring teachers to publicly choose a preference, we removed the stigma associated with wishing to participate in Spanish, since this choice could signal a lack of English proficiency for native speakers, and conversely, we eliminated the allure of convenience for learning in English for those teachers whose schooling has been mostly in English. We wanted teachers to know that their linguistic assets and expertise in working with bilingual students would not only be honored, but would be essential to collective learning.

As is often the case in bilingual classrooms, the levels of Spanish and English proficiency varied in these cohorts. This professional learning experience created an academic space for full Spanish immersion that supported teachers who preferred learning in Spanish, bilingual heritage speakers, and those who spoke Spanish as a second language. (A heritage speaker is someone who learned the language at home as a child, and didn't fully develop it because of insufficient input from the social environment. The speaker grows up with a different dominant language in which they become more proficient.)

These cohorts were doing more than just strengthening linguistic skills or accessing content in a familiar language. These PD sessions created spaces that celebrated the joy and healing power of being bilingual and biliterate in a professional setting. While there is a robust literature that exists documenting the wounds created for children when their home languages are not honored in school and conversely, the healing power of immersive and authentic bilingual education (e.g., Cummins, 2000; Santa Ana, 2004; Valenzuela, 1999), no one seems to talk about the unique challenges facing the *teachers* of bilingual children, much less what happens when bilingual children later *become* teachers. This chapter gives us the unique opportunity to explore these perspectives by creating meaningful cultural connection within an affinity cohort. In doing so, we hope to provide inspiration for healing bilingual teachers and teaching overall.

OUR LIVED EXPERIENCES AS BILINGUAL EDUCATORS

Our lived experiences inform our work. We are both bilingual teacher educators who were bilingual classroom teachers. Ivette Alvarez is the daughter of Mexican immigrants, and Rebeca Itzkowich is a Mexican immigrant herself. We understand the importance of challenging traditional PD practices that often push the cultural and linguistic identities of bilingual educators to the side. As bilingual teachers, we made a conscious decision to incorporate Spanish immersion pedagogy into these

Spanish affinity groups. We spoke in Spanish while creating a supportive environment that accepted teachers' full and dynamic use of their linguistic repertoire. Teachers were consistently exposed to key academic ideas and vocabulary in Spanish and encouraged to participate in Spanish regardless of their linguistic ability. These practices gently scaffolded their linguistic growth.

We led several Project Connect cohorts together in both English-only and in Spanish for three years. Although the program was effective for all participants, we had the unique vantage point of being able to compare the English- and Spanish-language cohorts and felt distinctly that the Spanish cohorts had greater teacher participation, engagement, and joyfulness. Our experiences as facilitators were validated by the analysis of the recorded sessions and the teacher satisfaction surveys. From the moment participants logged on, there was an immediate sense of warmth and relaxed banter, as if we were long-established friends, even though we were meeting virtually for the first time. It is possible that this stark difference was a product of the uniqueness of the experience, for all of us, since mainstream PD that does not intentionally address issues of teachers' language and identity was likely the only PD context that the teachers had experienced before.

"INFORMALITY" AND RELATIONAL LEARNING

Hickey & Riddle (2024) affirm that effective teaching and learning are rooted in relational, meaningful, and reciprocal interactions. They state that "informality" is the way to promote liberatory practices that do away with highly constricted and hierarchical educational practices. It was exactly this relational pedagogy, centering mutuality and trust among learners, that was fostered among bilingual teachers during our PLC sessions. Unlike what bilingual teachers encounter during English-only PD, every Spanish PLC session connected them authentically with colleagues, broke down linguistic and cultural barriers and helped them rediscover the power of their voice in a professional context. This emancipating space encouraged shared experiences, laughter, and risk-taking in a way that felt both validating and safe. In the following sections, we detail prototypical experiences of teachers in our Spanish language cohorts, from their childhoods, to their typical English-language PD experiences, to the "mechanisms of action" behind why Spanish-language PD ultimately created healing for them in their professional identity as a teacher.

LANGUAGE AND IDENTITY AFFIRMATION

Connection and shared experiences are especially important for bilingual teachers who navigate the complex intersections of language, race, culture, and professional identity. This constant negotiation can result in a fragmented sense of self. For many participating teachers we interviewed, this was the first time that their personal and professional identities did not feel separated. For instance, many bilingual teachers who arrived in the United States as children experienced linguistic assimilation into English rather than the promotion of bilingualism and biliteracy. Many of the Spanish cohort teachers spoke about these experiences growing up:

> *"My own experience as a student when my family came to join my father in the U.S. from Mexico in the late '80s was very difficult. I came at the age of 13 and entered a school system where my language was never valued. I had teachers who would tell us upon entering their classroom that we were in the U.S., so we needed to learn English. They wanted us to speak in English all the time. If we spoke in Spanish, we were punished. For students who are in their formative development years our self-esteem was greatly affected. We feared being embarrassed in front of our classmates because we couldn't speak English. Not knowing English was equated with being ignorant. Not that I think of myself as the most intelligent person, but I do like to communicate my thoughts and ideas, and I had always enjoyed participating in class. After hearing the warnings from the teachers about only talking in English, I thought to myself: 'I don't want to be punished, I don't want my teachers to stand me up in front of the class for speaking in Spanish.' The result was that I didn't participate in school. I preferred if I could not say it in English to stay quiet and say nothing so that I wouldn't get in trouble."* —Arcelia

Many Spanish speaking teachers have experienced "linguistic muting" of their home language in formal academic spaces. Even if Spanish continues to be the language spoken at home, if the school and community do not elevate Spanish as a worthy language for learning, they experience language erasure in the "educational" space. To lessen the daunting feeling of being an outsider, and as a protection from being discriminated against, they may choose to give up Spanish and assimilate to adopt hegemonic English-monolingual norms as the only way to succeed in the United States.

The pain Arcelia described is one that resonates across generations of bilingual children turned bilingual educators. The intergenerational harm of linguistic erasure doesn't fade with age. These effects can linger as doubts, compartmentalization, persistent feelings of not fully belonging in professional settings, or continuing to perpetuate the linguistic trauma by insisting that children learn English as fast as possible to avoid being discriminated against.

Linguistic muting is not confined to students' experiences in K–12 education settings. Native Spanish-speaking teachers shared stories of traumatic experiences during adult learning that reactivated linguistic scars and feelings of shame about their English proficiency or accent:

> *"When I am immersed in an all-English PD, my position is that of a listener. I am very attentive, trying to understand everything that is being said. If there is a word that I don't understand, my brain is working hard trying to figure out what it means.*

> *My voice is practically mute; if I do [speak], it's with very short and limited phrases because obviously my first language is not English. I would very much like to share what is going on in my classroom and my thinking behind it. I want people to know. But since I start thinking first in Spanish and then I need to translate it to English, as you can imagine the process is much slower. By the time I have gone through this process and I am ready to share, others have already participated and the conversation has moved on."* —Karla

The added cognitive load for a speaker in expressing herself in her nondominant language led to Karla's silence and her feelings of exclusion in an English-only PD. In contrast, when participating in the Spanish-language PD, Yuritzin describes the freedom that comes from not having the added cognitive burden of translating her ideas in her mind before speaking:

> *"Yes, I did feel more comfortable in the Spanish cohort because obviously I didn't have to worry if I was pronouncing the words correctly or if I was using the right professional words. I felt confident in myself and had certainty that I was going to be able to truly express what I really wanted. When I am among monolingual English-speaking teachers I often have the feeling of being judged. Like, 'They are going to notice that I can't speak English well. They are going to notice that I am not fluent in my second language, they will notice my accent.' So speaking in Spanish during the PLCs obviously was fantastic! To speak, to understand, we didn't have to think about or engage in double the mental work. It was like, I have an idea, I want to share it and I feel good about it, I felt liberated."* —Yuritzin

Although the Spanish-language PD did not erase the damage, through connections, laughter because of playful banter, and storytelling, this space created conditions where fragmented identities could be made whole again. Most importantly, participants experienced the kind of teaching they longed for as children. This feeling of well-being translated into a commitment to create parallel experiences for the children who walk into their classrooms every day. In doing this, they can help prevent the deep linguistic scars for the new generation and a path for the teachers to continue their own healing.

This "sequence" from harm to healing is at once simple, and yet rather profound. When at first children are muted—in *any* way, but in this case linguistically—they are harmed, because they receive the message that their very *self* is not OK. This is a wound to their identity, which is not easily healed. Learning requires fully jumping into experiences and letting go of fear, because not being in a state of mastery is uncomfortable even in the absence of major identity wounds. While learning in Spanish alone is not a cure-all, it provides teachers a rare, but powerful feeling of safety and relief. They could more readily invest their energy into the risk-taking required for learning instead of having to prove themselves to others or work in a less comfortable modality. This space paved a path toward the healing of intergenerational harm.

LINGUISTIC CONSIDERATIONS

Our Spanish immersion affinity group did more than facilitate learning. This program actively disrupted the systemic marginalization of Spanish in a society where English is the norm. By centering Spanish as the language of professional learning, we elevated its status and affirmed the professional contributions of those who speak it.

Elevating Spanish

Our space honored the spirit of bilingualism, positioning Spanish not as a deficit to overcome but as a powerful asset, which shifted the power dynamics between English and Spanish. As native Spanish-speaking bilingual teachers shared their ideas using their academic Spanish language proficiency, they were seen as language role models by heritage Spanish speakers, further boosting their confidence. By including instructional videos that were filmed in Spanish language classrooms with subtitles in English for all cohorts to see, bilingual teachers saw classroom instruction in Spanish being spotlighted as positive examples to be emulated. This not only elevated Spanish by recognizing it as a legitimate language for schooling, but bilingual teachers also experienced their full identities being validated and honored. In combination, these practices were experienced as healing because they did more than simply reverse early messages of "you are not OK" to "you are OK." While simply existing should always be enough and it should not be required to "be extraordinary," the rules of professional settings are different. Teachers are constantly being evaluated against not only their own metrics but those of their students as well. Having to perpetually prove oneself is a basic expectation, and thus the opportunity for *their* way of being to be viewed as the one to be emulated and admired—to be evaluated as "ahead" rather than in "catch-up"—was a balm for the soul.

Full Linguistic Expression

Teachers were encouraged to participate in our discussions using their entire linguistic repertoire. Heritage speakers sometimes shifted between Spanish and English as needed, while native Spanish-speaking teachers kept to Spanish. This provided all participants with the necessary space to focus on content and pedagogy and not be constrained by language. One heritage Spanish teacher shared how this welcoming climate gave him the courage to use his Spanish, bringing healing to his identity:

> *"Sometimes I felt frustration participating in the PD because English words come to my mind quicker. To be honest, all my life, in other Spanish settings I have had that fear of 'I don't want to get it wrong.' Because of how the sessions were facilitated I felt comfortable trying to use Spanish academic language during the PLCs. I have seen the changes in me, with the academic language and with my confidence in speaking in Spanish."* —Johnny

BUILDING COMMUNITY AND SOLIDARITY SPURS LEARNING

Despite the imagery of bustling school halls, teaching is a surprisingly solitary profession, with limited opportunities to collaborate among colleagues. For bilingual teachers, the challenge is typically greater, with most being either the only bilingual teacher in their school or their grade. In Project Connect, participants joined a community of bilingual kindergarten teachers where they did not need to constantly censor, explain, or justify their expertise and unique experiences. The typical reality of bilingual teachers' existence is being among educators who espouse hegemonic English language norms, are unfamiliar with bilingual learning trajectories, and question the complexities of bilingual education in the United States.

If you are not a bilingual educator in the United States, it might be difficult to imagine just how exhausting it is to be asked, even today, "Doesn't it confuse the kids to keep learning in two languages at once?" Participation in our PDs was a healing salve from these demoralizing and frankly boring exchanges. The experience ignited a renewed and collective commitment to bilingualism and biliteracy that reminded them that they were not alone in this work, but part of a greater movement that would also interrupt a cycle of intergenerational trauma and provide healing to future generations of children.

In this community, teachers felt safe to reflect on their practice. This gave them the courage to try new instructional strategies that at times ran counter to their existing curricula. Teachers candidly expressed successes, questions, and challenges resulting from trying the new classroom practices. The familial climate of the sessions was essential for holding uncomfortable, but necessary conversations that would lead to meaningful teacher growth that is empowering and healing. We cultivated the habit of seeing "mistakes" in student work as windows that reveal their current understandings and promising beginnings. During our exploration of emergent writing, bilingual teachers examined their students' nonconventional spellings of English words. The words "very," "hope," and "gum" were spelled: "beri," "jop," and "gam." After analyzing what at first seemed troubling, teachers were excited to see that students weren't just randomly stringing letters together, but they were making sensible approximations of how to represent English phonemes based on Spanish sound-letter correspondences. They were in fact demonstrating the flexibility that fosters sense-making. Engaging in discussions with bilingual colleagues with similar experiences allowed participants the opportunity to take pride in students' creative strategies for learning. It was an important counterpoint to the more common experience of being told that your students lag behind.

There is healing in being able to talk candidly about one's practice with colleagues who understand the bilingual context. There is such transformative power in being able to be inspired by and learn from colleagues in authentic ways through a language that speaks to your heart. There is a radical healing that happens when you realize that embracing the part of yourself that has been silenced as "less than" is an act of self-affirmation. Just as it is important to lift up the strengths of bilingual students, it is also important to be honest about their challenges, just like all other students. In this space, what used to be suppressed became a source of strength, pride, and professional empowerment.

CURRICULUM AND ASSESSMENT SUPPORT

The playful yet rigorous instructional routines explored in this program revitalized bilingual teachers' practices and brought the healing power of joy and laughter to their kindergarten classrooms. However, we didn't stop there. Teachers who teach in more than one language in the United States face specific linguistic and cultural challenges every day. For example, bilingual teachers struggle with finding curricular materials that are relevant for their students. Many of our teachers admitted they regularly needed to invest their own time to adapt and translate curricula. Therefore, teachers were thrilled to receive culturally relevant teaching materials in Spanish that they could use right away, allowing them to focus on the pedagogy of implementation. Educators who only speak English often do not consider this issue when working with bilingual colleagues; they merely think that if their colleague speaks English as one of their languages, they can do any translation work "on the fly." What a novel experience to feel that the materials were created with their students in mind and not just translated as an afterthought! Being provided these materials was at once a radical act of antiracism and a nurturing act of love and care.

Bilingual teachers also regularly experience a disconnect between what their students know and what they can demonstrate in mandated assessments. This is often due to linguistic and cultural mismatches. Because the instructional routines shared in this program honored the unique cultural capital and linguistic needs of Spanish-speaking students, the work that the students produced was a true reflection of their current understanding. Imagine the pain caused to children and teachers when children appear to be less capable than they are merely because they are speaking in two languages. Thus, it was healing for teachers to have accurate evidence of what children are capable of doing. Streamlining teaching and assessment was also healing on a practical level because time is a limited resource in classrooms.

RESTORING HUMANITY TO BILINGUAL TEACHER EDUCATION

Project Connect was more than a professional learning series. This journey highlighted that bilingualism isn't just a skill, but a force that binds people together across our shared cultural, linguistic, professional, and personal identities. Throughout the three years of Project Connect, the Spanish cohorts had over 95% attendance. We believe this level of participation reveals that providing content that is meaningful and rooted in teachers' realities within a safe professional community is the kind of learning that bilingual teachers need. This program supported healing the scars of linguistic and cultural othering and silencing that many have experienced as bilingual people. Healing conditions were created, including the pursuit of leadership opportunities that many had not considered before. Today, for example, Karla is mentoring new bilingual teachers in her district, Yuritzin is pursuing her principal license, and Arcelia has become the early childhood dual language coordinator at a public school. This experience was just as transformative for us as facilitators as it was for the teachers. Leading these sessions in Spanish allowed us to reconnect with our own cultural and linguistic roots as we engaged in professional dialogue in our heart language. This is an opportunity that is rarely afforded to us. In our reflections, we realized that we weren't just guiding teachers, we also saw ourselves in them. We realized that we were also educators who experienced a forced splitting of our identities in professional settings. The space we created wasn't just warm and affirming for participants. It was healing for us too as it reaffirmed why this work is so important. It validated our identities in ways we hadn't realized we needed.

CONCLUSION

If we want to create schools where all children thrive, we must also create spaces where all teachers, including bilingual teachers, can bring their full identities to their work without fear, shame, or erasure. This means creating professional spaces where bilingual educators are not asked to leave their language and culture at the door by educational policies and school structures. One way to do this for bilingual teachers is to create opportunities to break the isolation they experience at school and during professional development. As we explored in this chapter, offering language affinity groups, whether within or across schools, where teachers can learn together and from each other and where bilingualism is the norm and not the exception, is an important first step. Doing this gives bilingual teachers a path toward healing from the linguistic wounds and the discrimination they may have experienced as bilingual people in the United States. It also provides the solidarity necessary to counter the ubiquitous messages they regularly hear about the lack of competence of their students and instead develop the necessary strategies to cultivate the brilliance in their bilingual students.

REFERENCES

Cummins, J. (2000). *Language, power and pedagogy: Bilingual children in the crossfire.* Multilingual Matters.

Hickey, A., & Riddle, S. (2024). Proposing a conceptual framework for relational pedagogy: Pedagogical informality, interface, exchange and enactment. *International Journal of Inclusive Education*, *28*(13), 3271–3285. https://doi.org/10.1080/13603116.2023.2259906

Santa Ana, O. (Ed.). (2004). *Tongue-tied: The lives of multilingual children in public education*. Rowman & Littlefield Publishers.

Valenzuela, A. (1999). *Subtractive schooling: U.S.-Mexican youth and the politics of caring*. State University of New York Press.

PART III

EXPANSIVE SEL

HEALING LEADERSHIP AND HUMANIZING SYSTEMS

CHAPTER 10

Preparing SEL Systems to Sustain (and Support!) Educators

Addison Duane, Ashley N. Metzger, Kamryn S. Morris, Mai Xi Lee, Brent Malicote, and Valerie B. Shapiro

For many years, the status quo of social and emotional learning (SEL) has been to ask individual teachers to implement isolated programs and teach didactic lessons in their classrooms. The results we've seen from this approach to SEL have been quite impressive, showing many positive outcomes for students, such as improved academic performance, lower emotional distress, and more (Durlak et al., 2022). Recently, there have been calls for *systemic* SEL—efforts that expand implementation to encompass all levels of the education system—rather than asking more from teachers. Teachers are already tasked with the herculean work of teaching the next generation while simultaneously navigating inequities in the U.S. public school system. The COVID-19 pandemic made teaching more challenging and also exposed and exacerbated many of these inequities. The pandemic also made obvious how unsustainable it is for classroom teachers to carry the weight of supporting student well-being alone and raised important questions regarding supporting teachers' own well-being.

In response to these challenges, a community of educators and scholars in California came together with a bold goal: to disrupt the status quo by reimagining SEL as a shared responsibility, rooted in equity and support. In this chapter, we explore learnings from this state-wide endeavor and offer considerations for how teachers everywhere can participate in local SEL leadership teams and be supported in coconstructing solutions for lasting, systemic, and equity-oriented change. Consistent with the goals of this book, this chapter aims to explore how a shared, systems-level, and authentically supported implementation of SEL may be healing for teachers by reversing potential years of experiencing a "do as we say, not as we do" series of new initiatives from our profession.

CALHOPE STUDENT SUPPORT

While we understand that high-quality social and emotional learning (SEL) programs have been proven to prevent challenges and promote well-being among young people, we also know—from both research and practice—that there exist implementation and equity-related challenges. To overcome these obstacles, systemic and transformative implementation is needed. We draw upon Mahoney et al.'s (2021) conceptualization of *Systemic SEL,* which aims to engage each component of our complex educational system to support, integrate, and sustain SEL through building foundational supports, strengthening adult SEL, promoting SEL for students, and practicing continuous improvement. Additionally, *Transformative SEL* (tSEL) seeks to interrupt inequitable educational environments, address issues of power and privilege, and embed focal constructs as equity elaborations (e.g., belonging, identity) within SEL competencies (Jagers et al., 2019).

CalHOPE Student Support (CalHOPE) was developed to support the systemic and transformative implementation of SEL in PK–12 public schools across all 58 of California's counties. CalHOPE arose from a unique cross-sector partnership between the healthcare and education systems. Sacramento County Office of Education (SCOE) received funding in 2021 from the California Department of Health Care Services (DHCS), and worked in concert with California County Offices of Education (COEs), UC Berkeley, and The Center for Implementation to form a statewide network of experts to collectively augment SEL implementation across the state. Although "Student Support" is both in the name and the central aim of the initiative, CalHOPE has intentionally centered an "adults go first" model, focused on supporting educators in the system (for a brief overview of CalHOPE Communities of Practice, see Eldeeb et al., 2025). As members of the CalHOPE Statewide Planning team, we have had a front row seat—and participated in—the shifts happening across the state of California.

SHIFT-ING SEL

CalHOPE has expanded upon popularized approaches to SEL implementation with a logic model and vision called "SHIFT SEL" (see Figure 10.1; see Shapiro et al., 2025) that centers equity-oriented systems transformation. In applying the SHIFT SEL model, CalHOPE has endeavored to foster individual and systemic thriving where all people are engaged, highly performing, and well (individual thriving) *due to* favorable conditions for learning, teaching, and leading that catalyze, reinforce, and accelerate improvement (systemic thriving). This sequence is key for adult healing. Providing favorable conditions that ease the path for educators to take up caring and equitable practices (for themselves and others) actively disrupts the common practice of blaming teachers for poor implementation without providing requisite conditions for success.

This logic model is based on multiple years of practitioner insights and a systematic review of peer-reviewed research (see Shapiro et al., 2025) that integrates previously siloed branches of scholarship: (a) research on SEL implementation, (b) research on systemic SEL, and (c) research on equity and SEL. It includes three conditions for thriving: a foundation rooted in SEL competencies (e.g., social awareness) and embedded tSEL focal constructs (e.g., agency); positive climate (i.e., experiences of safety and connection, opportunities for voice and leadership, and culturally and linguistically responsive practices); and the right levers to transform the systems (i.e., partnerships, supports, capacities, structures, and routines of SEL implementation).

If we are intentional about nurturing favorable conditions (Figure 10.1), then we can actualize our vision to shift SEL "to be a process through which people coordinate and collaborate to improve their: (a) conditions for learning, teaching, and leading; (b) care and connection offered and experienced; and (c) respective social and emotional repertoires—to empower their collective well-being, engagement, and performance to thrive" (Shapiro et al., 2025).

So, what does all of this mean for teachers in classrooms? In the next section, we will describe three *Levers of System Transformation* (*Partnerships, Supports, and Capacities*) to explore how bolstering these levers is envisioned to contribute to the *Structures and Routines* needed for SEL implementation, cultivating more equitable learning environments, and promoting thriving in schools.

Partnerships

First, let's talk *partnerships*. CalHOPE begins with a deeply relational, colearning approach that relies on "developing trusting, equity-pursuing, and mutually beneficial partnerships across sectors and regions, between levels and divisions of the education

Figure 10.1. The Garden Model for Shifting SEL Statewide.

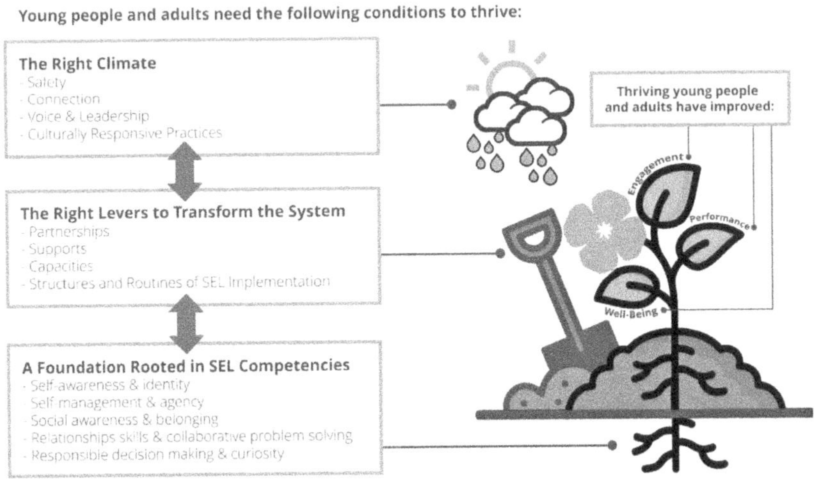

1. *Please inquire with CaliforniaSEL@berkeley.edu for permission to copy or reproduce images.*

system, with families, and allied to students" (Shapiro et al., 2024, p. 5). In the online resources for this book (refer to the Resources tab on the What Teachers Need page at www.tcpress.com), we provide examples of these partnerships, how they've contributed to CalHOPE, and recent lessons we've learned about partnerships from our research. Here, we offer a few examples to think about *who* teachers can lean on to support SEL implementation and about *how* partners can help share the work.

Research-Practice Partnerships

Recognizing early on that research and practice are too often disconnected, CalHOPE partnered with UC Berkeley to help bridge that gap. Among other things, UC Berkeley hosts Greater Good in Education, a website that makes research evidence useful for educators. Greater Good synthesizes research literature into practical strategies for teachers to use to promote their own well-being (https://ggie.berkeley.edu/my-well-being). We've had the opportunity to learn directly from Greater Good about how they help ensure that their translational work has real, applicable value for teachers. We found that the work of building bridges between research and practice is highly dependent on the bridge builders having advanced research training *and* experience as educators (see Metzger et al., 2024, for full study results). In other words, not just anyone can turn scientific discoveries into actionable strategies for teachers, which is why partnering with people who have these complementary skills can help ensure educators get effective tools, without having to become researchers themselves.

Partnerships Between Regions

CalHOPE also worked to establish partnerships between every county/region across the state of California. This collective decided to learn with and from each other in a statewide Community of Practice (CP). CPs are a powerful mechanism for cultivating partnerships and enabling shared learning because, as one leader said, the CP format addresses "the limited availability of high-level expertise" because "none of us were real experts . . . we needed to learn together" (Eldeeb et al., 2025, p. 711). The CalHOPE statewide CP has become a monthly gathering where educational leaders from across the state share learning from spotlights and successes, connect, and build solutions. Consistent with the theme of this book and CalHOPE, expectations are high for educational leaders to create the conditions for teacher uptake of SEL, but isolation may be a particular challenge for leaders' own well-being. Cross-region CPs are a valuable source to combat this challenge and assure once again that needed support filters through every level of the system.

Supports

High-quality partnerships lead to the second lever of transformation: *supports*. That is, the above partnerships, among others, generate, provide, and enable educators to take up supports. We conceptualize supports to include the training, coaching, tools, feedback loops, and funding that help educators implement SEL in a systemic and transformative way. Let's talk about two of them: tools and feedback loops (for more, refer to the Resources tab on the What Teachers Need page at www.tcpress.com).

Tools

As part of CalHOPE's efforts to support adults in implementing systemic and transformative SEL, we sought to provide a robust set of practical tools. In addition to sharing turn-key resources at each monthly statewide Community of Practice, CalHOPE funded the development and launch of UC Berkeley's SEL Foundations course, a three-unit graduate-level course for in-service teachers. Throughout each of the 12 modules and four live online sessions, course participants had the chance to explore, engage, apply, and expand existing SEL tools, including multimedia resources (e.g., videos, podcasts), reflection prompts, lesson plans, activities, guides, frameworks, and articles. In our research of teachers' pre- and postcourse survey responses, we found that participants demonstrated a large increase (effect size = .97) in having the tools needed to center, affirm, and sustain students' identities (see Duane et al., 2025, for the full study). These findings illustrate how providing concrete supports to teachers, such that teachers have what they need, can translate into meaningful SEL implementation.

Feedback Loops

Feedback loops, or the process of using information for continuous improvement, include collecting data from those at the center of the experience. CalHOPE has prioritized implementing feedback loops by collecting data at every level of the California education system—from superintendents to students. These feedback loops—such as self-evaluation frameworks, screening and assessment tools, surveys, empathy interviews, and focus groups—help guide improvement and on-the-ground practice. One example is a partnership with Tulare County Office of Education's Friday Night Live organization, which developed a series of SEL focus group protocols for young people around the state to participate in structured conversations to both build social and emotional competencies and provide important insights for improvement (visit the Resources tab on the What Teachers Need page at www.tcpress.com to access protocols). Youth who engaged in these focus groups appreciated the process and the dialogue that the protocols generated. In a postfocus group debrief, one youth shared, "It was really good to learn about what other people were interested in, you know, like 'Oh! we share the same goal or interest.'" Thus, feedback loops can amplify youth voices in ways that contribute to a culture of improvement, provide great insights, and inform meaningful decisions at all levels.

Capacities

With partnerships and supports in place, we turn to educator *capacities*—that is, the mindsets, knowledge, skills, and self-efficacy required to implement

SEL. In this section, we describe two elements of capacity: mindsets and knowledge.

Mindsets

Having an SEL mindset (positive beliefs, favorable attitudes, and sufficient motivation for SEL) is an important part of preparing for and sustaining SEL implementation. The field of education is a maze of competing priorities filled with obstacles and ever-changing demands, but having an SEL mindset means that even when considering all of those competing school priorities, teachers still believe SEL is important. In a recent qualitative study, we explored what motivated teachers to improve their SEL practice. Participants shared they wanted to: (a) strengthen their commitment to themselves, (b) be more responsive to their students' needs, (c) improve their classroom climate, (d) become a better teacher and leader, and (e) advance efforts toward equity (Morris et al., in press, p.16). Given these findings about teacher motivations, those who plan and provide professional learning should meet teachers where they are, incorporate more opportunities for educators to reflect on their "why," and provide opportunities for teachers to pursue SEL in ways that are consistent with their own goals.

Knowledge

Having knowledge about SEL is an important resource for overcoming the challenges of SEL implementation. Knowledge can include explaining SEL concepts like systemic and transformative SEL and describing how SEL intersects with other educational frameworks (e.g., Culturally Responsive Practices, Multi-Tiered Systems of Support). In the earliest days of CalHOPE (winter, 2021), we conducted a study in which we asked educational leaders to define SEL. Six months later, and after participating in several statewide Communities of Practice, we asked them to update or revise their definitions. In our qualitative analysis, we found that in their initial definitions, leaders emphasized popularized competency-based SEL definitions, skills rather than systems, and described SEL as an individualistic rather than a civic intervention. However, after six months of learning together, we found that many educational leaders shifted their definitions toward more systemic and transformative understandings of SEL (Eldeeb et al., 2025). These findings suggest that sustained and collaborative learning opportunities can help build knowledge, which in turn has real-world implications for SEL implementation.

CENTERING TEACHER WELL-BEING

When partnerships, supports, and capacities are in place, we believe that there may be positive impacts for teacher well-being. In fact, we've been lucky enough to learn from many teachers who have been involved in CalHOPE's efforts. As part of our work, we have had over 2,000 educators enroll in SEL Foundations. Participants complete a Capstone project where they (a) implement one adult SEL practice and two classroom-specific SEL practices and (b) reflect on that implementation. In a recent study, we qualitatively analyzed the adult SEL practices employed (for a digital repository of exemplar adult practices, see Duane, Hafen et al., 2025). Unsurprisingly, we found that when these participants had dedicated time to focus on themselves, an overwhelming number reported positive impacts on their well-being. Educators gave themselves "permission" to engage in (a) relationship building (e.g., attending social events, seeking out peer support); (b) lifestyle changes (e.g., sleep hygiene, movement); (c) self-reflection (e.g., journaling); (d) mindfulness (e.g., meditation, mindful awareness); and (e) boundary setting (e.g., leaving at contract time, limiting phone usage; Duane, Hafen et al., 2025).

The self-reported benefits to these teachers came from their thoughtful implementation and self-afforded "permission slips" to focus on themselves. Their success also shows up through statistical analyses, as educators' *resources for coping* significantly increased from the start to the end of the course (Duane, Caouette et al., 2025). Behind the scenes, each *Lever of System Transformation* was "turning its gear" to augment their success. *Partnerships* between the university, state, and practitioners across the state enabled the course to be developed and offered at no cost to participants. *Supports* included funding for the course, training via course content, a trove of tools and resources offered, and tailored feedback from expert SEL instructors. *Capacity*-building through knowledge sharing, skill development, motivation alignment, and confidence enhancement provided the foundation for teachers to implement adult SEL strategies. Taken together, these *Levers* created the conditions for transformation and healing.

CONCLUSION

The field of SEL has historically focused on asking teachers to *do* things differently without *supporting* the work differently. CalHOPE has offered an opportunity to think about—and more important, create the conditions for thriving in schools, systemwide. Challenges remain, and much work is left to do, but CalHOPE has provided a powerful blueprint for beginning this complex work that many believed couldn't be done. And, even for those not connected to CalHOPE or a state with robust SEL infrastructure, lessons from CalHOPE provide implications for any educator seeking to advance systemic and transformative SEL in ways that support teacher healing.

ACKNOWLEDGMENTS

CalHOPE Student Support has coordinated efforts across California to advance SEL implementation. We thank all participants, contributors, and champions, with a special acknowledgement of County Office representatives who have expanded their work and impact. CalHOPE research is enabled by the support of Megan Mitchell,

Esmeralda Michel, and Erika Hansen. Aspects of this work were funded by the California Department of Health Care Services. The contents may not necessarily reflect the official views or policies of the State of California. Valerie Shapiro would like to acknowledge her W. T. Grant Foundation Scholars Award.

REFERENCES

Duane, A. M., Caouette, J. D., Morris, K. S., Metzger, A. N., CalHOPE Research Committee, & Shapiro, V. B. (2025). Securing the foundation: Providing supports and building teacher capacity for SEL implementation through a university-based continuing education course. *Social and Emotional Learning: Research, Practice, and Policy, 5*, 100082.

Duane, A. M., Hafen, Q., McVeagh-Lally, P., & Shapiro, V. B. (2025). "It All Starts with Us": Exploring teachers' efforts to increase Adult SEL in practice. *Social and Emotional Learning: Research, Practice, and Policy, 5*, 100085.

Durlak, J. A., Mahoney, J. L., & Boyle, A. E. (2022). What we know, and what we need to find out about universal, school-based social and emotional learning programs for children and adolescents: A review of meta-analyses and directions for future research. *Psychological Bulletin, 148*(11–12), 765.

Eldeeb, N., Duane, A. M., Greenstein, J. E., Nuñez, A., Lee, J., Jones, T. M., CalHOPE Research Committee, & Shapiro, V. B. (2025) "I would add": Educational leaders' understanding of SEL during a statewide community of practice. *Educational Administration Quarterly, 61*(4), 701–738. https://doi.org/10.1177/0013161X2513504

Jagers, R. J., Rivas-Drake, D., & Williams, B. (2019). Transformative social and emotional learning (SEL): Toward SEL in service of educational equity and excellence. *Educational Psychologist, 54*(3), 162–184. https://doi.org/10.1080/00461520.2019.1623032

Mahoney, J. L., Weissberg, R. P., Greenberg, M. T., Dusenbury, L., Jagers, R. J., Niemi, K., Schlinger, M., Schlund, J., Shriver, T. P., VanAusdal, K., & Yoder, N. (2021). Systemic social and emotional learning: Promoting educational success for all preschool to high school students. *American Psychologist, 76*(7), 1128–1142. https://doi.org/10.1037/amp0000701

Metzger, A. N., Duane, A. M., Nash, A., & Shapiro, V. B. (2024). "Putting science into sction": A case study of how an educational intermediary organization synthesizes and translates research evidence for practice. *International Journal of Education Policy and Leadership, 20*(1), 1–19.

Morris, K. S., Duane, A. M., Metzger, A. N., & Shapiro, V. B. (in press). "I always want to learn more": Teachers' motivations for engaging in continuous professional development on social and emotional learning. The New Educator.

Shapiro, V. B., Duane, A. M., Lee, M. X., Jones, T. M., Metzger, A. N., Khan, S., Cook, C. M., Hwang, S. H. J., Malicote, B., Nuñez, A., Lee, J., McLaughlin, M., Caballero, J. A., Moore, J. E., Williams, C., Eva, A. L., Ferreira, C., McVeagh-Lally, P., Kooler, J., & CalHOPE Research Committee. (2024). "We will build together": Sowing the seeds of SEL statewide. *Social and Emotional Learning: Research, Practice, and Policy, 3*, 1–9. https://doi.org/10.1016/j.sel.2023.100014

Shapiro, V. B., Jones, T. M., Duane, A. M., Morris, K. S., & Metzger, A. N. (2025). SHIFTing social and emotional learning for equity: A systemic and humanizing implementation focused on transformation scoping review protocol submission. https://osf.io/nsmbx/?view_only=ee28a68db5844b62b4e5d88ac9b76103

CHAPTER 11

Caring for Educators by Addressing Their Psychological Needs

Recommendations for Policies and Systems

Patricia A. Jennings and Tara Hofkens

The "burnout cascade" among teachers is a phenomenon that Mark Greenberg and I (Patricia Jennings; Jennings & Greenberg, 2009) described long before the COVID-19 pandemic, but that global crisis further exposed the fragility of traditional education systems, amplifying stress and overwhelm among educators while spotlighting the misalignment between institutional expectations and the psychological needs of teachers and students. These challenges were not new, but the crisis brought them into stark relief. Consistent with the definition of the burnout cascade (Jennings & Greenberg, 2009), teachers reported feeling overwhelmed, unsupported, and increasingly disconnected from their professional purpose (Kurtz, 2022). The demands of the system and the classroom led to educator emotional exhaustion, which reduces their effectiveness in managing the classroom, creating a cycle that perpetuates exhaustion and ultimately leads to burnout. According to their Prosocial Classroom Model, teacher well-being is a critical cornerstone for managing stress, creating positive classroom climates, and nurturing student–teacher relationships. Addressing these systemic demands and shortcomings is not merely a moral imperative, it is foundational to building an education system capable of fostering resilience, engagement, and growth.

Our team has been deeply engaged in the domain of teacher well-being for over 15 years, most notably in the form of the Cultivating Awareness and Resilience in Education (CARE) program, the evaluations of which have demonstrated, among other findings, that a teacher-facing mindfulness program has positive cascade effects on classroom climate and student outcomes (e.g., Jennings et al., 2019; Brown et al., 2023). In the present chapter, we will both zero in on and zoom out from the teacher well-being component to dig more deeply into what gives rise to it, as well as imagine more broadly what may arise *from* it, in terms of healing the teaching profession as a whole, which is the aspiration of this book. Whereas the Prosocial Classroom

Figure 11.1. The Interconnectedness Among the Conditions for the Well-Being of Individual Teachers and the Teaching Profession Overall.

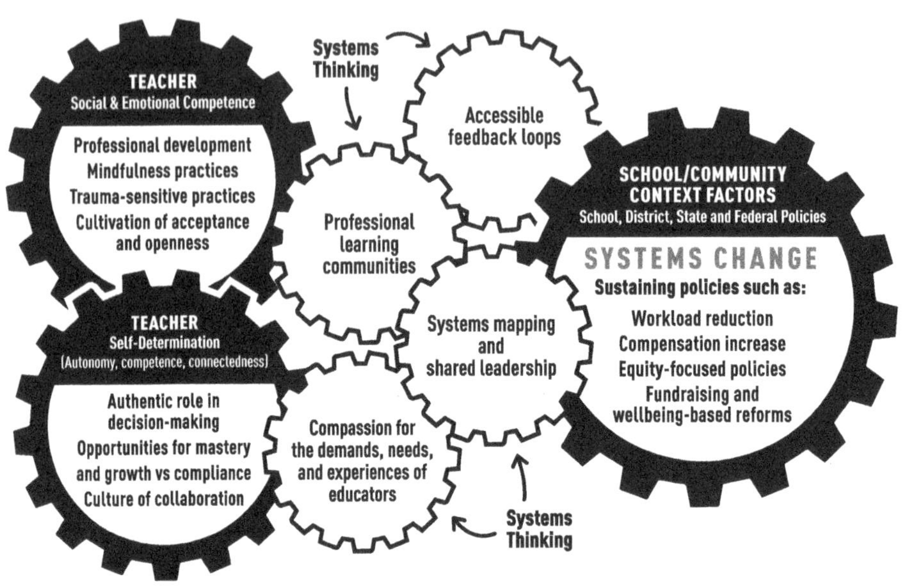

Figure created by Bourque Design

Model depicted in Jennings and Greenberg (2009) illustrates the pathway from teacher wellness and social competence to positive student outcomes, the model depicted in Figure 11.1, which we will discuss in the remainder of this chapter, illustrates the interrelationships and processes from individual- and psychological-level educator factors to broad-based, system-wide factors that could create healing and wellness for educators and therefore education writ large.

THE BURNOUT CASCADE: UNDERSTANDING THE PROBLEM

To fully grasp the urgency of addressing educator well-being, it is crucial to unpack the burnout cascade described in the Prosocial Classroom Model. This framework posits that stress among educators often originates from systemic factors, including unrealistic expectations, insufficient resources, and a lack of professional agency. These stressors erode teachers' capacity to form meaningful relationships with students and implement effective classroom management strategies leading to a breakdown in classroom climate and diminished student engagement. Over-stressed educators are prone to misinterpreting classroom situations, taking student behavior personally, or assuming behavior is intentionally provocative, rather than the result of normal child dysregulation. Over time, this creates a vicious cycle where struggling teachers inadvertently contribute to environments that further undermine their well-being. Furthermore, we now know that stress is contagious; when teachers are overburdened or unsupported, their stress can permeate the classroom, hindering learning and development for everyone involved.

The COVID-19 pandemic accelerated this cycle, pushing many educators to their limits. Teachers were expected to adapt overnight to remote instruction, often without adequate training or technological support. They navigated the emotional toll of supporting students who were themselves grappling with loss, isolation, and uncertainty. This dual burden—of meeting professional demands while managing personal stress—has led to an alarming rise in teacher attrition. A National Education Association (NEA; 2022) survey found that 55% of teachers were considering leaving the profession earlier than planned, with burnout being a leading reason. Additionally, a RAND Corporation report (Steiner & Woo, 2023) indicated that 23% of teachers were likely to leave their jobs by the end of the 2022–2023 school year, with those experiencing poor well-being more inclined to depart. This exodus poses a significant threat to the stability of education systems, underscoring the need for targeted interventions to support teacher well-being.

Teacher stress does not occur in isolation; it is deeply intertwined with the systemic structures and cultural expectations within education. High-stakes testing, punitive accountability measures, and rigid curricula often leave educators feeling powerless, undervalued, and disconnected from their professional purpose. These systemic issues are compounded by societal undervaluation of the teaching profession, which frequently manifests in inadequate compensation, limited career growth opportunities, and public narratives that frame teachers as failing rather than as professionals striving to meet impossible demands. Without systemic change, these patterns will continue to erode the foundation of the education system (Jennings, 2021).

SELF-DETERMINATION THEORY: A FRAMEWORK FOR HEALING

Self-determination theory (SDT; Ryan & Deci, 2020) provides a robust foundation for reimagining education systems that prioritize psychological well-being. At its core, SDT posits that humans are inherently motivated to grow and thrive when their basic psychological needs are met. These needs—autonomy, competence, and relatedness—are universal, transcending cultural and contextual differences. Autonomy refers to the need to feel a sense of control over one's actions and decisions. Competence involves the need to feel effective and capable in one's pursuits. Relatedness encompasses the need to feel connected to others and to belong to a supportive community. When these needs are met, individuals experience intrinsic motivation, greater engagement, and emotional resilience, key to effective teaching and learning.

For educators, however, these needs are often unmet in traditional school systems. Standardized curricula, rigid accountability measures, and top-down management structures can stifle autonomy, leaving teachers feeling like cogs in a machine rather than skilled professionals with agency. Similarly, a lack of resources and professional development opportunities can undermine competence, while isolation and adversarial relationships with administrators can erode relatedness. Addressing these gaps requires systemic change—an intentional shift toward policies and practices that create supportive communities that promote relatedness, empower educators, and foster their intrinsic motivation.

SDT also offers insight into how educational reforms can be framed to maximize buy-in and sustainability. Interventions that support teachers' autonomy by involving them in decision-making processes are more likely to succeed than those imposed from above. Similarly, professional development opportunities that emphasize mastery and growth, rather than compliance, can bolster teachers' sense of professionalism and competence. Finally, fostering a culture of collaboration and mutual respect among educators, administrators, and policymakers can strengthen relatedness, creating a more cohesive and supportive educational community.

TRAUMA-SENSITIVE PRACTICES: PATHWAYS TO HEALING

Trauma-sensitive frameworks help educators address the unique challenges faced by students while also fostering their own resilience. Building supportive relationships, creating safe spaces, and modeling emotional regulation are critical to creating a trauma-sensitive learning environment (Jennings, 2019). For example, a teacher who notices a student disengaging might approach the situation with curiosity and compassion rather than frustration. Instead of reprimanding the student, the teacher might say, "I've noticed you've been quiet today. Is there anything you'd like to share or anything I can do to help?" This approach not only supports the student but also reinforces the teacher's sense of efficacy and connectedness.

A key component of trauma-sensitive teaching is recognizing that behaviors often interpreted as defiance or disinterest may stem from underlying stress or trauma. Educators who adopt this perspective can shift their responses from punitive to supportive, fostering a classroom climate that prioritizes trust and emotional safety. For instance, one teacher restructured her classroom routines to include moments of reflection and mindfulness, creating a buffer for both herself and her students to reset after challenging interactions. This practice not only reduced disciplinary incidents but also strengthened her relationships with students, enhancing her overall job satisfaction (Jennings, 2019).

SUPPORTING EDUCATOR WELL-BEING THROUGH THE CARE PROGRAM

One way we have sought to enhance teachers' individual psychological resources drawing on the theorical frameworks just discussed is through professional development experiences. In particular, the Cultivating Awareness and Resilience in Education (CARE) program is a mindfulness-based professional development initiative specifically designed to enhance teachers' social and emotional competence

(SEC) while reducing occupational stress. Grounded in the Prosocial Classroom Model, CARE integrates mindfulness practices, emotional awareness, and stress management strategies to address the unique demands educators face daily (Jennings et al., 2017; Jennings et al., 2019).

Through 30 hours of in-person training and individualized coaching, CARE helps educators develop a nuanced awareness of their emotions and stress responses. This foundational skill enables teachers to recognize early signs of stress, regulate their emotional reactivity, and respond to challenging situations with greater composure and clarity (Jennings, 2016; Jennings et al., 2017). For instance, one teacher shared, "Rather than jumping in to take care of a situation, I realized the importance of pausing and allowing a student the space to process their feelings" (Schussler et al., 2015). Such mindful approaches not only enhance teachers' ability to manage their stress but also improve their interactions with students.

The program also includes mindful awareness exercises, which cultivate an open and accepting orientation to experiences—essential for maintaining balance in high-stress environments (Jennings, 2015). One participant described how focusing on their breathing during challenging moments helped them navigate high-stress situations with clarity and composure: "When I felt overwhelmed by the pressure of meeting deadlines or managing classroom behavior, I remembered to focus on my breathing and bring myself back to the present moment" (Schussler et al., 2019).

Research underscores CARE's effectiveness in improving teachers' capacity to manage classroom demands. Participants demonstrate significant increases in mindfulness, adaptive emotion regulation, and psychological resilience. These changes translate into more effective classroom interactions, as teachers who are emotionally self-aware and regulated can maintain positive classroom climates and model pro-social behavior for their students (Jennings et al., 2017; Jennings et al., 2019). One educator noted, "The program helped me become more empathetic and patient with my coworkers. It changed the way I approach teamwork, creating a more positive and collaborative environment" (Schussler et al., 2018). This improvement in workplace dynamics contributes to a supportive school culture, benefiting both staff and students.

Longitudinal studies further reveal that CARE's benefits persist over time, with educators reporting sustained reductions in psychological distress and improvements in emotional well-being nearly a year postintervention. A teacher reflected on the enduring value of mindfulness practices, saying, "The mindfulness practices taught me how to take a moment for myself during the day, which allows me to respond to challenges with greater calm and focus" (Schussler et al., 2018). This lasting impact highlights CARE's role not only in mitigating teacher burnout but also in fostering the emotional resilience necessary for effective teaching (Jennings et al., 2019).

By addressing the psychological needs outlined in self-determination theory—autonomy, competence, and relatedness—the CARE program provides a robust framework for enhancing teacher well-being. CARE promotes autonomy by equipping educators with tools to recognize and manage their stress, empowering them to navigate the challenges of teaching with greater self-efficacy and control. It fosters competence by enhancing teachers' emotional regulation and mindfulness, which translate into improved classroom management and higher-quality instruction. For example, a teacher explained, "Recognizing my emotional triggers and learning to disengage and recover quickly helped me stay more present and effective in the classroom" (Schussler et al., 2015). Finally, CARE strengthens relatedness by enabling teachers to build more supportive and empathetic relationships with their students and colleagues, creating a collaborative and positive school climate.

Another way CARE supports teachers' autonomy, competence, and relatedness is by positively influencing student outcomes. Research indicates that CARE promotes students' engagement, motivation, and reading competence, which directly reinforces teachers' sense of efficacy and purpose in the classroom. When students are more engaged and motivated, teachers experience fewer behavioral disruptions, allowing them to focus on high-quality instruction and relationship-building. Improved student outcomes also foster a sense of mutual respect and connection between teachers and students, enhancing the classroom climate and strengthening relational bonds. These positive feedback loops further reinforce teachers' autonomy, as they gain confidence in their ability to impact student success, and competence, as they witness the tangible results of their teaching efforts (Brown et al., 2023).

SYSTEMS THINKING: EMPOWERING EDUCATORS TO CHANGE THE SYSTEM FROM WITHIN SCHOOLS

While individual practices are a necessary part of the process, sustainable transformation in education requires a systemic approach. Systems thinking provides a powerful framework for educators to understand the interconnected dynamics of their schools, districts, and communities (Jennings, 2021). By viewing challenges through a systemic lens, teachers can identify root causes of issues, collaborate with stakeholders, and implement solutions that ripple through the broader educational ecosystem boosting their competence, autonomy, and sense of relatedness and connection with their students, colleagues, and leaders.

At its core, systems thinking invites educators to move beyond immediate symptoms of problems and examine the underlying structures and relationships that perpetuate them. We invite this process not to exploit teachers' labor further, but to engage their talents in ways that are meaningful to *them*. Generally speaking, educators choose their profession to make a meaningful impact on future generations (Bergmark et al., 2018). For example, a teacher noticing widespread disengagement in their classroom might initially attribute it to student apathy. However, adopting a systems thinking perspective reveals deeper systemic issues—such as rigid curricula, high-stakes testing pressures, or a lack of culturally relevant materials—that contribute to this disengagement. Recognizing these connections enables educators to advocate for structural changes while addressing immediate classroom needs.

One practical application of systems thinking involves using feedback loops to understand and address challenges. Consider a school grappling with high teacher turnover. Systems thinking reveals that factors such as heavy workloads, limited professional development opportunities, and insufficient administrative support are interconnected and mutually reinforcing. Addressing these issues requires a holistic approach: reducing unnecessary administrative tasks, investing in meaningful professional learning, and fostering a culture of trust and collaboration. By addressing the root causes rather than the symptoms, schools can break the cycle of turnover and create more sustainable and engaging working environments.

Collaboration is central to systems thinking. Educators cannot tackle systemic issues in isolation; they must engage with colleagues, administrators, families, and community members to cocreate solutions. For instance, a group of teachers in a large urban district used systems thinking to address chronic absenteeism. Rather than viewing absenteeism solely as a student or family issue, they explored systemic factors such as unreliable transportation, food insecurity, and unengaging curricula. Partnering with local organizations, they implemented solutions such as providing bus passes, establishing school meal programs, and redesigning lessons to reflect students' cultural contexts. These efforts not only improved attendance but also strengthened relationships within the community, demonstrating the power of collective action.

Another example of systems thinking in action is the use of shared leadership models in schools. In one rural district, teachers and administrators collaborated to address declining student performance in mathematics. Rather than assigning blame or implementing top-down mandates, they adopted a systems thinking approach, creating cross-functional teams to analyze the problem. These teams identified gaps in teacher training, misaligned instructional materials, and inconsistent assessment practices as key barriers. Through targeted professional development, resource alignment, and the introduction of collaborative lesson planning sessions, the district saw measurable improvements in both teacher efficacy and student outcomes. Some might view such an example and believe it to be just about academic achievement since it was in response to declining math scores, or a "cold" problem-solving analysis about lesson plan gaps and resource alignment. But the real "star of the show" here was the authentic power sharing that took place among administrators and teachers, which required multiple types of social and emotional competence, genuine listening, and humility for all involved.

Systems thinking also empowers educators to advocate for systemic change at the policy level. Teachers equipped with a systems perspective can articulate the interconnected impacts of policies on their daily practices, lending credibility to their advocacy efforts. For example, when lobbying for reduced class sizes, educators can use systems thinking to demonstrate how smaller classes lead to better student–teacher relationships, improved classroom management, and higher academic achievement—all of which reduce teacher stress and attrition. This holistic framing helps policymakers see the broader benefits of supporting teacher well-being.

Professional learning communities (PLCs) and networks are effective tools for embedding systems thinking into school culture. In these collaborative spaces, educators can share insights, identify patterns, and codesign solutions to shared challenges. For instance, a PLC focusing on equity might analyze disparities in student achievement and trace them to systemic factors such as unequal resource allocation or biased disciplinary practices. By collectively addressing these issues, PLC members can drive meaningful change within their schools and beyond.

To make systems thinking actionable, schools and districts can provide training and tools that help educators apply these principles in their daily work. Workshops on systems mapping, for example, can guide teachers in visualizing the interconnected elements of a challenge, while design thinking exercises can foster creative, iterative problem-solving. Importantly, systems thinking should not be positioned as an additional burden on already overstretched educators. Instead, it should be framed as a way to empower teachers to make sense of complexity, prioritize effectively, and advocate for the changes they need to succeed.

POLICY AND ADVOCACY: BUILDING A SYSTEM THAT SUPPORTS TEACHER WELL-BEING

While individual and systemic practices can significantly improve teacher well-being, the burden for this change does not rest primarily on the shoulders of teachers but rather requires facilitative policies at the school, district, and national levels. Advocacy for such policies must be grounded in evidence, emphasizing the interconnected benefits for teachers, students, and the broader education system. By aligning policies with the psychological needs of educators, we can create environments that not only prevent burnout but also foster professional growth and satisfaction. Foundational school-level programs such as CARE and practices such as professional learning communities that can catalyze teachers' systemic thinking are helpful in preparing educators to engage in a new path toward multisystemic healing. The following recommendations include systemwide supports that require vigorous and immediate strengthening, to make healing teaching possible:

- **Workload reduction:** One foundational policy recommendation is the reduction of teacher workloads. Many educators cite excessive administrative tasks, unrealistic expectations, and insufficient planning time as major contributors to stress. Policies that protect teachers' instructional time and limit nonteaching responsibilities are essential. For instance, a district in Finland restructured its schedules to include designated collaboration and planning periods during the school day, allowing teachers to focus on lesson preparation and professional development without sacrificing personal time. This change resulted in higher job satisfaction and better student outcomes, highlighting the value of prioritizing teachers' time.

- **Compensation increase:** Another critical area for policy intervention is compensation. Teachers frequently report feeling undervalued, a sentiment exacerbated by stagnant wages and limited opportunities for advancement. Competitive salaries and transparent pathways for career growth are vital for attracting and retaining talented educators. Moreover, innovative policies that tie compensation to holistic metrics—such as contributions to school culture or professional learning—rather than narrow performance measures can help shift the focus from punitive accountability to meaningful recognition.
- **Mental health services access:** Providing access to mental health resources is another cornerstone of teacher well-being. Policies that provide free or subsidized counseling services, stress management workshops, and wellness programs can help educators navigate the emotional demands of their work. For example, the state of New York launched a program offering mental health support to teachers during the COVID-19 pandemic, including virtual therapy sessions and stress reduction webinars. The program was widely praised for reducing stigma around mental health and providing timely assistance during a period of unprecedented challenges.
- **Equity-focused policies:** It is also essential to address systemic disparities that affect teacher well-being. Educators in underfunded schools often face greater stress due to larger class sizes, fewer resources, and higher rates of student trauma. Ensuring equitable funding across districts, providing grants for high-need schools, and supporting initiatives like trauma-sensitive training can alleviate these pressures. A case study from Massachusetts illustrates this approach: a statewide policy allocated additional resources to schools serving economically disadvantaged populations, enabling them to hire more staff, reduce class sizes, and implement SEL programs. Teachers in these schools reported significant improvements in their working conditions and student engagement.
- **Collective advocacy:** Stakeholders in education play a pivotal role in driving these policy changes with public demands. Teachers and administrators must work together to communicate the urgency of their needs to policymakers, using evidence and storytelling to make a compelling case. For example, a coalition of educators in California successfully lobbied for increased funding for professional development by sharing data on the correlation between teacher training and student achievement, alongside personal stories of how training improved their practices and morale. This dual approach of presenting hard evidence and human impact can sway decision-makers and build public support.

- **Professional organizations and unions:** Professional groups that are specifically set up to advocate and negotiate for educators are critical allies in this advocacy work. These groups can amplify teachers' voices, negotiate with policymakers, and ensure that proposed reforms are implemented effectively. For instance, the American Federation of Teachers (AFT) has been instrumental in advocating for teacher-friendly policies, such as increased funding for SEL programs and protections against punitive accountability measures. By joining such organizations, educators can strengthen their collective influence and gain access to resources that support their advocacy efforts.
- **Fundraising and reforms in support of teacher well-being and autonomy:** Finally, policymakers must consider long-term, systemic reforms that align education systems with the principles of self-determination theory and the Prosocial Classroom Model. This includes rethinking standardized testing mandates, investing in teacher leadership pathways, and creating policies that empower educators to design and implement innovative practices. For example, a pilot program in Colorado provided funding and autonomy to teams of teachers to develop project-based learning curricula tailored to their students' needs. This initiative not only enhanced student engagement but also reignited teachers' passion for their profession by giving them creative control. Systemic change also requires a cultural shift in how society values and supports teachers. Public awareness campaigns highlighting the critical role of educators can help counter negative stereotypes and build respect for the profession. Additionally, collaborations between schools, businesses, and community organizations can create networks of support that extend beyond the classroom. For instance, a partnership between a school district in Texas and local businesses provided teachers with discounts on wellness services, professional networking opportunities, and recognition events, fostering a sense of appreciation and community.

CONCLUSION

The challenges facing educators today demand systemic solutions that prioritize their well-being and professional growth. By both zeroing in on and zooming out from educator well-being as depicted in Figure 11.1, we can reimagine education systems that meet the psychological needs of teachers and students alike, and move toward a healed and healthy teaching profession. Addressing systemic stressors, fostering autonomy, competence, and relatedness, and promoting trauma-sensitive practices are essential steps toward creating sustainable and supportive school environments. Programs like CARE demonstrate the transformative potential of investing in teacher well-being, reinforcing the critical link between educator health, classroom climate, and student outcomes. Ultimately, a renewed focus on educators' social and emotional needs is not only a moral imperative but also the foundation of a resilient and thriving education system.

REFERENCES

Bergmark, U., Lundström, S., Manderstedt, L., & Palo, A. (2018). Why become a teacher? Student teachers' perceptions of the teaching profession and motives for career choice. *European Journal of Teacher Education, 41*(3), 266–281. https://doi.org/10.1080/02619768.2018.1448784e

Brown, J. L., Jennings, P. A., Rasheed, D., Doyle, S., Cham, H., Frank, J. L., Davis, R., & Greenberg, M. (2023). Direct and moderating impacts of the CARE mindfulness-based professional learning program for teachers on children's academic and social–emotional outcomes. *Applied Developmental Science, 29*(1), 14–33. https://doi.org/10.1080/10888691.2023.2268327

Jennings, P. A. (2015). *Mindfulness for teachers: Simple skills for peace and productivity in the classroom.* W. W. Norton.

Jennings, P. A. (2016). CARE for teachers: A mindfulness-based approach to promoting teachers' social and emotional competence and well-being. In K. A. Schonert-Reichl & R. W. Roeser (Eds.), *Handbook of mindfulness in education: Integrating theory and research into practice* (pp. 133–147). Springer.

Jennings, P. A. (2019). *The trauma-sensitive classroom: Building resilience with compassionate teaching.* W. W. Norton.

Jennings, P. A. (2021). *Teacher burnout turnaround: Strategies for empowered educators.* W. W. Norton.

Jennings, P. A., & Greenberg, M. (2009). The prosocial classroom: Teacher social and emotional competence in relation to child and classroom outcomes. *Review of Educational Research, 79*(1), 491–525. http://dx.doi.org/10.3102/0034654308325693

Jennings, P. A., Brown, J. L., Frank, J. L., Doyle, S., Oh, Y., Davis, R., Rasheed, D., DeWeese, A., DeMauro, A. A., Cham, H., & Greenberg, M. T. (2017). Impacts of the CARE for teachers program on teachers' social and emotional competence and classroom interactions. *Journal of Educational Psychology, 109*(7), 1010–1028. https://doi.org/10.1037/edu0000187

Jennings, P. A., Doyle, S., Oh, Y., Rasheed, D., Frank, J. L., Brown, J. L., & Greenberg, M. T. (2019). Long-term impacts of the CARE program on teachers' self-reported social and emotional competence and well-being. *Journal of School Psychology, 76*, 186–202. https://doi.org/10.1016/j.jsp.2019.07.009

Kurtz, H. (2022, January 12). Threats of student violence and misbehavior are rising, many school leaders report. *Education Week.* https://www.edweek.org/leadership/threats-of-student-violence-and-misbehavior-are-rising-many-school-leaders-report/2022/01

National Education Association. (2022). Teachers are burned out. Here's why there's no quick fix. *PBS NewsHour.* https://www.pbs.org/newshour/nation/teachers-are-burned-out-heres-why-theres-no-quick-fix

Ryan, R. M., & Deci, E. L. (2020). Intrinsic and extrinsic motivation from a self-determination theory perspective: Definitions, theory, practices, and future directions. *Contemporary Educational Psychology, 61*, 101860. https://doi.org/10.1016/j.cedpsych.2020.101860

Schussler, D. L., DeWeese, A., Rasheed, D., DeMauro, A. A., Brown, J. L., Greenberg, M. T., & Jennings, P. A. (2018). Stress and release: Case studies of teacher resilience following a mindfulness-based intervention. *American Journal of Education, 125*(1), 1–25. https://doi.org/10.1086/699808

Schussler, D. L., DeWeese, A., Rasheed, D., DeMauro, A. A., Doyle, S., Brown, J. L., Greenberg, M. T., & Jennings, P. A. (2019). The relationship between adopting mindfulness practice and reperceiving: A qualitative investigation of CARE for teachers. *Mindfulness, 10*(9), 1923–1935. https://doi.org/10.1007/s12671-019-01228-1

Schussler, D. L., Jennings, P. A., Sharp, J. E., & Frank, J. L. (2015). Improving teacher awareness and well-being through CARE: A qualitative analysis of the underlying mechanisms. *Mindfulness, 6*(4), 744–756. https://doi.org/10.1007/s12671-015-0422-7

Steiner, E. D., & Woo, A. (2023). *Job-related stress threatens the teacher supply: Key findings from the 2023 state of the U.S. teacher survey*. RAND Corporation. https://www.rand.org/pubs/research_reports/RRA1108-8.html

CHAPTER 12

The Role of the Superintendent in Systemic and Transformative SEL

Toward Critical Well-Being

Mai Xi Lee and Roberto Rivera

With the drumbeat for transforming schools getting louder, superintendents are at an inflection point. This is made more complex by ongoing conditions that keep systemic inequities in place as well as a rising mental health crisis amongst young people and adults. Teachers, in particular, are experiencing high levels of stress and burnout, resulting in many leaving the profession altogether (National Education Association, 2022). With teacher well-being and retention in crisis, coupled with inequitable student outcomes, expectations are high for superintendents to affect change. Superintendents, however, are not immune from ecological stressors and their well-being also needs attention (AASA, 2023).

Given these conditions, a system-wide, humanistic approach is needed. In recent years, implementing systemic social and emotional learning (SEL) has been one way schools have responded to the well-being crisis. Some schools have included Transformative SEL (tSEL; Jagers et al., 2019) to ensure equity elaborations are embedded. While systemic SEL & tSEL (defined further in the Key Terms section) have improved climate/culture and student outcomes (Cipriano et al., 2023; Durlak et al., 2022; Mahoney et al., 2018), they are still fringe initiatives that are dependent on funding and staff "buy-in." Furthermore, the siloing of SEL/tSEL implementation from other change efforts (e.g., DEI, climate, etc.) fragments resources, promotes initiative fatigue, and is unsustainable. As such, a paradigm shift that centers Critical Well-Being (CWB), a humanistic approach that incorporates the promise of SEL/tSEL alongside critical consciousness and participatory engagement, may be needed to transform systems. How superintendents understand their role in this new paradigm will have a significant impact on their organizational well-being.

This chapter explores the role of the superintendent within this paradigm shift. We acknowledge the complexity of the superintendency, uniqueness of organizations, and the nuanced challenges faced by superintendents. Accordingly, this chapter is not intended to essentialize superintendents and their roles. Rather, our aim is to ignite curiosity and critical reflection for superintendents as they navigate well-being for themselves and their organizations.

WHO WE ARE AND WHAT HAS INFORMED OUR WORK

Our collective experiences researching, developing, facilitating, and leading change efforts across school systems have informed our current work and understanding of systemic transformation. Mai Xi Lee's role as a district and statewide SEL leader has contributed to her understanding of systemic implementation and sustainability. Roberto Rivera's experience as a youth facilitator, researcher, and SEL expert have coalesced to inform the field of CWB. Specifically, Roberto's engagement with this topic is deeply rooted in his personal experience working with adolescents in out-of-school time programs, where he utilized strength-based, holistic, and culturally relevant pedagogical practices. Subsequently, Roberto's research with First Nations communities affirmed the importance of culturally sustaining and holistic well-being strategies, which he coined as Critical Well-Being (Rivera, 2021).

In our experience, even systemic and transformative SEL, which themselves have attempted to overcome some of the shortcomings of the early SEL framework, have nevertheless been vulnerable to a scarcity approach. A scarcity approach is characterized by understaffing teams (e.g., a team of one "champion" expected to carry the load), insufficient resources and unsustainable funding, and superficial support. The scarcity approach relegates humanistic approaches, like tSEL and CWB, to temporary statuses that are vulnerable to budget cuts and shifting priorities. Coupled with complex political dynamics and high leadership turnover, tSEL and CWB remain at the fringe of educational priorities. This scarcity paradigm undermines systemic transformation toward critical well-being.

Authentic CWB adoption involves an asset-based approach that includes seeing and activating the community cultural wealth that lies within one's school community (Yosso, 2005). When superintendents implement tSEL with a CWB paradigm and clearly articulate their expectations for working together, they create space for meaningful stakeholder participation, welcoming diverse cultural perspectives and voices, which strengthens momentum and makes realistic system change possible. For example, Mai Xi's work accelerated when one superintendent decided to reconceptualize a two-day leadership institute to prioritize a *culture of care*. Senior leadership, including the superintendent, coconstructed the two days with the SEL team and actively participated alongside their leaders. This radical approach to pausing transactional activities and prioritizing personal well-being for leaders was unprecedented and effective. The feedback was overwhelmingly positive, with many leaders remarking how refreshing it was to feel cared for and to have no expectations other than to "breathe and take care of myself." Thus, a superintendent's role is crucial to ameliorating the scarcity approach and improving organizational well-being.

KEY TERMS THAT BOLSTER SYSTEMIC AND TRANSFORMATIVE SEL TOWARD CWB

- ***SEL and tSEL:*** SEL is defined as the process through which adults and young people acquire and apply skills to develop healthy identities, manage emotions, achieve personal and collective goals, show empathy, establish supportive relationships, and make responsible decisions (Collaborative for Academic, Social, and Emotional Learning, n.d.). This is operationalized through five interacting competencies: *Self-Awareness, Self-Management, Social Awareness, Relationship Skills, and Responsible Decision-Making*. The tSEL constructs are equity elaborations that expand on the competencies to focus on *Identity, Agency, Belonging, Collaborative Problem-Solving, and Curiosity*. Beyond the specific construct additions, the key difference between SEL and tSEL is that whereas SEL is focused more on intra- and interpersonal relations, tSEL brings in more of a focus on students' civic responsibility, and standing up for others, especially in the face of unfairness and injustices (Jagers et al., 2021). Research indicates that SEL/tSEL can improve school climate, culture, academics, mental health, and prosocial skills (Cipriano et al., 2023; Durlak et al., 2022; Mahoney et al., 2018).
- ***Systemic and Transformative SEL:*** SEL practitioners generally understand systemic implementation to be a *wall-to-wall* approach where SEL is integrated into all organizational policies and practices. Systemic implementation consists of four areas: *Build foundational support and plan; Strengthen adult SEL competencies and capacity; Promote SEL for students; and Reflect on data for continuous improvement* (Collaborative for Academic, Social, and Emotional Learning, n.d.). When implemented with intentionality, these focus areas interact to maximize SEL development and outcomes for people, classrooms, schools and communities.

  Transformative SEL implementation expands on systemic implementation to amplify conditions that are necessary for change. To shift conditions, transformative SEL implementation prioritizes the calibration of the right climate levers (i.e., *safety, connection, voice and leadership, and culturally responsive practices*), the right levers to transform the system (i.e., *partnerships, supports, capacities, structures, and routines of SEL implementation* as referenced in the previous chapter), and a foundation rooted in SEL and tSEL practices (Shapiro et al., 2024). These calibrated levers and foundational roots enable a systemic *and* transformative SEL implementation that shifts conditions to improve student engagement, academic performance, and well-being so that students and adults can collectively thrive.
- ***Critical Well-Being (CWB):*** CWB serves as a north star for SEL and tSEL. Where SEL shines a light on the path for all and tSEL insists on a path that is equitable and inclusive, CWB seeks to counter systemic oppression

and create the conditions for healing and well-being through three key tenets: *cultivating a beloved community; sustaining holistic well-being; and amplifying staff, youth, and community voice.* CWB emphasizes the need for safe and inclusive spaces for individuals to develop racial literacy, cultural awareness, and the ability to challenge dominant narratives through critical engagement (Paris & Alim, 2017; Sealey-Ruiz, 2011). Furthermore, CWB cultivates organizational collaboration and participatory engagement to establish culturally sustaining policies and shared decision-making in order to ensure long-term changes to well-being efforts (Rivera, 2023). Through this humanistic approach to education, CWB nurtures an educational system that prioritizes personal and collective well-being as *a way of being*, and an ecosystem that honors community assets and voice, leading to a more healthy, whole, and just society.

WHY THE ROLE OF THE SUPERINTENDENT MATTERS

The superintendent's positional power and authority significantly impact systemic and transformative SEL toward CWB. Superintendents lead, shape, and inspire district culture, policies, and strategies, and can set the tone for systemic and transformative change (Collaborative for Academic, Social, and Emotional Learning, 2020). Although the students in a district may often not even know who their superintendent is, teachers and principals certainly will, and the culture and attitudes that they convey day-to-day in the classroom and school hallways will be a reflection, at least in part, of the superintendent's communications, directives, and most importantly, *way of being* when inhabiting their role.

Superintendent capacity and influence may buffer against the scarcity approach. Superintendents can work with their board and executive cabinet to embed tSEL and CWB into organizational policies including budget, academics, and climate/culture goals. Superintendents can hold their communities accountable for moving the needle on authentic and sustainable change. In particular, during stressful times, the community relies on the superintendent to embody authentic vulnerability and model emotional intelligence. While these expectations may place undue stress on the superintendent to be all things to all people, they are important reminders of the significance and critical hope endemic to the role, the value of authentic and humanistic leadership, and the critical need for superintendents to attend to their own well-being.

AN ECO-HUMANISTIC APPROACH TO THE SUPERINTENDENT'S ROLE

Applying an ecological systems lens (Bronfenbrenner, 1977) helps to elucidate how superintendents are situated within systems and how they support humanizing systemic and transformative SEL toward CWB. In this section, we describe the embodied stance and practices that support well-being at the personal level, the capacity-building and partnerships necessary at the relational level, and the importance of values alignment at the organizational level. Figure 1 conceptualizes this approach.

Superintendents Embody Critical Well-Being

Superintendents humanize and operationalize systemic and transformative SEL by embodying CWB. One way superintendents embody CWB is by doing regular P.I.E.S check-ins with staff, where everyone, including the superintendent, shares how they are doing *physically, intellectually, emotionally, and spiritually*. Mai Xi and Roberto have done this with county, district, and school leaders, and have received feedback that this simple practice signals integrity, vulnerability, and authenticity while humanizing the leadership team. In addition, Roberto has worked with superintendents who have gathered leadership teams together and engaged in personal storytelling, such as talking about a time one demonstrated courage, vision, strength, or compassion. Further, engaging leaders to identify their community cultural wealth has been instrumental in developing a sense of collective agency in the work Mai Xi and Roberto have done. These types of *intentional* activities and prompts, when shared with vulnerability, can lead to fostering a sense of beloved community, where rather than having the solutions all of the time,

Figure 12.1. The Role of the Superintendent Across an Ecological System

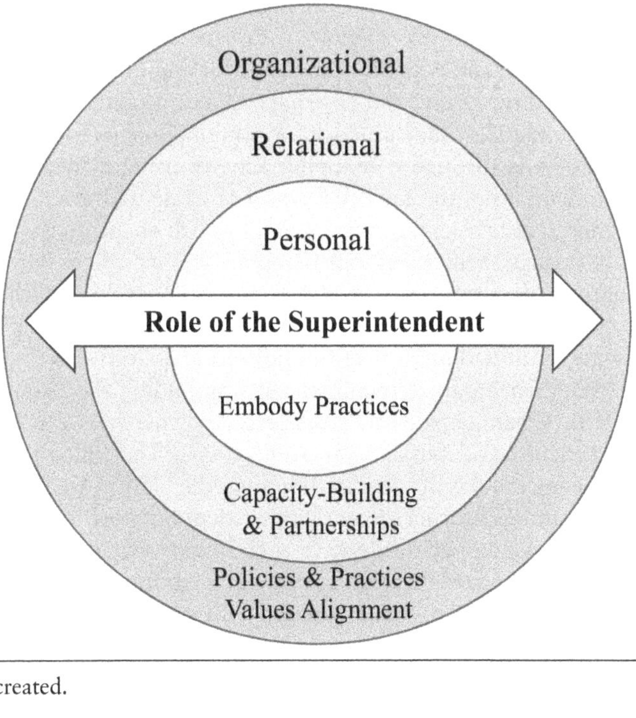

Note: Author created.

the superintendent models and embodies leading with humanity and leveraging strengths to take critical risks collectively.

Embodying CWB paves the way for a paradigm shift grounded in critical consciousness and critical hope, both of which are essential for enacting meaningful change. As Prilleltensky (2008) notes, power and well-being are deeply interconnected: those who hold power are often able to meet their well-being needs in culturally relevant ways, while marginalized groups frequently experience diminished well-being as a result of systemic exclusion and injustice. By deepening critical consciousness, superintendents are better positioned to examine their role in advancing well-being, interrogate their own power and privilege, and embody values that foster collective thriving. Superintendents may consider fortifying their CWB embodied practices with reflections such as:

- Why does my personal well-being matter for others?
- What dead-end beliefs do I have that continue to hold the problems of inequities in place? Am I willing to be uncomfortable while I examine those areas?
- What are the critical issues facing my school-community and what are the collective cultural assets that are present that could address these issues?

Superintendents Build Capacity and Partnerships Toward CWB

Shifting toward CWB requires superintendents to be intentional in building capacity and fostering partnerships. CWB promotes a holistic approach to well-being (emotional, physical, spiritual, and cognitive) and calls for alignment between internal systems (e.g., policies and resources) and external collaborations with community-based organizations (Rivera, 2023). One practice for superintendents to build capacity with their systemic leaders is through a mapping activity using a medicine wheel. This activity utilizes a diagram of the medicine wheel (a circle with four quadrants), with each quadrant representing mental, emotional, physical, or spiritual well-being. From here, leaders can engage their teams in a mapping activity where they identify all of a district's initiatives, departments, and efforts and collectively map them onto some aspect of the wheel. By viewing all initiatives, whether explicitly related to SEL or not, as potentially interconnected and unified in bolstering collective well-being, superintendents can strengthen organizational capacity by finding the "connective tissue" representing CWB. Where gaps exist, cross-sector partnerships can deepen support for educators, students, and families (Warren, 2005). The following section highlights two humanizing models of capacity-building: the Native American Community Academy (NACA) and California's CalHOPE Student Support.

At NACA, leaders mapped all departments, initiatives, and efforts toward supporting staff, student, and parent/caregiver cognitive, emotional, physical, and spiritual needs and where gaps existed, they partnered with youth and parents in identifying community-based organizations that could meet these needs in culturally relevant ways. As a result of these efforts, 33% of NACA staff are alumni of the school, and the school has become a national model for academic achievement. The experiences at NACA demonstrated to Roberto (Rivera, 2021) that coconstructing an equitable education system required systems leaders to engage staff in aligning intra-institutional initiatives and collaborating with youth and communities in identifying and connecting with relevant community organizations as partners.

The CalHOPE project leverages capacity-building and cross-sector partnerships to transform systemic SEL/tSEL (see Chapter 10 for a fuller description of CalHOPE). Through CalHOPE, 56 of California's 58 county offices of education (COE) are engaging in monthly communities of practice (CoP) where they regularly learn, network, collaborate, and share resources. The CalHOPE CoP is bolstered by a logic model that seeks to shift systemic conditions in order to improve engagement, performance, and well-being for adults and students toward collectivist thriving (Shapiro et al., 2024). Some early indicators point to improvements in adult SEL (i.e., improvements in *teacher attitudes, mindsets, efficacy, skills, and knowledge*), leadership capacity to implement systemic SEL structures and routines, and student outcomes for chronic absenteeism (CalHOPE Chronic Absenteeism, December 2024; Duane et al., 2025). Teachers are also finding healing through CoP participation, as exemplified by this feedback:

> "The SEL seminars [CoPs] were so amazing; a fantastic opportunity to network with other like-minded individuals from around the area. Of special note were the Empathy Interviews, Dimensions of Belonging, Walk and Talks, info about implementing school-wide SEL, and from the final session, Flash Consultancy. On a personal note, I was the person presenting the problem for the Flash Consult, and my two listeners were exceptionally adept at breaking down my problem and allowing me to reach my own decision. This was so meaningful to me as my mother had just passed away, and I needed clarity on speaking with authenticity, with my own voice, at her memorial service, which was the very next day. Through this process, I was able to sit right there after our seminar [CoP] and write out my speech (which granted had been percolating in my head for days, but after the Flash Consult, I was grounded enough to get it all down on paper!). Thank you for the opportunity to participate in this important work." —CoP Participant

To build capacity and partnerships, superintendents may consider how they are:

- Engaging with diverse partnerships across educational and noneducational spaces *(Example: Cross-sector partnerships between education, healthcare, higher education, and county leaders)*
- Allocating and communicating resources to support SEL/tSEL implementation *(Example: An accessible digital and turnkey-ready compendium of resources)*
- Developing the capacities (beliefs, attitudes, skills, efficacy, mindsets) of educators across all systems *(Example: Humanizing practices that support personal and collective well-being)*
- Establishing structures and routines of SEL implementation *(Example: A community of practice dedicated to well-being)*

Superintendents Align Values to Practice

Aligning values to policies/practices deepens and authenticates the work of tSEL and CWB. Aligned values and practices can garner trust, confidence, and promote sustainability. Conversely, stakeholders detect very quickly when values and practices do not align, and the broken trust from such ruptures is not regained easily, taking resources and time to rebuild.

One way that superintendents can align values to practice is by setting clear expectations about their humanizing intentions. These clear expectations are actualized through regular communication, resource and budget allocations to support the work, and intentionally integrating into organizational practices. For example, the CalHOPE Student Support community of practice was actualized through initial seed funding from the Sacramento County Office of Education (SCOE) superintendent, whose ongoing support can be seen through the development of a statewide SEL leadership and technical support team. At SCOE, SEL is regularly communicated regionally and statewide, and practices are integrated into meetings and learning spaces, including leadership team meetings.

In addition, superintendents may also leverage personal practice to activate tSEL and CWB. Personal practice involves actively engaging with diverse partnerships and coconstructing CWB together. To actualize this approach, superintendents may initiate multipartnership convenings (e.g., parents, young people, staff, community members, and leaders) to dialogue about what matters to them, including values and assets intrinsic to community/cultural groups and what well-being means to them. These coconstructed conversations should be dynamic and generative with all participants sharing power and voice. These initial CWB conversations can become synergistic spaces of care, connection, and wellness, which can expand to be spaces of solution-building and working through emerging community tensions. Research supports this approach—youth participatory action research (YPAR), for instance, has been effective in empowering students to shape systemic policies related to mental health and well-being by aligning district, school, and community efforts with meaningful, stakeholder-driven data (Rivera, 2023; Skoog-Hoffman et al., 2024). Through these intentional, participatory practices, school systems can move toward sustained, equity-driven transformation that centers well-being, cultural responsiveness, and collective agency.

IMPLICATIONS

There are several implications to enacting change with systemic and transformative SEL and CWB. Prioritization toward sustainability is one implication. Given varying and persistent needs (e.g., teacher shortage, mental health crisis, chronic absenteeism, and achievement gaps), superintendents will have to decide which issues receive priority. This prioritization is made more complicated with leadership attrition and diminishing resources. A second implication is how superintendents navigate humanizing systems in the face of increasing polarization, toxic discourse, and sociopolitical tensions. Schools are microcosms of the harmful effects of socioenvironmental and sociopolitical strife, and communities will look to the superintendent for reassurance and care. How superintendents navigate these tensions will have tremendous implications for personal, relational, and organizational well-being, particularly for marginalized families, students, and staff. Finally, there are implications for the role of tSEL and CWB in education. Amid a growing mental health crisis, superintendents may need to rethink traditional definitions of school success. This shift creates an opportunity to embrace a CWB paradigm that centers authentic stakeholder voice and participation. While such redefinition may challenge existing structures, it offers the potential to humanize education and establish a sustainable, shared leadership model beyond any one leader's tenure.

RECOMMENDATIONS

In the spirit of future-dreaming and critical hope, we offer these recommendations to support healing and humanizing educational systems and conditions, with specific attention to our front-line teachers:

- **Prioritize people over content.** If leaders and teachers are unwell, they cannot care for students. If students are unwell, they cannot learn and a cycle of disparate outcomes persists.
  - » Coconstruct ongoing healing spaces *with* teachers.
- **Integrate into academics.** Emphasize the *how (classroom routines, relationships, culturally-responsive practices, etc.)*. The revised 2024 California Standards for the Teaching Profession (CSTP) provides a good example.
  - » Incorporate well-being practices in teacher evaluations, along with the necessary supports.
- **Cultivate diverse partnerships,** including healthcare and universities that may be better resourced to support humanizing structures.
  - » Leverage local health and sports organizations to support teacher well-being.
- **Use an asset-based approach** to honor the cultural and community wealth that already exists in your community.
  - » Conduct empathy interviews and focus groups to learn about the cultural and community wealth that your teachers have.
- **Enact the duality of critical hope:** interrogate systemic inequities *and* reimagine a better way of being at the same time.
  - » Maximize meetings to build relationships, collaborate, and codream a better way of being for teachers.

- **Practice a stance of curiosity** by inviting opportunities for CWB coaching and support, personally and organizationally.
    - » Provide affinity spaces and journey-partnerships for teachers.

CONCLUSION

Superintendents are well-positioned to adopt a paradigm shift and support a humanistic approach to education. Through embodied leadership, superintendents can model a human-centered approach toward CWB and deepen their capacity to care for their organizations. Embodied practices, however, are just starting points toward systemic and transformative change. To promote trust and confidence, superintendents will need to align CWB values to intentional actions. Furthermore, a humanistic approach to education requires collective action, and this means superintendents must leverage cross-sector partnerships to build capacity across organizations. Finally, in order to actualize the promise of SEL, tSEL and CWB, superintendents will need to liberate themselves from the hero complex and shift toward a paradigm of host leadership (Wheatley & Frieze, 2011). This will require superintendents and their communities to leverage the cultural and communal wealth that already exists, and work to coconstruct a better future together.

REFERENCES

AASA. (2023, May 18). *How well-being bolsters superintendents amid district challenges* [Webinar recording]. AASA, The School Superintendents Association. https://www.aasa.org/resources/resource/how-well-being-bolsters-superintendents-amid-district-challenges

Bronfenbrenner, U. (1977). Toward an experimental ecology of human development. *American Psychologist, 32*(7), 513–531. https://doi.org/10.1037/0003-066X.32.7.513

CalHOPE Chronic Absenteeism. (2024, December 20). *CalHOPE student support: Initial findings of successful reductions in chronic absenteeism within low resource communities.* [Unpublished brief]. Sacramento County Office of Education.

Cipriano, C., Strambler, M. J., Naples, L. H., Ha, C., Kirk, M., Wood, M., Sehgal, K., Zieher, A. K., Eveleigh, A., McCarthy, M., Funaro, M., Ponnok, A., Chow, J. C., & Durlak, J. (2023). The state of evidence for social and emotional learning: A contemporary meta-analysis of universal school-based SEL interventions. *Child Development, 94*(5). https://doi.org/10.1111/cdev.13968

Collaborative for Academic, Social, and Emotional Learning. (2020). *Districtwide SEL for superintendents.* https://drc.casel.org/superintendent/

Collaborative for Academic, Social, and Emotional Learning. (n.d.). *What is the CASEL framework?* https://casel.org/fundamentals-of-sel/what-is-the-casel-framework/

Duane, A. M., Hafen, Q., McVeagh-Lally, P., & Shapiro, V. B. (2025). "It All Starts with Us": Exploring teachers' efforts to increase adult SEL in practice. *Social and Emotional Learning: Research, Practice, and Policy,* 100085.

Durlak, J. A., Mahoney, J. L., & Boyle, A. E. (2022). What we know, and what we need to find out about universal, school-based social and emotional learning programs for children and adolescents: A review of meta-analyses and directions for future research. *Psychological Bulletin, 148*(11–12), 765–782. https://doi.org/10.1037/bul0000383

Jagers, R. J., Rivas-Drake, D., & Williams, B. (2019). Transformative social emotional learning (SEL): Toward SEL in service of educational equity and excellence. *Educational Psychologist, 54*(3), 162–184. https://doi.org/10.1080/00461520.2019.1623032

Jagers, R. J., Skoog-Hoffman, A., Barthelus, B., & Schlund, J. (2021). Transformative social emotional learning: In pursuit of educational equity and excellence. *American Educator, 45*(2), 12–17.

Mahoney, J. L., Durlak, J. A., & Weissberg, R. P. (2018). An update on social and emotional learning outcome research. *Phi Delta Kappan, 100*(4), 18–23. https://doi.org/10.1177/0031721718815668

National Education Association. (2022, February 1). *Survey: Alarming number of educators may soon leave the profession* [Report]. Retrieved October 1, 2022, from https://www.nea.org/advocating-for-change/new-from-nea/survey-alarming-number-educ

Paris, D., & Alim, H. S. (2017). *Culturally sustaining pedagogies: Teaching and learning for justice in a changing world.* Teacher's College Press.

Prilleltensky, I. (2008). The role of power in wellness, oppression, and liberation: The promise of psychopolitical validity. *Journal of Community Psychology, 36*(2), 116–136. https://doi.org/10.1002/jcop.20225

Rivera, R. (2021, August 1). *Transitioning away from a social and emotional learning program to a critical well-being paradigm.* Medium. https://medium.com/transitioning-away-from-social-emotional-learning/transitioning-away-from-social-emotional-learning-programs-to-a-well-being-paradigm-aa8ba6337587

Rivera, R. (2023). *School and community leaders' experiences implementing critical well-being during the dual pandemics* [Unpublished doctoral dissertation]. University of Illinois at Chicago.

Sealey-Ruiz, Y. (2011). Learning to talk and write about race: Developing racial literacy in a college English classroom. *English Quarterly Canadian* 42(1–2), 24.

Shapiro, V., Duane, A., Lee, M., Jones, T., Metzger, A., Khan, S., Cook, C. , Hwang, S., Malicote, B., Nunez, A., Lee, J., McLaughlin, M., Caballero, J., Moore, J., Williams, C., Eva, A., Ferreira, C., McVeagh-Lally, P., & Kooler, J. (2024). "We will build together": Sowing the seeds of SEL statewide. *Social Emotional Learning: Research, Practice, and Policy, 3.* 100014. https://doi.org/10.1016/j.sel.2023.100014

Skoog-Hoffman, A., Miller, A. A., Plate, R. C., Meyers, D. C., Tucker, A. S., Meyers, G., Schlund, J., & Jagers, R. (2024). *Social and emotional learning in U.S. schools: Findings from CASEL's Nationwide Policy Scan and the American Teacher Panel and American School Leader Panel Surveys.* [Report]. RAND Corporation. https://www.rand.org/pubs/research_reports/RRA1822-2.html

Warren, M. R. (2005). *Communities and schools: A new view of urban education reform. Harvard Educational Review, 75*(2), 133–173. https://doi.org/10.17763/haer.75.2.m718151032167438

Wheatley, M., & Frieze, D. (2011). Leadership in the age of complexity: From Hero to Host. *Resurgence & Ecologist, 264*, 1–10. https://www.resurgence.org/magazine/article3282-from-hero-to-host.html

Yosso, T. J. (2005). Whose culture has capital? *Race, Ethnicity and Education, 8*(1), 69–91. https://doi.org/10.1080/1361332052000341006

CHAPTER 13

Healing by Principals, Healing for Principals

A Conversation with Maurice Swinney

Amanda Moreno and Maurice Swinney

The principal's point of view forms critical connective tissue between teachers and the larger systems we have represented in other chapters in this book. It felt like so much was riding on our one chapter from a principal's perspective, and that readers would be eager to hear how a healing-centered principal has been able to create meaningful change. Given how many questions we had for Dr. Swinney, it seemed that a real-time conversation would help assure we could provide dynamic and in-depth answers, and thus we decided to conduct this chapter as an interview.

Dr. Swinney's professional tagline is that he is an educational leader focused on supporting students who are "furthest from opportunity." He was a teacher and a freshman principal in his home state of Louisiana and has been in Chicago since 2012, where he served as a principal for several years, then as Chicago Public Schools' (CPS) inaugural Chief Equity Officer, then Interim Chief Education Officer, before moving into his current position as Chief Innovation Officer at Chicago Beyond. He intersected with Chicago Beyond during his time at CPS, as part of the development of the *Healing-Centered Framework* (see CPS website or Resource Tab for What Teachers Need at www.tcpress.com) initiative that began in 2016 as a response to the high levels of trauma in the district, but by 2021 had grown into a broader effort to proactively address "collective healing and wellness" (Portilla, 2022, p. 5).

I was greatly interested in speaking with Dr. Swinney for purposes of this book because, as you can hopefully begin to sense, he holds a number of vantage points that are critical to healing teaching. In my view, the fact that he is a *former* principal while now holding a leadership role in a philanthropic organization that still partners with the public school sector provides a unique combination of empathy, wisdom, and perspective on this topic that few could authentically inhabit as he does. In preparation for this conversation, Dr. Swinney also spoke with Dawn

Ramos, who was the Assistant Principal during Dr. Swinney's time at Tilden High School and took over as Principal when he left for his position as Chief Equity Officer in the district. He wanted to get her perspective on the continued and current work with the healing-centered framework, both at Tilden specifically and the district at large.

School buildings are worlds unto themselves (he likens the principal role to being mayor of a small town), and thus, healing philosophies and work must live there, or, frankly, they will die. As you will read in our conversation, Dr. Swinney demonstrates that this both essentializes and distributes the role of the principal simultaneously. They must embody healing, but not manage it alone. They must radiate healing, but not perform it. They must speak healing into being, inside the school walls and in their own life, but not define what it means for the community.

Amanda Moreno (AM): *Heavy on my mind today are the teachers I know in my personal life who are at once burned out and doing the "countdown" of days left in the year, seriously considering not returning next year, calling themselves "situationally depressed," all due to their job as a teacher, but at the same time are gifted instructors, whose principals know this and always send the outside observers to their rooms and come out with "no notes." Their principals are competent and kind—they don't have adversarial relationships, but still, these teachers I know are at the end of their rope. What advice would you give to their principals, to give their gifted instructors the best chance of sharing at least one more year of their talent while staying well?*

Maurice Swinney (MS): The very first step is for principals to hold up the mirror to themselves and say, how am *I* doing, and what supports do *I* need to be a better person? I've been telling all principals, "You need a therapist, full stop." There is no way you can set the conditions for the school community without having a separate space where you can say what you need to say, unfiltered. Those principals who create room in their lives for both therapy and executive coaching are by far the most successful in their own well-being and therefore their own leadership. Second, principals need to have a vision that is spoken out loud. For example, "At this school, we will become better at trauma-informed practices," or "We will create a welcoming space for everyone in this building." The responsibility becomes public, shared, and open dialogue. Schools are unique places where hundreds of people come together to have hundreds of interactions around a common purpose. It's a lot, so someone has to be there guiding that ship in a direction. Third, a common mistake I see principals make is to not have teams, or to not know how to assign or work well with teams. Who is the team who is going to lift up and make this vision real? I call this holding change rather than holding power. If the principal tries to enact change in a way that the burden is on himself alone, then the teachers are going to think that is the correct way, and that is what leads to burnout for all.

AM: *Okay, but let me interrupt you for a minute because the concept of "scarcity mindset" in leaders was brought up in the previous chapter. A principal could go to either extreme—I do it all myself, or, I delegate it to one "champion." We've seen this a lot in the SEL world, where the school finally gets the funding for an SEL coordinator, but the effort fails because it's too much for one person and it's not embedded. So, we know that, but what do you say to principals when there may be some truth to their scarcity mindset, for example, maybe there's only enough funding for a psychologist one day a week, or you can't build a team from existing teachers because their plates are already full?*

MS: I think that is a lie that principals tell themselves, born out of the weight of the responsibility. You can call that the savior complex, hero complex, whatever you want to call it, but there are people all around you including custodians, families, and staff, who want to help and get involved. But you have to create the conditions, and extend the invitations, and do so from your own place of knowing that people want to be a part of something meaningful. This "champion" concept is a real trip-wire for schools. It doesn't work. Once you have a team, they can help you look into: What's the professional learning journey we need as a school? What practices do we want to implement? What do we want to change about our discipline policies? What supports do we have for adults and students? What are the *fun* things we want to do? What services do we need to provide and advocate for? All of these questions can be responded to, and other questions will emerge, once we have a team. Let people choose which areas they are motivated to plug into, and how much time they want to lean into it instead of saying, this person is here only one day a week. They might choose to be a part of the greater good anyway. I really push principals on the mindsets and beliefs that they have in their own heads. Allow yourself to be surprised at the amount of complexity these teams can really grapple with. The solution is in the gathering. The outcome is the process—the figuring it out together.

AM: *We've covered the principal's mindsets and what they need to do at the school level and the team level to set the vision and the tone, but what about at the individual level with the teacher? What would you say to a principal to engage directly with a teacher who has hit that burnout wall?*

MS: It was always important to establish a culture of fun, of liveliness, of taking a breath, of appreciation, of joy. Of course we have these academic strongholds, and they're important, but the brain does it so much better when there's some oxygen, some space for human connection. That way, when it comes time for some more serious one-on-one interactions, they know that I care about them more than I care about the content.

AM: *Person-centered rather than content-centered.*

MS: For sure, for sure. If I had teachers who were hitting that wall, I would meet with them and say, let's create some space and make your "to STOP doing list." We'd look at their calendar for the next two weeks, and I would learn things! Like, you've got after school commitments three days a week, or you're doing special tutoring on Saturdays—you're never walking away from the thing! I developed this rule of "36 hours or two sleep cycles" where teachers had to put down their work. It's an easy way to remember—two sleeps before you can pick it back up. I would say, "Stop!" "Stop pushing paper around!" Sometimes these obvious solutions are blocked by weariness, but you begin to realize it benefits the work too, because your brain needs to step away, it is processing in the background, but if you never step away, you won't be able to see clearly. I also tell principals to encourage your teachers say no to *you*. Don't always rely on the competent teachers for the classroom observations—encourage them to tell you they need their space that day. Tell them to let you know when they cannot fit one more thing on their plate. Teachers need to be reminded to use the supports they have—such as their insurance. Our insurance covers therapy, sometimes it might cover massages or even acupuncture. Teachers should be encouraged to take their time off that's due to them. You don't have to fake it, we don't have to stay in a space of high tension like that. If you tell me in advance—you don't have to tell me why—then I can get the best sub for you, and you can feel better about being away, and it's a win-win. Stop shooting for perfect attendance, that's not real. So I feel like there are different things that are implied here that I know are covered in the book—teachers' joy and lightness, showing them love, respecting their time, their agency, their voice, their mental and physical health, being real and authentic with them. These are the ways I have seen principals help teachers come back from very real cases of burnout.

AM: *If someone had no idea what healing-centered engagement was, and they walked into a school where the practices were being lived and breathed, what would they see and hear, and what might they be able to describe as their understanding of the concept?*

MS: You would see quotes and images on the walls that were uplifting. You would see billboards signaling that "there is life here." You would see people greeting each other and people would greet you. You would see people talking to each other. The environment might not be fancy, but it would be neat and cared for, welcoming spaces, colorful, well-lit. One of the most favorite things I ever did as Principal was to print out huge pictures of students and have them all over the hallways, with their friends, engaging in their activities, almost like a living yearbook. That was transformational because it said so much that kids took care of these posters and what it meant about belonging to the space and the space belonging to them. If you were to go to a classroom it would feel cordial and inviting. You would see the event schedules so you wouldn't have to ask. Students' lives and activities are openly exalted. There are plants, fresh flowers sometimes, in offices and in the hallways, fresh air, that was encouraged. People know each other's names—the principal would know all the students' names. If a student comes in angry, you would always find out if they were hungry first, ask if they want an apple or a banana, because so often, that's what it's about, and healing-centered means getting curious about the underlying needs of the kids.

AM: *OK, talk more about that because obviously a top concern of teachers is difficult emotions and behavior challenges with students. What would you see during a behavioral or emotional challenge in a school that was carrying out the healing-centered framework? In particular, how would we know that teachers were being supported in those moments?*

MS: An observer wouldn't see much as far as the student is concerned because I think the whole problem with traditional approaches is too much public humiliation and combativeness. If there were a disruption in a healing-centered school, you would not see the teacher constantly questioning the student in front of everyone—in fact, you would see the teacher subtly trying to get the attention *off* that student. They might just whisper or pass a sticky note and ask to see them in the hallway to just speak about what's going on with them. For support for the adults, especially if we're talking about a more serious kind of infraction where the teacher is just finding themselves unable to engage and needs a break . . . I'm from New Orleans and we say, "I'm going to the 'stoh'" so at our school the code was "I need to go to the STO," for Staff Time Out, which means, "I'm about to lose my shit, and somebody would step in." Whoever was closest, whether that was support staff or another teacher, and that person would alert someone on leadership. I would ask the teacher what they needed to come back to their body whether that's stepping off school grounds to get a coffee, a cigarette, or listen to their favorite song. We would collect that data on these "pauses" so we would know, and be able to examine, if there are 20 pauses, is there something we need to look into further with a teacher or with a classroom.

AM: *You mentioned earlier that principals need therapy and executive coaching for their own wellness. What other practices did you engage in, both within and outside of the school setting for your own wellness, and perhaps that of others?*

MS: I modeled a practice of having an evening during the work week with "nothing to do." For me, it was Tuesday, and faculty and staff knew. They would tell me: "Why are you answering my e-mails, isn't it Tuesday?"

So it became a collective wellness practice to remind each other to disconnect and do things you enjoy in your personal life. For me, that was going to the barbershop. That was my therapy. Sometimes twice a week. Even though people like to make fun of that self-care stuff sometimes, something that you have as a ritual is very important. I had a ritual of quiet time in my office as well. A few times a week I would tell my executive assistant that I needed 20 minutes of quiet time in my office to just chill, or process.

A lot of times my wellness practices in the building were more social too. Sometimes I would just go and situate myself in the cafeteria. I know this meant a lot to students to see me there—fist bumps, handshakes, high fives, playing Uno—and it did me good too, to get away from that bureaucratic weightiness and just be in community. We had "Fried Fridays" where we would have fried fish or chicken at lunch time, as well as a salad, getting some greens in there. These meals were made by students from the culinary school, so we got to experience their art in that way.

AM: *You're reminding me of a recurring theme in the book that Jeanette calls "hospitality." She says that hospitality is more than comfort and helpfulness, it is a practice of openness that invites new possibilities, interrelatedness, and care. As a principal, you created a hospitable school.*

MS: Yes, and again, these are shared practices. These kinds of community partnerships, like with the culinary school, can be an easy "hack." Some of your teachers are going to be great at that stuff—we got furniture, coffee makers, plants, and we now have this beautiful teachers' lounge, all because of just asking. Teachers wrote the letters, and now with AI you can write the letters much faster, so you just reach out, and you'd be surprised what people donate. These simple practices of kinship in public spaces in your school, beautifying the school, engaging in partnerships that allow outside organizations to demonstrate that they care about your kids too—these are all community wellness practices that a principal can model.

AM: *Speaking of outside partnerships, I have a final, selfishly motivated question for external partners such as me. What is your advice for folks like me who work in the teacher professional development space who have good intentions, maybe do have some wisdom to share, but a few of us in our chapters have made reference to our awareness that we get made fun of on social media or that teachers will roll their eyes—understandably—if a PD facilitator engages in silliness like "What is your why?," when we know that teachers are coping with the most serious challenges and professional—not to mention federal—gaslighting, on the daily. So how should we speak more genuinely to the lived experiences of teachers to support them in being more well in their jobs?*

MS: I'm going to use a kind of clinical term for lack of a better word here, but: "diagnostic." PD folks can be better received and more effective with their work if their agenda is less canned, so to say, and more fitted to the diagnosis of what is going on at that particular school. From a principal's lens especially, it is ideal to have a prerelationship and a series of premeetings with the principal where this diagnosis can occur. Our best SEL providers, we would have lunch meetings, and we would talk over lunch and plan for what we thought was needed in the PD. I would invite a couple of different teachers in each time and just say, hey, can you come in and download a few thoughts on where your kids are at. I learned this from the equity work, that this was the way to gather the best thinking, and avoid that eye-rolling, to get the buy-in. Then the PD person can say, OK, this is what I heard, this is what is needed at this school. Even if not every teacher was a part of that particular download, they can confirm or not if that aligns with their needs. This boosts the credibility of any outside partner dramatically because you are showing that you listened, and you made your choices on what to talk about based on that listening.

AM: *That makes a lot of sense because it's not like there's a shortage of things to talk about. And if there is some wellness-based work that is "diagnosed" that falls outside your expertise, that's OK, too—you can call on others to step in.*

MS: Right, and that builds your credibility further, rather than trying to pretend you have knowledge that you don't have.

AM: *That is very helpful advice, thank you. Any final words you would like to share on the healing-centered work from a principal's lens?*

MS: My conversation with Principal Ramos reminded me of some of the foundational work that we did, that really speaks equally to both teachers and school leaders. First, just how key the *self*-work is as a starting place. I was reminded that as part of the development of the equity toolkit, we engaged in some very careful and arduous work to develop what ended up being this seemingly simple tool called the "Liberatory Thinking Tool," (see CPS website or Resource Tab for What Teachers Need at www.tcpress.com) which includes concepts of self-care, identity, disposition, bias, and actions. It touches on many of the concepts from our conversation today, including the importance of basic ideas such as sleep and medical care, and the idea of modeling what I expect to see from others. The idea being, how can I engage in the complex work of equity and wellness of a community if I'm literally not rested or caring for myself or living these principles in my own life? It was a good reminder that some of these tools are no-cost and can be a great way to reduce the overwhelm of where to start. You can do this in a private, quiet space, and just reflect on it on your own first. You have to liberate your own thinking before you can help steward the wellness of a community. Then, it was just beautiful for me to hear Principal Ramos voice some of these things in her way, to remind me of the continuation of the work, like, "Oh yeah, we started that, and that. . . . " But to hear how they were keeping it going, not necessarily with some new special formula, but they were still *working it*, you know? She was really seeming alive, and she was modeling that for her community, and it highlighted that generative cycle for me, where the ideas get born and reborn, worked and reworked, forgotten and reremembered. No matter what "level" of educator you are, someone is looking to you for care or guidance or inspiration, and your superpower—which costs nothing—is *your* agency to activate *their* agency.

REFERENCES

Chicago Public Schools. (n.d.). *CPS equity framework liberatory thinking tool.* https://www.cps.edu/sites/equity/tools/liberatory-thinking/cps-equity-framework-liberatory-thinking-tool/

Chicago Public Schools. (n.d.). *Healing-centered framework.* https://www.cps.edu/strategic-initiatives/healing-centered/framework/

Portilla, X. A. (2022). Healing school systems. Solutions for educational equity through social and emotional well-being. *MDRC.* ED623974

PART IV

HEALING TEACHING THROUGH INNER AND OUTER HARMONY

SELF, OTHERS, EARTH

CHAPTER 14

Peace Education as a Path to Healing in Crisis-Affected Regions

Dody Wibowo

Education is not merely a process of imparting academic knowledge and technical skills; it is also a powerful medium for shaping individuals who contribute positively to community well-being and work toward achieving social justice. This dual role of education underscores the moral responsibility of teachers to go beyond teaching facts and skills (Toh & Floresca-Cawagas, 1990). Teachers must nurture their students to become agents of peace and justice, cultivating a society where every individual experiences fairness, dignity, and harmony (ILO/UNESCO, 2016). If peace is understood as the state where justice prevails for all, then the role of teachers as peace educators becomes even more critical (Reardon, 1999; Harris & Morrison, 2013).

Unfortunately, this moral responsibility is often overlooked or inadequately addressed within the current educational landscape. Teacher professional training rarely emphasizes the importance of instilling values of peace, justice, and social responsibility in their students, which represents a tragic missed opportunity to ensure a more peaceful society. In some cases, such as in Bosnia and Herzegovina (Clarke-Habibi, 2018), teachers who have experienced past trauma, such as those who have lived through periods of violent conflict, may still be struggling to heal themselves. Thus, a lack of focus on peace education results in both students and teachers without adequate tools to process, heal, and make positive change.

Schools represent the primary context teachers and students spend in community with others, except for their own families. If the need for peace and mutual healing is ignored, especially in regions in which collective trauma exists, such as war-torn nations or areas prone to natural disasters, even further harm could be caused. Without intentional efforts to integrate peace education into teaching practices, schools risk producing individuals with technical skills and academic knowledge but without the integrated capacity needed to navigate the world's complex social challenges. This disconnect contributes to the perpetuation of social injustices, conflicts, and inequalities, thereby undermining the potential for long-lasting peace in society.

The situation outlined is common across various world regions. Since 2010, I have faced such challenges in areas of Indonesia impacted by natural disaster while delivering peace education training in six schools across three provinces. It became clear during this experience that many teachers viewed peace values as an issue outside their domain, perhaps suited only for certain subjects like religion or civics. These misconceptions arose because local education authorities offered peace education training only once, without follow-up or assessment. School leaders failed to encourage teachers to share their new knowledge or integrate it into classes and school events. This lack of support led to minimal practice and sharing of training outcomes.

I was profoundly moved by the difficulties these teachers experienced, and I felt a strong urge to design and test a method for more effective, system-wide implementation. After completing my doctoral studies, which focused on teacher professional development for peace education, I had the chance to apply my knowledge when I joined the Sukma Foundation, which manages Sukma Bangsa Schools. My role involved designing and implementing strategies to support teachers as authentic and effective peace educators. The goal of my position was to create a concrete, comprehensive strategy aimed at helping teachers become effective peace educators. This chapter discusses the strategies I adopted at Sukma Bangsa Schools between 2021 and 2024, shares essential lessons learned, and offers guidance on how these strategies can be generalized to other schools and world regions.

THEORETICAL FOUNDATIONS

Peace education should be viewed as a vital element in educational practices, anchored in the belief that a major obligation of education is to nurture nonviolence, community cohesion, and resolution of conflicts (Counts, 1978; Harris & Morrison, 2013). Peace education encourages a critical examination of social inequalities while equipping learners with the necessary skills to promote enduring peace. Nevertheless, the successful implementation of peace education heavily depends on teachers, who serve as catalysts for change in both formal and informal learning environments (Reardon, 1999).

Teachers play a vital role as facilitators of student-centered learning experiences and peace education (Freire, 2000; Girardet, 2018; Harris & Morrison, 2013). Yet, inadequate teacher training often deprioritizes the moral and social dimensions of education (Avalos, 2011). Carter (2008) proposed essential skills to support teachers in developing competence in peace education. These include guiding students to construct their own understanding of peace, embracing cultural diversity, practicing inclusive communication, and creating safe and nurturing classrooms. Teachers are encouraged to engage with families, model nonviolence, and utilize restorative practices to foster peaceful school communities. Rather than working in isolation, teachers benefit from a broader network of educators, researchers, and communities who care deeply about their well-being and are dedicated to accompanying them on a shared journey of healing and peace-building for both themselves and their students.

A comprehensive approach is essential to effectively incorporating peace education into teacher development programs. This entails structured training, hands-on learning experiences, and institutional policies emphasizing ethical and social responsibility. Without these vital components, teachers are unlikely to fully assume their roles as peace educators, thereby hindering the potential of education to contribute to collective healing and foster a just and equitable society.

BACKGROUND OF THE SUKMA BANGSA SCHOOLS

The Sukma Bangsa Schools were founded in Aceh following two significant disasters in Indonesia: the 2004 Aceh earthquake and tsunami and the 2018 earthquake and liquefaction (i.e., when loose ground loses its strength as a result of the shaking, which can cause landslides and destruction of buildings) in Central Sulawesi. The devastating 2004 earthquake caused a tsunami and over 200,000 deaths, marking one of the worst natural disasters in history.

Established by Sukma Foundation, a foundation associated with the Media Group, three schools were built in Pidie, Bireuen, and Lhokseumawe for children affected by the tsunami and the conflict with the Free Aceh Movement. These schools serve as peace education hubs, offering quality academic instruction and promoting nonviolence and social harmony. They aim to reduce conflict and foster an environment where violence is not viewed as a means to express emotions or resolve disputes. These schools were created through public contributions to aid postdisaster education and recovery initiatives and as such, they exhibit a strong commitment to peace education and the professional growth of teachers. In 2018 another school was added after a 7.7-magnitude earthquake devastated Palu and Donggala in Central Sulawesi. This school prioritizes earthquake victims and underprivileged children, offering full scholarships, while self-funded students are also welcome, fostering economic diversity.

The Sukma Bangsa Schools aim to create a positive learning environment that fosters academic excellence and moral integrity (Baedowi et al., 2015). They follow a holistic educational approach that emphasizes research, collaboration, and community empowerment for promoting peace. Peace education principles are central to the school's culture, integrating the 5S philosophy (Senyum, Sapa, Salam, Sopan, and Santun), which advocates for friendliness, respect, and patience, and the 4NOs policy (no cheating, violence, smoking, or littering) to uphold integrity and environmental stewardship (Baedowi et al., 2015). To promote nonviolent conflict resolution, the schools utilize a School-Based Conflict Management system that addresses conflicts through mediation and peace-focused curricula (Panggabean et al., 2015).

THE IMPLEMENTATION PROCESS

Since its founding, teachers at Sukma Bangsa School, especially in Aceh, have undergone training in peace education. However, this training has been inconsistent, leaving some later joiners without the chance to participate. In July 2021, I was invited to join Sukma Foundation, tasked primarily with overseeing the implementation of peace education at Sukma Bangsa Schools. Improving peace education at Sukma Bangsa Schools involved a progressive process that began with foundational learning, deepened through everyday engagement, and was reinforced by collective and institutional support.

Laying the Foundation for Peace Education

As a starting point, I ensured that all staff at Sukma Bangsa Schools, including teachers, administrative personnel, maintenance crew, and security, were introduced to the core principles of peace education. This was crucial because the entire school community grasping these fundamental concepts provides a foundation for any learning endeavor. These concepts serve as a framework, enabling individuals to interpret their experiences, emotions, and observations methodically, leading to more strategic and informed decision-making based on their understanding.

Participation in at least one introductory session was mandatory to foster a shared understanding of peace education among all school staff. These discussion-oriented sessions served as an initial step to introduce participants to the fundamental concepts of peace education. The introductory session lasted two hours and included a structured presentation, followed by a Q&A segment that allowed participants to clarify their doubts and engage in meaningful dialogue. The session covered key concepts, including conflict, violence, peace, and peace education. For instance, the discussion on conflict included definitions from peace studies and explored why individuals may have different feelings and perceptions about conflict. Some may fear and avoid it, while others may view it as neutral or manageable. Approximately 15 teachers and staff participated in each session. I provided handouts and reading materials, and participants were invited to contact me if they wished to engage in a deeper discussion.

To evaluate the effectiveness of these sessions, I conducted interviews with participants. The feedback was largely positive, with many noting that the discussions broadened their perspectives on conflict, peace, and violence. One particularly impactful topic was the concept of conflict. During the sessions, I explained that in peace studies, conflict itself is not inherently negative; rather, it is a natural and often necessary part of human interaction. I emphasized that it is not the presence of conflict that matters but how we respond to it, which ultimately determines whether it leads to constructive change or destructive outcomes.

This framing challenged many teachers' prior assumptions. Several participants from Aceh shared that their understanding of conflict was shaped by the violent history between the Indonesian government and the Free Aceh Movement, leading them to associate all conflict with violence and harm. The sessions encouraged a shift in this thinking, opening the possibility of viewing conflict as a neutral event that, when handled peacefully, can lead to growth and reconciliation. Although this initial phase was only a single session, it was nonetheless an important first step. I firmly believe that cultivating teachers as peace agents necessitates sustained and continuous efforts. By starting these conversations, I laid the initial groundwork for further development in future training and implementation stages.

Encouraging Mindful Engagement

To help peace education take root beyond theory, I designed a series of activities that encouraged teachers to reflect deeply and observe their surroundings through a peace-oriented lens. I implemented a year-long process to support gradual and meaningful habit formation. This extended timeframe was essential for fostering lasting change. I initiated a sequence of reflective practices that began with a sensitivity exercise and gradually expanded into more sustained personal journaling and collective reflection.

The objective of the first activity was to enhance teachers' social awareness and help them analyze daily situations through the lens of peace education. I invited teachers to take a 15-minute walk outside the school premises, asking them to observe their environment and pinpoint one notable social phenomenon they had previously overlooked. After their walk, the teachers noted their feelings and thoughts about the phenomena that intrigued them in their notebooks. Some decided to share their reflections, igniting vibrant discussions. For example, one teacher observed an elderly couple residing in a dilapidated house near the school, something he had previously missed. He shared his concern about the social injustice happening so near to his workplace. This prompted several other teachers to engage in the discussion, exploring potential reasons behind the situation. This is not to suggest that teachers were previously blind to their surroundings, or had not previously thought about local injustices, but the exercise added a level of intentionality, time to reflect in community, and the new lens of peace education to support them "seeing" their environment in new ways despite their typically busy lives and likely task-based walks only for the purpose of getting to work.

A different teacher highlighted a damaged road often traveled by Sukma Bangsa School's students, questioning why local officials had not fixed it and expressing worries about possible traffic accidents. Several teachers offered their views on the government's duty to provide safety and comfort for its citizens. These conversations showcased the teachers' increasing attention to peace education principles and incorporating the assessment of real-world social challenges as more of a daily habit than previously.

Recording observations from the 15-minute walk was a foundational step in the development of habits incorporating peace values into everyday practices. By writing about their experiences during the walk, teachers engaged in reflection, a process where individuals thoughtfully analyze their encounters to gain new insights and appreciations. This self-examination allows them to derive meaning from their lives, assess their personal growth, and acknowledge their connections with others (Boud et al., 1985; Wibowo, 2020).

Three months after the activity, I revisited it to conduct follow-up interviews and evaluate impact. One teacher mentioned that since the activity, she had become more aware of her surroundings, especially during her commute. She now noticed social issues she had previously glossed over, such as street vendors, poor infrastructure, and marginalized communities. This feedback indicated that the training was starting to change teachers' perspectives, nurturing a deeper sense of social responsibility, which is essential for embracing peace education.

Personal reflection through journaling is crucial for internalizing peace education values. To start institutionalizing reflective practices, I also engaged school leaders, including directors and principals, in regular journaling activities. I encouraged daily reflections in a shared Google Drive, where I provided feedback and motivated others to participate. After a month, during an evaluation, the school leadership team noted increased awareness of daily events, stemming from the reflective journaling process. One reflection revealed that he had overlooked early arrivals, focusing more on latecomers and neglecting those who demonstrated punctuality. Through reflection, he learned to acknowledge and value positive behavior, recognizing that affirming early arrivals could encourage good habits and inspire others.

I continued this initiative exclusively with the school leadership team for three months before inviting them to encourage teachers at their respective levels to participate as well. This incremental strategy demonstrated its effectiveness. With school leaders having already witnessed the benefits of reflection, they successfully persuaded their colleagues of its importance. They reported several benefits, including a greater sensitivity to their emotional responses. Reflection taught them to pause and assess situations holistically before reacting, particularly during conflicts. This enabled them to respond with self-regulation and intention, avoiding impulsive reactions that could harm themselves or others. Such emotional awareness and self-restraint are crucial for their healing. I kept track of the development of this habit-forming process by frequently consulting with the school directors for updates on its effects.

Over time, this practice of reflection led to significant outcomes. Teachers noted a greater comprehension of their instructional strategies and became more sensitive to shifts in their students' behaviors and emotions. The school had actively provided opportunities for reflection, including regular group sessions and a shared Google Docs document where school leaders regularly offered encouraging feedback. Even so, participation in journaling remained a personal choice. Some teachers may have had other responsibilities or time constraints that limited their ability to contribute regularly, and this was understood without judgment. It was hoped that through consistent exposure to a supportive and reflective school culture, primarily as modeled by the school leadership, teachers would gradually develop the awareness and motivation to engage in personal reflection at their own pace. Reflection is crucial in both peace education and healing, enabling teachers to process their emotional experiences, address past traumas, and cultivate a more empathetic and nonviolent teaching approach (Reardon, 1999).

Collective Growth and Institutional Support

To sustain momentum and expand impact, the next step involved a yearlong process of creating systems of peer support, mentorship, and institutional backing. Throughout this habit formation process, I noticed substantial improvements among the teachers at Sukma Bangsa Schools. They grew increasingly aware of peace-related issues and began to weave peace values into every subject. A striking instance involved a teacher from Sukma Bangsa School in Sigi, who successfully published an article in a national newspaper detailing how he incorporated peace education into his physics classes.

From his story, he shared that he had been a victim of bullying for more than 16 years, which left him with deep trauma and a lingering sense of anger. When he began learning about peace education, he gained a deeper understanding of the issues he was facing. Consciously, he chose to transform the negative energy resulting from his experiences as a bullying victim into positive energy to manage his anger. He stated that he has since been able to regulate his mood effectively. For instance, if he is in a bad mood at home, he deliberately does not bring that energy to school. He intentionally adopts a positive and professional attitude at school, aware that his emotions can impact his students.

His painful experience of being bullied also became a strong motivation for integrating peace education into his physics classes. He noticed some of his students were experiencing bullying, and he wanted them to learn that such behavior is unacceptable. He further shared that after several sessions, he observed changes. A student who had previously been quiet and withdrawn began to speak up, and their peers also began to show more positive attitudes. This clearly illustrates that peace education is applicable across all subjects when educators acknowledge its importance, and it also reflects a meaningful journey of personal growth for this teacher.

Building on these results, I introduced an embedded and ongoing mentoring strategy for teachers at Sukma Bangsa Schools. The primary approach was to designate selected teachers as focal points for peace education at each location. Our first activity consisted of monthly gatherings with these four focal point teachers. During these 90-minute Zoom meetings, we addressed progress in each school and examined national issues, such as the increasing incidence of bullying in Indonesian schools. Furthermore, the focal point teachers outlined next steps to enhance peace education initiatives in their schools, followed by conversations with their colleagues at their respective institutions. This tiered communication framework facilitated the broader exchange of knowledge and best practices, amplifying peace education's impact across the Sukma Bangsa Schools community.

After four months, I realized that monthly meetings were inadequate for momentum for our progress, and a switch to weekly meetings yielded immediate, substantial results. Teachers could more promptly address emerging issues, showed a better understanding of peace education, and more easily engaged in deeper self-reflection. One teacher in Aceh shared a personal reflection about a student whose emotional struggles had gone unnoticed despite appearing cheerful. The experience left a deep impact on her. However, through ongoing reflection and peer support, she shifted from self-blame to learning and began developing more intentional ways to recognize and respond to students' emotional needs, something she viewed as part of her own healing journey.

Additionally, the peace education initiatives led by focal point teachers became more organized and tailored to address the unique challenges of each school. At Sukma Bangsa School in Sigi, for example, one teacher sparked a dialogue with students about sexual violence. This activity uncovered numerous instances of sexual violence faced by students, particularly within their families. This insight proved crucial for the school in formulating strategies to safeguard students and enhance family awareness regarding child protection against sexual violence. Another example of systemic embedding of peace values occurred at Sukma Bangsa School in Bireuen, where a teacher initiated discussions with colleagues on nonviolent communication. This topic drew considerable interest, prompting teachers to engage actively and reflect on their own communication styles. As a result, many teachers became more conscious of their interactions with peers, and some even supported each other in adhering to nonviolence principles. This process improved communication and facilitated emotional healing, helping teachers build stronger, more compassionate relationships with one another.

CONCLUSION

Teachers play a vital and challenging role in creating a better world. Through education, they can steer students to actively promote global peace and social justice while simultaneously embarking on their own journey of healing and personal growth. If teachers do not embody and pass on to students values of peace, education as a context for making the world a better place will go unrealized. Worse, school could serve as a reinforcer of harm to self, others, or the environment.

To teach peace effectively, teachers require opportunities for capacity building. However, they must first internalize these peace values and have the opportunity to begin to heal within a supportive community, particularly from the traumas they may have experienced before passing them on to their students. Supporting teachers through this intricate process cannot be accomplished quickly or superficially. During my mentorship of teachers at Sukma Bangsa Schools, I discovered four essential elements that serve to create a deep and authentic pathway to peace values:

1. **A well-defined and articulate school vision.** When a school embraces peace values as part of its identity, it guides teachers in integrating these principles into their teaching. Maintaining this vision requires ongoing

curriculum updates and practices like group discussions or journaling. School leaders should model these values and foster collaborative planning, ensuring the vision remains integral to the school culture.

2. **Effective school leaders.** When school leaders recognize teachers as vital peace educators, they are inclined to establish policies and frameworks that promote and support peace education in the school setting. This may include practical steps such as allocating specific time in the school schedule for reflective activities and regular team discussions focused on peace-related themes.
3. **Access to learning opportunities and resources.** These resources may be available within the school or through partnerships outside it. If a school does not have enough internal resources for peace education training, it can collaborate with other institutions, such as a university that has a program on peace studies or peace education.
4. **Teachers supporting each other.** A meaningful peace education journey supports teachers in realizing that the work of peacebuilding is not theirs to carry alone but is a shared path of healing, rooted in solidarity with their school community. However, this sense of solidarity does not emerge automatically. It must be intentionally nurtured within the school environment. In this regard, school leaders play a critical role in cultivating a culture of collaboration and mutual care. This involves creating dedicated time and space for shared reflection, encouraging peer support structures, and modeling the values of empathy and cooperation. By doing so, leaders help build a beloved community where teachers feel supported in their healing and empowered to bring peace values into their classrooms.

Alongside promoting peace within their classrooms, teachers' personal healing journeys are vital, particularly in regions affected by conflict or disaster. Through peace education, teachers uplift their students and aid their own emotional recovery and development. The earlier mentioned reflective practices, peer support, and institutional support are crucial for helping teachers process their traumas and build resilience. As teachers recover, they are more capable of leading their students toward a more just and peaceful world, creating a continuous cycle of healing that resonates throughout the school community.

REFERENCES

Avalos, B. (2011). Teacher professional development in teaching and teacher education over ten years. *Teaching and Teacher Education*, 27(1), 10–20. https://doi.org/10.1016/j.tate.2010.08.007

Baedowi, A., Azhar, K., Sarlivanti, Sansrisna, Zen, S. P., & Yasadhana, V. (2015). *Manajemen sekolah efektif: Pengalaman Sekolah Sukma Bangsa*. PT Pustaka Alvabet.

Boud, D., Keogh, R., & Walker, D. (1985). Promoting reflection in learning: A model. In D. Boud, R. Keogh, & D. Walker (Eds.). *Reflection: Turning experience into learning* (pp. 18–40). Routledge Falmer.

Carter, C. C. (2008). Voluntary standards for peace education. *Journal of Peace Education, 5*(2), 141–155. https://doi.org/10.1080/17400200802264347

Clarke-Habibi, S. (2018). Teachers' perspectives on educating for peace in Bosnia and Herzegovina. *Journal of Peace Education, 15*(2), 144–168. https://doi.org/10.1080/17400201.2018.1463209

Counts, G. S. (1978). *Dare the school build a new social order?* (Vol. 143). SIU Press.

Freire, P. (2000). *Pedagogy of freedom: Ethics, democracy, and civic courage.* Rowman & Littlefield Publishers.

Girardet, C. (2018). Why do some teachers change and others don't? A review of studies about factors influencing in-service and pre-service teachers' change in classroom management. *Review of Education, 6*(1), 3–36. https://doi.org/10.1002/rev3.3104

Harris, I. M., & Morrison, M. L. (2013). *Peace education.* McFarland & Co.

International Labour Organization (ILO) / United Nations Educational, Scientific and Cultural Organization (UNESCO). (2016). *The ILO/UNESCO recommendation concerning the status of teachers (1966) and the UNESCO recommendation concerning the status of higher-education teaching personnel (1997)—Revised edition 2016.* International Labour Office, Sectoral Policies Department, ILO.

Panggabean, R., Baedowi, A., Yasadhana, V., Hanafiah, S., & Firawati, T. (2015). *Manajemen konflik berbasis sekolah: Dari Sekolah Sukma Bangsa untuk Indonesia.* PT Pustaka Alvabet.

Reardon, B. A. (1999). *Educating the educators: The preparation of teachers for a culture of peace.* School of Education.

Toh, S. H., & Floresca-Cawagas, V. (1990). *Peaceful theory and practice in values education.* Phoenix Publishing House.

Wibowo, D. (2020). *The role of school culture in teacher professional development for peace education: The case of three schools in post-conflict Aceh, Indonesia.* [Unpublished doctoral dissertation]. University of Otago.

CHAPTER 15

Healing Teaching and the Earth Through Nature Companionship

Jeanette Banashak

> "Action on behalf of life transforms. Because the relationship between self and the world is reciprocal, it is not a question of first getting enlightened or saved and then acting. As we work to heal the earth, the earth heals us."
>
> —Macy (n.d., as cited in Kimmerer, 2013, p. 340)

I invite the reader to read this chapter outside, by a window, with a pet on your lap, or next to a plant.

While no one would likely dispute the concept that time spent in nature can be healing, readers might be skeptical about what this has to do with teaching specifically, especially for urban teachers whose schools' recess areas are more blacktop than greenspace. According to a recent national survey, K–12 public school teachers work about 53 hours a week (Steiner et al., 2023), so we know that whatever interventions are offered, these will need to lighten their burdens rather than add to them—so is it realistic to ask teachers to seek out and add nature to their day?

Through my experiences facilitating urban educators in *forest bathing*, as well as a training program I designed entitled Nature Companionship, this chapter seeks to demonstrate how, for school leaders and teachers, being in ecorelationship with the more-than-human world can help bring them closer to themselves via their ecological self, bringing lasting restorative effects on wellness. The opposite of an add-on, cultivating relationship, reciprocity, and eco-justice with the natural world *opens up* physical and psychological space, thereby healing the natural world *and* humans. The chapter will include specific suggestions for principals, culture and climate deans, and teachers to begin to incorporate Nature Companionship in schools, creating parallel processes for healing and mutual decreasing of burdens.

MY BUDDING RELATIONSHIP WITH CHICAGO'S NATURAL ENVIRONMENT

Several years ago, I experienced my first gently guided *forest bathing* experience as I was cofacilitating a social and emotional learning (SEL) project with early childhood educators in partnership with my coeditor, Amanda Moreno. Though I had been a hiker and backpacker for decades, this quiet, slow outer and inner journey transformed my relationships with the natural world: I became more intentional building and nurturing relationships and offering a gift in return for nature's generosity (Kimmerer, 2024); I developed an attitude and practice of respect for nature and "culture of responsibility that makes us accountable and responsive to Earth others" (Krause, 2023); and I grew in my knowledge of the natural world through training as a *shinrin yoku* (forest bathing) and mindful outdoor guide.

My relationships with the mourning doves on the roof next to my house, the trees out front, and Lake Michigan three blocks away changed, deepened. I began to think about and live differently in Chicago. Even for many people who are from here and are aware that we have 578 parks and 32 beaches, the word "Chicago" first conjures up images coming from negative news stories and stereotypical TV shows. I began to consider *nature access* in the city more expansively as I guided small groups of educators, children, and caregivers in urban forest bathing, or what I now call Nature Companionship, curating multidisciplinary experiences in Chicago for educators, environmentalists, birders, forest bathing guides, biologists, geologists, and many more to cocreate community around the natural environment in our complicated, complex, and beautiful city.

This humble project is preceded and joined by the efforts of so many others in Chicago who have implemented a range of initiatives to green the city and protect Lake Michigan. With nearly 9,000 acres of parkland, including almost 2,000 acres of nature areas, 26 miles of lakefront, and 16 lagoons, advocates within the Park District, city, and local communities are restoring river habitats, protecting the Lake's shoreline, planting thousands of trees yearly, removing dams, greening schools and playgrounds, expanding native plants, protecting birds, and building climate-resilient and sustainable infrastructures, among many more initiatives. What if there were a solution that helped to solve multiple pandemics, from the climate crisis to loneliness to poverty? Nature Companionship is one possibility: Healing teaching is interwoven with, and mirrors, healing the Earth.

* * *

Before I get to the next section, I'm going to go outside, find a stone, and consider the history of wind and rain it may have seen.

THE BURDEN OF BEING INDOORS

It is a burden for educators to be inside all day. Indoors, there is little to no access to the feel of the sun (or rain), the sounds of birdsong and wind in the trees, or awareness of the visible changes and movements happening outside. In the West, indoor environments are typically motivated by utility and protection, cost and function, with light and sound emanating from fluorescent bulbs. The changelessness of the indoor atmosphere, over-stimulation of the urban environment, and resulting lack of connection and relationship with the wild world outside (Weiss et al., 2023), or the more-than-human world, create a host of psychological and physiological illnesses.

No doubt, adults' alienation from the outdoors is a direct cause of the fact that children in the United States spend less than 10 minutes of unstructured outdoor play each day, while they spend over 7 hours looking at screens (Gray et al., 2015; Rideout et al., 2010). Adults create policies, such as one that eliminates recess for kindergarteners, to use the time instead for testing preparation (Patte, 2006). Even considering recent efforts to preserve and legally require recess (Slater et al., 2012), children are still subject to adults' regulations and structure, resulting in a restriction of environmental knowledge and restoration (Thomson, 2007).

On the bright side, some teachers have eliminated insignificant activities and fine-tuned their teaching to increase daily recess to up to four times each day (Bauml et al., 2020). SEL skills that improve or increase through outside time in recess include prosocial behavior, listening, and concentration. Furthermore, recess allows for problem-solving and creativity, which may translate inside the classroom to "improve[d] academic achievement and classroom behavior" (Bjornsen et al., 2024). For humans of all ages, time outside helps decrease anxiety, depression, and stress, and improves mood and focus (Tsunetsugu et al., 2007; White et al., 2019). It lowers blood pressure, supports the immune system, and decreases the risk of chronic disease.

Clearly, adults and children alike need their own authentic nature-centered experiences to nurture appreciation and curiosity of the natural world, build relationships of respect for and responsibility to the more-than-human world, and work toward healing nature as an act of reciprocity. When school leaders individually and communally take the lead to get back into alignment with nature, healing spreads throughout the school context and back to nature. Yet, burdens exist that restrict wellness and restoration.

Species loneliness, which feels like a sorrow and sadness and is a result of isolation from the natural world, also increases with a lack of outside time. The scarcity of being outdoors results in a lack of relationship with the plants and animals of the land, air, and water. The absence of connection with the natural world can translate into assumptions about our separateness from nature. Yet, we are deeply reliant on nature for many essential aspects of life, including food, energy, healing, every breath we take, our very existence, and our relationships. Equally, nature is deeply reliant on humanity for improving biodiversity, telling its story, and ensuring its right to exist, heal, thrive, and restore itself.

Humans have coexisted with the natural environment since the dawn of humanity and connect with it as part of our DNA (Olson, 1984). When we are exposed to nature, our preference for it increases; conversely, when we lack contact with nature, our preferences may decrease. Time spent in nature has been shown to produce higher attentional functioning (Kuo & Sullivan, 2001); improved performance in working memory and cognitive flexibility (Stevenson et al., 2018); reduced stress (Ulrich, 1983); and better mental health (Jimenez et al., 2021).

Shinrin yoku (forest bathing) was originally conceived as a reaction to improve the stress level of Japan's workforce. Some research studies, like those of Qing Li (2022), have demonstrated that psychological and physiological benefits occur with nature immersion. Another line of inquiry relates education and nature immersion, such as forest schools, which locate teaching and learning (mostly) outdoors. However, the framework in this chapter centralizes the fact that resources for enrollment in special schools or even living near a forest are not required to increase our connections with the natural world. Research documents improved attention with greater greenspace surrounding a school, students feeling more relaxed by looking out of windows showing natural landscapes, or positive effects on students' mood and well-being with the addition of plants or pets (e.g., Dadvand et al., 2015; Zhang et al., 2024).

* * *

Would you like to join me for a walk around the block to listen to the birds before proceeding?

NATURE COMPANIONSHIP

Nature carries our burden, and humans can carry nature's burden: Nature facilitates healing for both humans and the beings of the land, water, and sky in urban, suburban, and rural settings. Joyful, awe-inspired, and wonder-filled contemplative activities/exercises/invitations encourage reciprocity between humans and greater-than-humans. The term I use to describe gentle, mindful, slow, justice-and-love-centered, playful walks (or kayaks, swims, rock climbs, etc.) outside is Nature Companionship.

Inspired by the Association of Nature and Forest Therapy's standard sequence of forest bathing, Kripalu's nine steps of a mindful outdoor experience, the practices and philosophies of forest schools, various Indigenous wisdoms, contemplative pedagogy and andragogy, and the science behind nature immersion activities, the *Nature Companionship flow* I created is a framework, process, practice, and way of being. The flow provides a structure for a continuous experience outdoors; as a process, it is a series of contemplative invitations to build and nurture relationship, reciprocity, and compassionate presence with the more-than-human world; as a practice, it is an intentionally sequenced 30-minute to multiple-day experience in the outdoors; and as a way of being, it is a lifelong commitment to eco-justice, deep listening to self, others, and the land and beings on the land, and care for the wider world of community.

Nature Companionship is an antidote to the climate crisis that humans—particularly in the global North—have caused through burning fossil fuels, cutting down forests, farming livestock, and overconsumption. When humans spend time getting to know who is around us in the natural world, we develop our capacity for compassion and knowledge that we have and are, enough.

The following is an outline of the flow *as a practice and process*. School leaders and educators might consider incorporating relevant aspects of the flow or receive training for facilitation (see suggestions in the following steps). It may not be realistic for educators or school leaders to facilitate an entire Nature Companionship flow, yet, there are aspects of it that can be incorporated as a "one-off" experience, or shorter activities at various points throughout the day.

Step 1: Attunement With Stories and Ancestors

A foundational exercise for empathy, the main idea of step one is about attuning to the past and present, or giving one's attention to who and what were present 500 or 5,000 years ago on the particular land that participants are on. A paleoecological perspective allows us to grow in our appreciation for the lives lived and stories shared outside our consciousness. This perspective can help us imagine the different kinds of biodiversity that might be possible in our climate crisis. In the first step, the facilitator acknowledges the myriad ways that the Indigenous people have related to the land and continue to in spite of dispossession and settler colonialism. Participants may spend a few moments in quiet gratitude to anyone who has encouraged them to spend time in the natural world, including to their ancestors.

Step 2: Attunement With Beings

In this transition, participants shift their awareness to the moment and the presence of the more-than-human world. In a traditional forest bathing sequence, this step is called the pleasures of presence: The senses become awakened and expanded through invitations/contemplations of singling out one to five of the "traditional" senses: sight, sound, touch, taste, feeling. Participants observe their surroundings, deepen their breathing, and feel the aliveness of the land; they tune in to the external landscape, while simultaneously tuning in to their internal landscape.

Step 3: Attention to the Earth

In step three, the facilitator continues to offer invitations/contemplations that are centered in embodiment and awareness of the present moment. Though attention takes mental effort, it can be restored by time in this gently guided, communal experience in the natural environment. Drawing on Kaplan's attention restoration theory (1995), these exercises promote renewed focus and concentration, which creates an opening for new mental pathways that are primed for reflection. Participants spend moments of "soft fascination," such as allowing the gaze to move from one flower to the next in an effortless way, observing the patterns and textures of a leaf, or looking up at the clouds.

Step 4: Sitting With and On the Land

The basis for this step comes from an Aboriginal practice of deep inner listening or contemplation, *dadirri*, that encompasses respect. First Nations people have participated in *sit spots* for centuries as a way to nourish relationship with the more-than-human world as well as the self. Apache grandfather and shaman, Stalking Wolf, passed on his wisdom and knowledge to now famous tracker and survivalist, Tom Brown, Jr. (1999), who taught and practiced observation and awareness. Sit spots involve sitting with what and who are present with eyes open and noticing with the senses *what or who is here*? In a Nature Companionship experience, participants may choose a location in the natural world that they are drawn to or, alternatively, indoors by a window or plant. The instructions are simply to find the spot that feels safe and comfortable, sit (or stand, slowly walk, or lie down), and notice.

Step 5: Responding to Self, Others, and the Needs of the Natural World

Nature Companionship experiences enable deepened observation of both the exterior world and interior landscape. Yet, beyond the noticings is an invitation to respond—to the self and our inner teacher or wisdom, to the community that has *withnessed* the current natural landscape, and to the natural world through a consideration or commitment to reciprocity, respect, and responsibility. *Withnessing* is a Bayo Akomolafe phrase (2020) that emphasizes the sense of me as part of a larger whole.

Responding to the wisdom of the self and the inner source of truth is a trust-building exercise that is supported in community. In this fifth step, participants are invited to pause and contemplate what they are appreciating, what they are noticing, or what brought them joy and wonder—and then *respond back* with these noticings. As the facilitator asks questions for debriefing and processing, they may hear stories of a dynamic moment where a participant felt the sense of everything relying on everything else, or they delighted in a spider's web, watched a mother racoon care for her baby, built a relationship with a tree, committed to care more for the land, sang a song to a stream, or enjoyed the sensations of rain on the face for the first time.

At the end of any of the steps or invitations/contemplations, participants may feel a deepened sense of belonging in and friendship or kinship with the natural world. A follow-up question to promote healing the land is *How can I reciprocate back the gifts I've received from this experience?*

* * *

Before reading about the impact of nature immersion in the city and a list of requests for school leaders, I invite the reader to turn your attention to take a sip of water and consider its source.

NATURE COMPANIONSHIP IN YOUR SETTING

After a two-hour Nature Companionship experience in Chicago, educator participants reported physiological and psychological well-being, though the benefits go much further: They consider and often re/commit to reciprocal relationships with Earth others, including increased respect and responsibility for them as well as working toward elevating the rights of the natural environment. Health and wellness effects last up to 30 days in their professional contexts after just one experience, and educators increase their incorporation of nature, pets, and animals in their curricula well into their academic year. On their own or with their families, participants often return to the joy and wonder-filled urban nature spaces, like bird sanctuaries, Lake Michigan, the Chicago River, pocket parks, and nature preserves. Weeks and months after a Nature Companionship experience, participants share stories with me about connecting with the maple, European buckthorn, green ash, American elm, and black cherry trees outside their homes and other city wildlife such as birds, squirrels, turtles, beavers, raccoons, and maybe even rats and pigeons.

It is clear that educators become more well with a one-time nature immersion experience. And further, one-time experiences with teachers have turned into multiple times that turn into habits and life-long commitments to new nature-centric ways of being. With recovered relationships in the natural world, the practices and ways of being get taken into the classroom and other educational spaces. Children enjoy and need authentic encounters with the outside world, and they receive more of such immersion when school leaders not only encourage it with the teachers, but when they create a climate and culture through practices, spaces, and policies around it. Teachers "catch the vision" when school leaders prioritize the wellness of the planet and engagement in the natural world not as secondary, but as a primary way of being and learning together in an educational context.

Before I move on to more specific suggestions, I want to speak for a moment to the school gardeners and nature lovers who have advocated for similar ideas for years, mostly on their own time, and even on their own dime. It's a familiar story: One, maybe two teachers known to have green thumbs are tasked with being the school garden "champions," and while there may be some appreciation for the work, after one or two seasons of sampling the vegetables, if those one or two gardeners don't continue literally tilling the soil, the effort dies out. To all such advocates, allies, and arborists, thank you. But it is time to take nature out of the realm of a "special interest" and integrate it with the other wellness work being recognized as critical to education.

Increasingly, it is understood that SEL is only a complete intervention when it nurtures teachers' and students' care for others, the community, and the planet, and thus I call upon school leaders to recast their view of nature activities as smooth terrain toward SEL outcomes. No longer is it on the shoulders of the "outdoorsy ones" to find the time and the resources "in between" the sanctioned educational activities. School leadership can set the tone and lead the way, creating ways of being consistent with a Nature Companionship-based wellness in their educational spaces. As you consider these possibilities, you can think of them on at least three possible levels: (a) bringing the outside in; (b) bringing the inside (teachers and students) out; (c) creating catalyzing conditions for either (a), (b) (e.g., funding, partnerships, advocacy), or nature-based habits of mind.

- Begin and maintain a regular morning or afternoon sit spot or nature meditation for teachers.
- Partner with local nonprofits, for-profits, libraries and other after-school educational spaces, and families who currently prioritize teaching and learning outdoors.
- Incorporate curricula that focus on relationship with, reciprocity to, and justice in the natural world.
- Beginning in preschool, encourage loose parts play and child-led outside activities.
- Work together to clean up, make accessible, and beautify the outdoor spaces and plant trees and bushes.
- Bring the natural environment inside—listen to nature sounds, play nature videos, diffuse essential oils such as Douglas fir, cypress, frankincense.
- Read nature-themed poetry, such as that from Camille Dungy, Ada Limón, Emily Dickenson, and Mary Oliver, and incorporate nature-themed visual art throughout the school.
- Procure funding for day- and week-long nature immersions for educators.
- Include two-hour forest bathing or Nature Companionship experiences for faculty and staff wellness throughout the academic year.
- Work together around eco-anxiety, or distress about environmental degradation.
- Promote nature-based professional development and outdoor activities throughout the year.
- Incorporate more outside time into the school day—advocate for an additional recess and supervised unstructured time or hold class outside.
- Hold meetings outside as walk and talks.

- Bring purifying plants into the classroom and school, such as golden pathos (devil's ivy), peace lily, chrysanthemum, mother-in-law's tongue, gerbera daisy, azalea, or spider plant.
- Take care of pets in the classroom, such as bearded dragons, hamsters, fish, as well as in the school office.
- Tend a school garden (with a team!).
- Your ideas . . .

CONCLUSION

Through conversations and encouragement from the participants of Nature Companionship experiences, we are slowly cocreating a community of like heart-minded people around the natural environment in Chicago. If you'd like to train in guiding nature immersion experiences, options exist on the websites of the Association of Nature and Forest Therapy, Kripalu's Outdoor School of Mindful Outdoor Leadership, or my Nature Companionship training program (https://www.forestbathingchicago.com/training). When school leaders "plant seeds" for their school communities to connect with their eco-selves, they are easing the paths to SEL and wellness. Our care for the Earth reflects our care for our educators and students; with a commitment to relationship, reciprocity, and eco-love-and-justice, Nature Companionship promotes mutual healing for both humans and the natural world.

* * *

Let's go see what those brilliant crows are up to!

REFERENCES

Akomolafe, B. (2020). *Making sanctuary.* Jung Platform. https://jungplatform.com/store/making-sanctuary

Bauml, M., Patton, M. M., & Rhea, D. (2020). A qualitative study of teachers' perceptions of increased recess time on teaching, learning, and behavior. *Journal of Research in Childhood Education, 34*(4), 506–520. https://doi.org/10.1080/02568543.2020.1718808

Bjornsen, M. A., Perryman, K. L., Cameron, L., Thomas, H., & Howie, E. K. (2024). The impact of recess on students: A scoping review of developmental outcomes and methodological considerations. *Journal of Research in Childhood Education, 38*(4), 649–664. https://doi.org/10.1080/02568543.2024.2313021

Brown, T., Jr. (1999). *The science and art of tracking.* The Berkley Publishing Group. https://www.originalwisdom.com/wp-content/uploads/bsk-pdf-manager/2019/03/Brown_1999_the-science-and-art-of-tracking.pdf

Dadvand, P., Nieuwenhuijsen, M. J., Esnaola, M., Forns, J., Basagaña, X., Alvarez-Pedrerol, M., Rivas, I., López-Vicente, M., Montserrat de Castro Pascual, Su, J., Jerrett, M.,

Querol, X., & Sunyer, J. (2015). Green spaces and cognitive development in primary schoolchildren. *Proceedings of the National Academy of Sciences*, *112*(26), 7937–7942.

Gray, C., Gibbons, R., Larouche, R., Sandseter, E. B., Bienenstock, A., Brussoni, M., Chabot, G., Herrington, S., Janssen, I., Pickett, W., Power, M., Stanger, N., Sampson, M., & Tremblay, M. S. (2015). What is the relationship between outdoor time and physical activity, sedentary behaviour, and physical fitness in children? A Systematic Review. *International Journal of Environmental Research and Public Health*, *12*(6), 6455–6474. https://doi.org/10.3390/ijerph120606455

Jimenez, M. P., DeVille, N. V., Elliott, E. G., Schiff, J. E., Wilt, G. E., Hart, J. E., & James, P. (2021). Associations between nature exposure and health: A review of the evidence. *International Journal of Environmental Research and Public Health*, *18*(9), 4790. https://doi.org/10.3390/ijerph18094790

Kaplan, S. (1995). The restorative benefits of nature: Toward an integrative framework. *Journal of Environmental Psychology, 15*(3), 169–182. https://doi.org/10.1016/0272-4944(95)90001-2

Kimmerer, R. W. (2013). *Braiding sweetgrass: Indigenous wisdom, scientific knowledge, and the teachings of plants*. Milkweed Editions.

Kimmerer, R. W. (2024). *The serviceberry: Abundance and reciprocity in the natural world.* Scribner.

Krause, S. (2023). *Eco-emancipation: An earthly politics of freedom.* Princeton University Press.

Kuo, F. E., & Sullivan, W. C. (2001). Aggression and violence in the inner city: Effects of environment via mental fatigue. *Environment & Behavior*, *33*(4), 543–571. https://doi.org/10.1177/0013916012197312

Li, Q. (2022). Effects of forest environment (Shinrin-yoku/Forest bathing) on health promotion and disease prevention. *International Journal of Environmental Research and Public Health, 19*(21), 14140. https://doi.org/10.3390/ije

Olson, E. O. (1984). *Biophilia: The human bond with other species.* Harvard University Press.

Patte, M. M. (2006). What's happened to recess? Examining time devoted to recess in Pennsylvania's elementary schools. *Play and Folklore, 48,* 5–16. https://doi/epdf/10.3316/informit.T2024042000008601052532010

Rideout, V. J., Foehr, U. G., & Roberts, D. F. (2010). *Generation M2: Media in the lives of 8- to 18-year-olds.* Kaiser Family Foundation.

Slater, S. J., Nicholson, L., Chriqui, J., Turner, L., & Chaloupka, F. (2012). The impact of state laws and district policies on physical education and recess practices in a nationally representative sample of US public elementary schools. *Archives of Pediatrics & Adolescent Medicine*, *166*(4), 311–316. https://doi.org/ 10.1001/archpediatrics.2011.1133

Steiner, E., Woo, A., & Doan, S. (2023). *All work and no pay—Teachers' perceptions of their pay and hours worked: Findings from the 2023 state of the American teacher survey.* RAND. https://www.rand.org/pubs/research_reports/RRA1108-9.html

Stevenson, M. P., Schilhab, T., & Bentsen, P. (2018). Attention restoration theory II: A systematic review to clarify attention processes affected by exposure to natural environments. *Journal of Toxicology and Environmental Health, Part B*, *21,* 227–268. https://doi.org/10.1080/10937404.2018.1505571

Thomson, S. (2007). Do's and don'ts: Children's experiences of the primary school playground. *Environmental Education Research, 13*(4), 487–500. https://doi.org/10.1080/13504620701581588

Tsunetsugu, Y., Park, B. J., Ishii, H., Hirano, H., Kagawa, T., & Miyazaki, Y. (2007). Physiological effects of Shinrin-yoku (taking in the atmosphere of the forest) in an old-growth broadleaf forest in Yamagata Prefecture, Japan. *Journal of Physiological Anthropology, 26*(2), 135–142. https://doi.org/10.2114/jpa2.26.135

Ulrich R. S. (1983). Aesthetic and affective response to natural environment. In I. Altman I. & J. F. Wohlwill (Eds.), *Behavior and the natural environment* (pp. 85–125). Springer.

Weiss, T., Kahn, P. H., & Lam, L.-W. (2023). Children's interactions with relatively wild nature associated with more relational behavior: A model of child-nature interaction in a forest preschool. *Journal of Environmental Psychology, 86,* 101941. https://doi.org/10.1016/j.jenvp.2022.101941

White, M. P., Alcock, I., Grellier, J., Wheeler, B. W., Hartig, T., Warber, S. L., Bone, A., Depledge, M. H. & Fleming, L. E. (2019). Spending at least 120 minutes a week in nature is associated with good health and well-being. *Scientific Reports, 9*, 7730. https://doi.org/10.1038/s41598-019-44097-3

Zhang, Y. O., Tang, Y., Wang, X., & Tan, Y. (2024). The effects of natural window views in classrooms on college students' mood and learning efficiency. *Buildings, 14*(6), 1557. https://doi.org/10.3390/buildings14061557

CHAPTER 16

Dismantling Toxic "Professionalism" to Liberate Schools and Ignite Healing

Kamilah Drummond

Walk into any school building and you'll likely encounter an adult population caught in a storm of competing priorities. Stress is the air they breathe—unavoidable, constant, and suffocating. In my experiences as a Social Emotional Learning (SEL) coach, principal, and professional development provider, I've spoken to countless teachers who haven't had time to eat lunch, use the restroom, or catch their breath. Leaders, similarly, are buried under the weight of systemic demands. This relentless pace has profound effects. Educators, who dedicate their lives to nurturing others, often find themselves depleted, isolated, and disconnected. This is a reality that compromises their well-being and their ability to create a thriving environment for students.

To truly support educators, we must recognize the real toll stress takes on their bodies and minds. Chronic stress and elevated cortisol are linked to serious health issues like immune dysfunction and heart problems (James et al., 2023; Hannibal & Bishop, 2014; Seiler et al., 2020). Since most public school educators are women—and women are more prone to stress-related illnesses (Halbreich, 2021)—the urgency is clear. What makes this even harder is the message many women, especially women of color, receive: that their worth is tied to self-sacrifice. Many enter teaching to help others, not realizing they'd be blamed for the system's failures. They're told to give more, go faster, feel less, and stick to rigid formulas—all in the name of "student success." But these demands aren't just unsustainable, they're harmful. That's why I use the term *toxic professionalism*, and why healing isn't just a metaphor—it's a physical, social, and moral necessity.

While it cannot independently solve all of teachers' challenges, when designed intentionally, the professional development (PD) context can serve as an imaginative and "future dreaming" space to model what a path to healing could look like for educators and leaders. By centering healing, reflection, and connection within the context of adult learning, we create pathways for educators to reclaim their humanity and, in turn, model that humanity for their students. In this chapter, I share a three-part Professional Development (PD) model I created to dismantle toxic "professionalism." I'll offer stories of how this model has fostered healing for educators, along with practical examples that can be adapted to other settings to help cultivate the more humanizing culture of education we all envision.

HOW DID I GET HERE?

I am a Black woman raised by proud Caribbean immigrants. I am the first person in my family born in the United States and spent most of my summers in my parents' homeland of Jamaica, which became a place where I saw myself reflected in all levels of life from the prime minister to the banker to the teachers to the janitors—mirrors of my beautiful Blackness shone bright. I am a mother of Black children, a wife of a Black Muslim man, and a sibling to many.

My parents raised me to be identity-conscious and justice-centered in how I carry myself and interact with others. I am a trained dancer, poet, and singer. My background in psychology and counseling ultimately led me to the realm of education, deciding to found my own consulting company where I combine the passions that I bring to my facilitative approach: social and emotional learning (SEL), equity-focused work, and embodied practices.

My approach to PD is shaped by my training with the National SEED (Seeking Educational Equity and Diversity) Project and my work as an SEL coach, PD facilitator, and director of a nationally recognized SEL program. I've also been a charter school founder and now serve as an interim middle school principal—roles that keep me closely connected to the real challenges educators face in prioritizing wellness in often toxic environments. As a principal, I've had to learn that I won't get everything done each day, but if I center humanity for myself, my staff, and my students, then I'm on the right path. That's the heart of my work with educators: creating space for reflection, storytelling, and connection, all grounded in love and compassion. These practices foster empathy, self-awareness, and healing.

A LIBERATORY MODEL OF WHAT IT MEANS TO BE A PROFESSIONAL EDUCATOR

For every narrative, there is a counternarrative, and for too long, the narrative of professionalism for educators has been an unhealthy, even toxic one that has led to the crisis of burnout, turnover, and ill-being discussed in this chapter and throughout this book. My approach to PD is intentionally disruptive to toxic professionalism and creates a counternarrative that has the impact of igniting a path toward healing, even in small doses. The basic concepts are summarized in Table 16.1.

Table 16.1. Liberatory Model of Educator Professionalism

Toxic Professionalism Narrative	Liberatory Professionalism Counter-narrative
Stoicism, neutrality, masking	Vulnerability, emotionality, authenticity, embodiment (CONNECT)
Going fast, auto pilot, productivity and efficiency at all costs	Slowing down, introspection and imagination, pausing and resting, sacrificing of the self is never a price worth paying (REFLECT)
Formulas, isolating, jargon, policies	Stories, accessible language, funds of knowledge (RECLAIM)

Connect

How often, when someone is having trouble making a decision, have we heard the cliché, "Take your emotions out of it"? From neuroscience, we know that this is not only bad advice but impossible. Tuning into our emotions helps, rather than hurts, our ability to make wise decisions. Even decades after the publication of Daniel Goleman's *Emotional Intelligence* (1995) and the establishment of the field of social and emotional learning (SEL) in education, U.S. culture remains at its core averse to shows of genuine emotion and connection. This is true in all fields that require "professionalism," even in settings that rely on relationships to function, such as hospitals and schools. In the Connect, Reflect, Reclaim PD model, we encourage connecting to self and others via the open sharing of emotions, and explain how welcoming emotions regulates them better than suppressing them.

Tuning into one's authentic feelings enables us to tap into vulnerability in a manner that allows us to center individual and collective humanity. This is the counternarrative to perfectionism. While individuals always retain the final say over what they choose to share or keep private, our PD sessions work toward building trust and safety, discarding perfectionism, and connecting to aspects of our personal selves that inform and impact how we experience our professional lives. This model disrupts the notion that the personal is not professional. We acknowledge that we must connect to self, others, emotions, and personal experiences in order to gain insight into the work we do in school communities. This model asserts that disconnection is toxic and creates disconnected communities that impede growth, learning, and healing. As a facilitator, I model this for participants by bringing my whole self to the room as well—my emotions, my Jamaican accent, my experiences, and my stories—and by doing so, I give participants permission to do the same.

Reflect

If there's any one factor that is most emblematic of toxic work culture, it might be the relentless pace toward the "altar" of productivity, and schools are no exception.

As the liberatory counternarrative, many educators (including me) have been inspired by the principles of Tricia Hersey's Nap Ministry and her books, *Rest is Resistance: A Manifesto* (2022), and *We Will Rest!: The Art of Escape* (2024). On her website, Hersey states, "Rest pushes back and disrupts a system that views human bodies as a tool for production and labor. It is a counter narrative. We know that we are not machines. We are divine . . . . It is not a joke nor anything to make light of. Black people are dying from sleep deprivation and our resistance to rest is a social justice and public health issue" (Hersey, 2022).

While no one would openly argue against the critical needs for rest and reflection, having them on full display in a professional context is still a deeply uncomfortable concept in U.S. culture. Incorporating ample time for a sacred pause to reflect deeply during PD is a deliberate component to this model. At first, reflective practices during PD can feel awkward, but with consistent use and clear framing, educators and leaders start to value the "a-ha" moments and insights that come from this intentional work.

While PD alone can't create all of the structural shifts a school may need, I've seen small shifts spark big ideas. When educators slow down and reflect together, it becomes a powerful catalyst, giving them space they rarely have to explore their inner landscape. This opens the door to real change, helping them lead with more self-awareness, resilience, and compassion.

Reclaim

All workplaces will typically involve some kind of written policies, structures, and jargon that staff must know and follow. Our counternarrative does not require that educators reject these things, rather, that they acknowledge that the path to healing takes place "in the spaces between." As noted throughout this book, it is incumbent upon the supporters of educators to widen these spaces, that is, create buffers for teachers around the necessary administrative burdens they have, and make more room for their stories, funds of knowledge (Gonzalez et al., 2005), autonomy, and power to do their work in the way they know best. Administrative work and top-down policies are a necessary part of teachers' work, but they are not *why* teachers come to work. As their supporters, we need to be careful to not offload our stress about these matters onto them, thereby making the space for what matters smaller and smaller.

Storytelling is a powerful but often overlooked tool for healing and connection in education. It helps us move beyond jargon and policy by grounding our work in real human experiences. In PD sessions, we share stories of struggle, resilience, and joy—not to vent, but to challenge the idea that personal experiences don't belong in professional spaces. Educators are natural storytellers, and anyone who says there's no place for stories in schools misses the point of what education is truly about. We must resist that thinking, unlearn the harmful belief that our humanity has no place in our work, and reclaim the rightful place of stories as a natural part of the healing that teaching can do.

Language is another powerful tool that can be used in both formal and informal ways to deepen and enrich professional work in schools. For me personally, I shift fluidly between dialects—my Jamaican Patois, Black vernacular, and so-called "professional" English. This intentional code-switching disrupts the idea that intelligence and professionalism look or sound one specific way. It signals to educators that their authentic voices are welcome, valued, and essential to the conversation, and that they can demonstrate their knowledge of their vocation in multiple ways. This *reclaiming* has parallel ripple effects on parents and students as well, who are also victims of an onslaught of messages that their ways of speaking and demonstrating knowledge are not good enough. We are all in an active journey of deprogramming ourselves.

STORIES OF HEALING

In the following two examples from my work with schools, I demonstrate the implementation of my model at two levels: one with teachers and one with school leaders.

Calling Myself In: How We Treat Youth Impacts Our Own Wellness

When we're asking teachers to change their thinking or their behavior, it can be very helpful for them to hear a facilitator first vulnerably "call themselves in," which is why I often share the following story about me and my daughter (shared with permission). As mentioned, I come from a Caribbean culture, and one of the ways we show our elders respect is by greeting them with a hug and sometimes a kiss on the cheek. For my daughter, however, anytime someone would approach her to hug, she would immediately stiffen and pull away, often adding a side eye or annoyed look. I share with my teacher groups how horrified and flushed with shame I would feel in these moments, for not raising my daughter "right" or as a "good Caribbean child." I explained that my follow-up would often include apologizing for her behavior to family and friends, scolding her for not being respectful and embarrassing me, asking her "What is wrong with you?" or saying, "Stop making a big deal out of this."

Often, knowing looks would begin to develop among the teachers around the room, perhaps with feelings of recognition from their own families or classrooms (whether as children or adults). I would tell the group I believed that the solution to this problem was so "simple"—just do this harmless thing that is expected of you! Then one day, I happened to see a Girl Scouts of America commercial that asserted "Stop forcing your daughters to hug people" that stopped me in my tracks. This public service announcement compelled me to slow down and realize that I never asked my daughter why she didn't want to hug people. When I finally did, she revealed that she does like physical affection—she reminded me she loves hugs from me—but just not from people she is not in close relationship with. I share with the group how my daughter's simple answer brought me back to the times as a young girl when I hugged elders when I didn't want to out of compliance. I realized that my socialization as a child made me perpetuate the expectation that my daughter overstep her personal boundaries for the comfort of others.

Now that I was no longer locating the problem in my daughter but instead in the messages I received as a child, it enabled me and my daughter to heal. I described how my daughter and I came up with ways to respect community elders without compromising her personal boundaries (e.g., putting her hand to her heart and smiling). After sharing this story, prompts I use in teacher groups have included: (a) Do you recognize yourself in any stories of finding a student's behavior inconvenient or reflecting poorly upon you, and perhaps "going on instinct" rather than slowing down to ask for their viewpoint? (b) In such a story, how are aspects of your identity or your childhood socialization influencing these different perspectives? (c) As you reflect now, what new insights are coming up? What clarifying questions could you have asked? What assumptions did you make?

Educators often share that they can relate to this idea of "going too fast to ask." Although their level of busy-ness is not their fault, the culture of toxic professionalism, which doesn't allow time to reflect, is what causes them to revert to their "default modes" from childhood or other quick fixes that harm relationship-building. This story also seems to support teachers in becoming more aware of how their childhood socialization is playing out in their interactions with students and families. As I learned—or rather remembered—with my daughter, she and I were not so different. This consciousness raising helps teachers "come back to" themselves and their students and therefore is a potent pathway for mutual healing within the school setting.

When Leaders Listen to the Margins: Healing School Communities Through Story

School leaders are in a unique position to impact the collective experiences within their school communities. I once co-led a session with a group of school administrators focused on early gender messages—those formative lessons about what it means to be a boy or girl. We asked the leaders to state the messages they received growing up, like "stop being a sissy" or "good girls always smile." The emotional weight in the room grew as these familiar narratives were shared.

At one point, a male administrator became visibly emotional. A deep, reflective silence filled the space—not out of discomfort, but because everyone felt the gravity of what had just been named. We didn't rush past it. We stayed with the moment. That stillness became a turning point. Participants began to realize these weren't just personal experiences—they were part of a larger narrative of systemic gender norms. As people reflected, they connected those early messages to the way toxic masculinity had shaped their own leadership spaces, limiting women and marginalizing men who didn't fit a narrow mold. Moments like this do more than create awareness—they build essential adult SEL skills. Sitting with discomfort, honoring vulnerability, and engaging in honest reflection strengthen self-awareness, social awareness, and relationship skills. It's in these pauses that real growth and healing begin.

In that moment I made the decision to make a facilitative pivot to deepen the work that was occurring in the room. I shared a current event regarding a young,

Black, queer dancer by the name of O'Shea Sibley who was recently murdered. I displayed his name and picture on the screen in an elegant dancer's pose. No one in the room knew who he was. I shared that he and his friends were dancing and full of joy as they stopped at a local gas station and a group of teenage boys began hurling racist and homophobic slurs at them. A tussle ensued and one of the teenagers stabbed O'Shea to death. Again, a hush fell upon the room, this time reflecting the pure horror at this brazen act, as well as the many questions swirling through everyone's minds, especially, "Why didn't I know about this?" We maintained the silence for participants to feel whatever might come up, and one of the male administrators began to audibly weep. The group appeared to "hold space" for that moment in a way that created healing and broke through the toxic masculinity that had riddled the district's upper administration's culture.

To reflect on these stories, I asked the leaders the following prompts: What is our responsibility to know the stories of the members of groups we are not a part of? What guidance of the teenagers in this story was needed for them to show more empathy, tolerance, and humanity? Who are the people in your school community who might have been affected by this story? Who are the groups of students and educators who hold these racial and sexual identities that need to hear they are safe and protected in your school communities? How might you leverage your role as a school administrator to be intentional about slowing down and helping the community feel deeply when needed as a path to healing?

Many BIPOC and LGBTQIA+ educators experience systemic oppression in their schools—they often feel unseen, undervalued, and disconnected. They're asked to create safe, supportive spaces for students, even when they haven't been given the same care themselves. This is where school leaders must step in to *connect*—to truly see and hear their educators, especially those with marginalized identities. By taking time to *reflect* on the disproportionate burdens placed on these educators and the harm caused by ignoring injustice, leaders begin to create space for healing. And when educators feel supported and valued, they're better able to *reclaim* their sense of purpose, belonging, and professional agency.

While the examples I've shared come from individual sessions, change doesn't have to take years. When the conditions are right, consciousness can shift quickly. In the rest of this chapter, I'll explore concrete actions that can move us from awareness to sustainable healing.

A NOTE ON BUILDING A CONTAINER

Prompts alone don't create healing. What really makes the difference is *building an emotional container*—a supportive, trust-filled space where people feel brave and authentic. Creating this kind of container involves setting clear norms (and holding folks accountable to them), starting with low-risk activities before moving deeper, and using structured conversations like the constructivist listening protocol to foster genuine reflection and deep listening. It also means facilitators must *embody*—not just model—the liberatory and healing practices they're inviting others into. That embodiment is where the work truly lands. Building a container means creating the emotional and relational conditions that allow people to show up fully, listen deeply, and take real risks. Without it, learning spaces will fall flat or, worse, cause harm. But with it, the Connect, Reflect, and Reclaim model has the power to truly take root.

SUPPORTING ONGOING LIBERATION AND HEALING IN SCHOOLS

Toxic professionalism is one way to name the culture crisis in schools—one that enfolds broader societal issues like racism, grind culture, individualism, and digital burnout. These messages exhaust and compromise our well-being. Thus, healing isn't just about balancing things out with a bit of liberation talk; it requires intentionally centering liberatory practices in both our daily interactions and in how we design policies that promote equity and well-being. As PD providers, many of us are filling gaps—supporting the holistic needs of schools that the system itself often overlooks. But our reach has limits when it comes to shifting deeper culture and policy. That's why stepping into the unexpected role of interim middle school principal this year was so powerful for me. It gave me the chance to try these ideals out in the midst of a school community that was going through rapid change and culture shifts. In this call to action, I'll share practical moves I've made that can support both PD providers and school leaders looking to create meaningful, lasting change. Examples of practices we used to uphold the ideals of *connect*, *reflect*, and *reclaim* included:

- Getting to know the teachers (or participants) first; asking them what is going well and what isn't; listening to their stories (formal meetings and hallway chats) before putting my agenda out.
- Changing the schedule to add more breaks or remove working sessions if needed. Emphasizing that sometimes the "work to be done" is actually rest, can mean a lot to, and do a lot for, educators.
- Proactive encouragement of, and getting comfortable with, silence.
- Using a constructivist listening protocol during meetings that accounts for equal time or "serial sharing," noninterruption, emotion, and reframing (e.g., Weissglass, 1990).
- Coconstructing action plans when concerns are raised and always doing what I say I will. Openly stating, "I have your back," and follow up with action.
- Attention to hospitality and space curation (e.g., seating arrangements, lighting, snacks, respect for original start and end times).
- Putting the original agenda items on hold when urgent concerns arise. Note how this is different than respecting start and end times—both practices show respect for educators' humanity.
- Creating space and time for reflection, relationship-building, personal growth, and fun.

- Working in peer group teams that are replicable and helpful outside of the meeting times. For example, I do not force different grade teams to "get to know each other better" if this is not something they are requesting.
- Making myself visible in public spaces and available for connection. Proactively working to maintain an "on front lines with my team" culture.

CONCLUSION

It has been surprising what has been accomplished in the few short months I have been in the role of principal, just by listening to the pain points, and by enacting many of the lessons I learned in my various roles supporting schools as an outsider. I don't claim to be creating miracles, and no doubt, readers who are veteran principals might have a lesson or two for me after the honeymoon period is over. The point is, dismantling toxic professionalism in schools is an active, ongoing, communal practice in which everyone, whether old pro or newbie, has an important role to play. In some cases, as the stories from my PD sessions demonstrated, we all need help being awakened to the unintentional roles we are playing that we don't want to play anymore. The liberatory model helps us remember to *connect* with our emotions and each other, slow down, rest, and *reflect* on whether our actions are having the impact we intend, and lastly to *reclaim* the messages from our childhoods and our cultures, restoring a fully valued and whole version of ourselves and our students, which is the vision of wellness we all want.

REFERENCES

Goleman, D. (1995). *Emotional intelligence*. Bantam Books, Inc.

Gonzalez, N., Moll, L. C., & Amanti, C. (Eds.). (2005). *Funds of knowledge*. Routledge.

Halbreich, U. (2021). Stress-related physical and mental disorders: a new paradigm. *BJPsych Advances*, *27*(3), 145–152. https://doi.org/10.1192/bja.2021.1

Hannibal, K. E., & Bishop, M. D. (2014). Chronic stress, cortisol dysfunction, and pain: A psychoneuroendocrine rationale for stress management in pain rehabilitation. *Physical Therapy*, *94*(12), 1816–1825. https://doi.org/10.2522/ptj.20130597

Hersey, T. (2022, February 21). *This is about more than naps*. The Nap Ministry. https://thenapministry.wordpress.com/2022/02/21/this-is-about-more-than-naps/

Hersey, T. (2022). *Rest is resistance: A manifesto*. Brown Spark.

Hersey, T. (2024). *We will rest: The art of escape*. Little, Brown Spark.

James, K. A., Stromin, J. I., Steenkamp, N., & Combrinck, M. I. (2023). Understanding the relationships between physiological and psychosocial stress, cortisol and cognition. *Frontiers in Endocrinology*, *14*, 1085950. https://doi.org/10.3389/fendo.2023.1085950

Seiler, A., Fagundes, C. P., & Christian, L. M. (2020). The impact of everyday stressors on the immune system and health. In A. Choukèr (Ed.), *Stress challenges and immunity in space: From mechanisms to monitoring and preventive strategies* (pp. 71–92). Springer.

Weissglass, J. (1990). Constructivist listening for empowerment and change. *Educational Forum*, *54*(4), EJ411326.

CHAPTER 17

Healing the Givers

Addressing the Link Between Emotional Labor and the Feminization of the Teaching Profession

Alexander Enrique Parker

> *"Historical scholarship on the feminized profession points to several categories of teacher representations . . . for example, teachers as mothers and teachers as selfless saviors, show the historic assumptions that teachers should not be in the profession to further their own goals but to support the achievement of their pupils (even to their own detriment). Teachers were encouraged to regulate their minds and emotions in order to better meet the needs of their students. Teachers were structured as (White) saviors . . . fulfilling a patriotic duty to their country, sacrificing themselves for the greater cause of educating children." (Dunn et al., 2020, p. 5).*

This quote is a part of a larger discussion centered on the feminization of the United States' teaching profession that began during the 19th century. At the time of reading this quote, I was already eight years into my teaching career and had yet to sit with the role emotions played in the profession. I suddenly began to play back the innumerable times in my career that I needed to suppress, alter, or hide my emotions while teaching, and wondered if there was a name for this experience. It was not long into my search that I discovered there was, as I was experiencing emotional labor firsthand.

Emotional labor can be viewed as the emotion requirements, emotion regulation, and emotion performance that permeate employees' vocational experiences (Grandey & Gabriel, 2015). These experiences may include the ways in which individuals display or hide their emotions from others, the ways individuals modulate their emotions and expressions, as well as the ways an individual's emotions are aligned or misaligned with the emotion-based expectations at their place of employment. When one engages in emotional labor, they are "held accountable not only for the expression of their own feelings but the feelings of others" (Hackman, 2023, p. 4). The dual affective accountability that emerges from emotional labor, where an individual carries the weight of their own emotions and the feelings of others, increases one's emotional burden. Although emotional labor may present subtly or invisibly, the pervasive need to account for the emotions and sentiments of others can take a toll on individuals as they navigate their vocational lives.

The introductory quote succinctly described the early emotional labor expectations for teachers. During the 19th century, new entries into the teaching force were viewed as "angelic public servants motivated by Christian faith; wholly unselfish, self-abnegating, and morally pure" (Goldstein, 2014, p. 26). In a sense, these self-sacrificing women were seen as willing to give their all to students and their role as educator. This slowly led to the belief that teachers should engage in mental and emotional suppression or inauthentic affective displays, with their dedication to students superseding the educator's desires or aspirations. As this was during a time when women taught students only when they were single and childfree, they were expected to leave the profession once they were married and had children (Kim & Taso, 2024).

With legal and macrosystemic limitations being placed upon women's ability to work as teachers, their careers were often short-lived. Thus, the challenge of a teacher masking and contorting their emotions to meet students' needs can be viewed as a sprint: teachers would often give their all to students for a fleeting timeframe and then would shift to domestic duties, perhaps making the unrealistic emotional labor expectations within the vocation easier to bear. Presently, the profession has become a marathon (for those who do not leave), yet teachers are still held to a modern equivalent of the same affective expectations. Teachers are still expected to suppress, alter, and feign their emotions to meet the needs of students and place students' outcomes above their own.

As the historical expectations of the teaching profession have perseverated into the present day, emotional labor expectations are ever-present for teachers of all gender identities. Although the seemingly inexorable nature of emotional labor affects male educators across teaching contexts, the profession is still overwhelmingly made up of women (76% of U.S. public educators and 89% of U.S. public elementary educators; National Center for Education Statistics, 2021). Moreover, some research has suggested that emotional labor impacts women educators to a greater extent than male educators (e.g., Akin et al., 2014).

Challenges that may arise regarding educators' emotional labor experiences include the potential for depersonalization (Yilmaz et al., 2015), emotional exhaustion (Taxer & Frenzel, 2015), turnover intentions (Lee, 2019), and teachers losing sight of their identity (Dunn et al., 2020). Without a centralized focus on healing the emotional labor challenges in the teaching profession, educators will continue to struggle (often silently), and we will continue to have an unwell profession composed of unwell people.

POSITIONALITY

As a cisgender, heterosexual man, whose mixed race background encompasses both Black and Mexican American identities, I am always in constant reflection whenever researching gender issues in the teaching profession. I hesitate to fall into a trap of being a man writing about women's issues, lauding himself an expert about an identity I have no experience living. So, why do I contain a degree of trustworthiness in this realm?

Presently, I am in my 11th year of teaching in a public elementary school. During this time, I have been my school's only male classroom teacher, and the only Black or Latine teacher. Early in my career, I found myself grappling with my racial identity as it related to my (mostly White) students. I began to recognize I was teaching with an ever-present façade, leaving elements of my identity at home. Daily, I would hide my true self while at school, afraid to say the wrong thing or express the wrong emotion. In essence, I felt the limitations of my racial and ethnic background on my identity and expression. I rapidly began to see how these challenges I navigated had a salient overlap with the vocational marginalization that exists for many women. This, in turn, motivated my desire to research gender-based issues in my doctoral studies. I am using the qualitative portion of my research as an opportunity to listen to, learn from, and understand the stories of women educators. In short, the combined experiences of being a teacher, being a racial and gender minority among teachers, and speaking directly to those most affected by the demands of emotional labor in our profession, has helped me to get as close as possible to an insider perspective.

EMOTIONAL LABOR, WOMEN, AND INTERSECTIONALITY

The teaching vocation, like many service industry jobs, is person-facing, making it disproportionately burdened with emotional labor. Service workers are expected to please those they are serving, leading to employees engaging in emotional labor (Hochschild, 1983). In doing so, employees often alter, suppress, or mask their emotions, expressions, and sentiments to meet the needs of those they are interacting with, increasing the affective burden they take on. The presence of occupational segregation in the United States only further contributes to this phenomenon, as the five most held vocational roles for women are service-based (U.S. Department of Labor, 2024). Centuries-old stereotypical beliefs about women promulgate the idea that women are more nurturing and, thus, are turned to for their maternal energy (Hochschild, 1983). Such stereotypes have permeated into the vocational space, creating a workforce where employees in service-based roles are expected to display stereotyped behaviors and take on emotional labor more frequently relative to roles that are male dominated (Martin, 1999).

The result of the teaching profession being structured around gender-based beliefs means that all educators are operating under historically-based assumptions about the role. For women educators, these challenges are palpably exacerbated due to the construct of outlaw emotions, which are emotions the dominant majority deems to be unacceptable to express, especially by marginalized groups (Jaggar, 1989). As such, women educators often find that certain emotions or forms of emotional expression, such as anger or overly strong affective displays, are deemed less favorable (Olson et al., 2019). With outlaw emotions impacting all marginalized identities, it is critical to note that women are not alone in being impacted by limitations in emotional expression. For other historically and racially marginalized identities, the same affective limitations exist (e.g., Neary et al., 2016; Stevenson, 2024). Moreover, as identity is intersectional, there are a great deal of women educators who simultaneously belong to multiple marginalized communities and are faced with even more intense scrutiny from society based on the limitations of outlaw emotions.

THE PATH TO HEALING THROUGH THE HEALING JUSTICE FRAMEWORK

The healing justice framework can provide a structure to address the emotional labor-related difficulties teachers face. The framework, credited to the Kindred Healing Justice Collective, "Recognizes that collective traumas, whether arising from particular events or ongoing circumstances, are rooted in oppressive histories and perpetuated by existing structures and systems" (Raffo, 2019, as cited in Shaw et al., 2022, p. 27). Although not all engagement in emotional labor is inimical to teachers, its ubiquity in the teaching profession is borne out of a patriarchal and White-dominant system that holds expectations for educators to consistently deploy emotional masking and carry the weight of others' sentiments, disregarding the affective toll on teachers. Such a system provides a pathway to stress, burnout, intention to leave the profession, and the disruption of one's personal identity.

To address such difficulties, healing justice can help ensure that steps are taken to engender repair and care in individuals and the collective community (Pyles, 2020). Recently, there has been an increase in the presence of self-care being promoted to address personal and vocational difficulties. For teachers, there are several benefits to self-care in the face of affective challenges (e.g., Taylor et al., 2021). While potentially beneficial, a singular focus on self-care often overlooks the etiology of emotion-based challenges for teachers, shifting healing responsibilities to teachers while simultaneously neglecting the prominent role that systems and organizations play in such difficulties (Pyles, 2020). As a counterweight, healing justice can give rise to collective healing for issues that impact women and for women-dominated professions (Pyles, 2020; Raffo, 2019; Shaw et al., 2022).

To put healing justice into action for teachers, schools and school systems need to engage in intentional and focused dialogue. The Dialogue, Awareness, Belief, Action, and Social Change Model (DABAS model) can be engaged with to "dismantle gender inequality" (Dunson, 2024, p. 3709) and elucidate a path toward healing for the teaching profession. The model encourages structured and equitable dialogue that holds space for all to have their voice heard, creating space to converse across gender lines in ways that often do not occur, with a goal of each individual seeing others in a different light. Using dialogue to increase awareness can alter power, conceptualizations, and beliefs about gender ideologies to foster change.

The DABAS model serves as a guide in varying examples below and this model, along with healing justice, synthesizes well with the writing of many other of this book's chapters, as we collectively invoke a Freirean focus on equitable dialogue, with the aim to traverse educational chasms, heal teachers, and do so in a manner that does not require an untenable level of energy to lead to obtainable change. Along with use of the DABAS model, I interviewed and spoke to teachers or teacher candidates from across the United States. These individuals (as well as the countless others whose words did not make this chapter) shed light on the pressing affective needs of today's teachers and helped frame the proceeding recommendations.

Bring Emotional Labor Out of the Shadows

A 5th grade teacher, Maggie, stated the following about emotional expression at her school:

> *"When women express their emotions, you're viewed as soft, and not in control of your emotions. But you are, you're expressing them. And I've seen where my male counterparts have, you know, lost their cool or are annoyed by something, and they get action as a result of their expressing their emotions. And I feel like I've had my emotions dismissed. And kind of like, 'Oh, well, you know, we'll look into that,' or it's kind of written off as, 'Oh, you're having a bad day,' or, 'You know, must be that time of the month' kind of stuff, and that's not the case with men. The men that I work with at my building, you know, they complain, and there's change that happens right away."*

The experience of Maggie points to a larger issue at hand, as there are differing levels of acceptability for emotional expression by gender (and more broadly, identity) engrained in teaching. Maggie's anecdote also highlights the ways in which emotions are received, as the men's use of emotions generated their desired action, whereas Maggie, a woman, saw her expression of emotions resulting in a devaluing of her perspective, chalked up to emotional or physiological factors. To address this, administrators, schools, and school systems need to begin with an education for themselves and their staff about the role emotional expression and emotional labor play in teaching, along with an examination of emotions and emotional expression amongst staff. Following the DABAS model, a structured dialogue is a starting point. The structured nature of these conversations is important as, without guidance, conversations about identity may lead to stagnation or will continue to uphold the current systems and beliefs regarding emotional expression. To begin, school staffs can establish safety and candor in conversation by developing coconstructed community agreements. Next, the following questions can serve as an initial structural guide:

- "Do you feel you have to hide or change your emotions when teaching or speaking with staff? Can you share some examples?"
- "What are the reasons you feel you have to hide or change your emotions?"
- "What does being a 'professional' mean to you? How does this belief play into the ways in which you express your emotions here at school?"
- "Thinking about your gender identity, do you think this factors into emotion expression?" (The same question can be asked for questions related to other identities.)
- "Think about your colleagues who have a different gender identity than you. How do you think their experiences may be different than yours when it comes to emotions and emotional expression?" (The same question can be asked for questions related to other identities.)

School leaders should also aim to sit down to meet one-on-one with their teachers who belong to racially or historically marginalized identities. As I quickly learned through interviews with teachers, educators are rarely given the chance to express challenges they have regarding emotion regulation or emotional labor. For a school leader, holding space to hear the experiences of their educators, regarding emotional labor, and offering support for any difficulties they face, is an additional and necessary step. Without this step, a school leader may be unaware of how their teaching staff are impacted by emotional labor, rending them only partially capable of addressing challenges.

Creating Community

In another interview, Morgan, a 4th grade teacher, shared with me how she and her teaching team handle emotional labor challenges:

> *"Once we walk them (the students) out, there is typically just like a little get together with either, you know, all of our team or one or two of us and just kind of like venting like just for 5 or 10 minutes. You know, I think it's needed. Or sometimes it's a phone call on the way home. Like, it's just because you can't do it during the day."* A similar sentiment was shared by Divya, a high school math teacher, who stated she felt that she could best navigate the emotional labor hurdles she faced in her teaching career with support such as the following: *"I would benefit from a community of educators to non-judgmentally share experiences and struggles with, ideally already set in place."*

For both teachers, the idea of a community of teachers, to candidly express emotions and emotional labor, is a clear path to healing and wellness. Morgan was able to create this kind of space and community through organic means. While resourceful, ad-hoc spaces also run the risk of exclusivity, and many teachers may be left out of these organically developed healing spaces. In addition, teachers who are experiencing stress or burnout might engage in withdrawal from their colleagues and work environments (Guerrero et al., 2011; Kidger et al., 2016), or not feel they have the personal resources to find such improvised healing spaces. Instead, school leaders, instructional coaches, or mental health support staff can work in tandem to create teacher-centric spaces.

Although teachers may have established spaces to share their emotional labor difficulties, perhaps turning to a friend, family member, or a romantic partner, these individuals are often approaching challenges from an outsider perspective. Conversely, fellow teachers can provide support via their institutional and recondite knowledge that cannot be found anywhere else (Halbesleben, 2006). Due to the ability of education colleagues to understand one's role and professional context, they are more likely to be able to help each other craft solutions and implement new practices, both of which can lead to reductions in burnout (Fiorilli et al., 2019). Teacher-centric spaces, instead, can be intentionally designed for teachers to express their difficulties regarding emotional labor. In addition to expressing difficulties, space should be held for teachers to develop action steps for addressing their challenges. The action steps should then be considered by administration, looking to put such steps into action, continuing the efforts to disrupt the present system.

Healing Starts at the Beginning

During a recent conversation with a preservice teacher, Grace, who was in her final year of undergraduate studies, stated: *"I wish I had a better model for all of this (in reference to emotional labor) during this student teaching semester."* The sentiment shared by Grace exemplifies the experiences of teacher candidates, as it has been stated that preservice teachers often miss out on having an effective role model regarding emotion management and emotional labor (Burger, 2024). A similar thought was shared by Molyneux (2021), who felt that university programs need to make changes to address emotional labor for teacher candidates, deeming this the "missing piece" of teacher education. To address the missing elements, professors and instructors of preservice teachers should work to reimagine coursework, incorporating emotional labor in meaningful ways. Faculty can then help teachers in the development of their teacher identity, ensuring that their burgeoning vocational identity accounts for emotional labor experiences (Molyneux, 2021).

One such way would be for coursework to follow the DABAS model and hold discourse about the role of emotions in relation to teaching and gender, aiming to change beliefs and create action steps for a healthier teacher candidate. Faculty can discuss the origins of emotional labor and how it may present within the classroom, while also providing students with methods to effectively use their emotions as a resource in the classroom. In addition, faculty can work with cooperating teachers to ensure that the assignments and activities teacher candidates are engaging in are not treated as "busy work" but, instead, are valuable opportunities to share methods to manage emotional labor, and how to address any identity-related challenges that may arise. For example, a course's assignment may ask candidates to complete a reflection after instructing a lesson. In the reflection, the inclusion of a question about the affective state of the candidate while teaching ("How did you find yourself managing your emotions while teaching the lesson?") can serve as an initial step. Then, the answers to the reflection question can be discussed with the cooperating teacher or faculty, with feedback being provided, as well as ways the cooperating teacher or faculty would address the emotions and emotional regulation during a similar lesson.

WHERE TO NOW?

There are several messages I want readers to take away after engaging with this chapter. The relationship between emotional labor and burnout (along with other negative impacts on teachers) must remain as a key piece of this chapter's message. Now, more than ever, we need to ensure that our teachers are emotionally healthy and supported, so they may pursue long and joy-inducing teaching careers, for both themselves and the students they serve.

Another salient message centers on the ways emotional labor is experienced differently within the profession, based upon teachers' identities. To move forward means the disruption of a system that retains many of its beliefs from centuries past. To move forward also means the disruption a system that operates under the guise of outlaw emotions, creating a vocation where women and other historically or racially marginalized identities are restricted to a finite range of emotions that are deemed appropriate to express.

CONCLUSION

In the spirit of healing justice, I call upon the education community to rally in the pursuit of collective wellness. This call first extends to school systems and leadership. The steps I have outlined in this chapter encourage a reframing of discourse amongst school staffs. Conversations about emotional labor, identity, and teachers' affective experiences may well be uncomfortable. Persevering through the difficult moments, though, can change beliefs, create actionable items, and push toward social change. Along with having difficult conversations, developing spaces for teachers to create community can also attenuate emotional labor challenges, a much needed step toward healing.

I also call upon those working at the postsecondary level. I believe we need to fill the emotional labor knowledge gap that exists, and this can begin with preservice teachers. Intentional effort to incorporate emotional labor into the teacher preparation process, in ways that resonate with the teachers of tomorrow, can be of ineffable value. Teacher candidates can begin to feel that the emotional labor role models they have been lacking will have emerged. I acknowledge that this plan is ambitious, but I don't believe it is overly idealistic. Instead, it emerges from a palpable desire to heal the profession in a way that brings increased joy to its practitioners and addresses the challenges of women and other marginalized identities in particular experience. Like the collective call to action that this book implies, it is time to get serious about looking for ways all across the teacher pipeline and profession to reduce emotional labor, and place the responsibility for doing so not on teachers themselves, but on those responsible for creating their work conditions, such as principals, administrators, district leaders, and teacher preparation faculty and administration.

REFERENCES

Akın, U., Aydın, İ., Erdoğan, Ç., & Demirkasımoğlu, N. (2014). Emotional labor and burnout among Turkish primary school teachers. *Australian Educational Researcher, 41*(2), 155–169. https://doi.org/10.1007/s13384-013-0138-4

Burger, J. (2024). Constructivist and transmissive mentoring: Effects on teacher self-efficacy, emotional management, and the role of novices' initial beliefs. *Journal of Teacher Education*, *75*(1), 107–121. https://doi.org/10.1177/00224871231185371

Dunn, A. H., Moore, A. E., & Neville, M. L. (2020). "There isn't an easy way for me to talk about this": A historical and contemporary examination of emotional rules for teachers. *Teachers College Record, 122*(9), 1–36. https://doi.org/10.1177/016146812012200915

Dunson, K. (2024). Closing the gender gap: Women and men creating social change through dialogue. *Advances in Social Sciences Research Journal, 11*(8), 161–183. https://doi.org/10.14738/assrj.118.17356

Fiorilli, C., Benevene, P., De Stasio, S., Buonomo, I., Romano, L., Pepe, A., & Addimando, L. (2019). Teachers' burnout: The role of trait emotional intelligence and social support. *Frontiers in Psychology, 10,* Article 2743. https://doi.org/10.3389/fpsyg.2019.02743

Goldstein, D. (2014). *The teacher wars: A history of America's most embattled profession.* Penguin Random House.

Grandey, A. A., & Gabriel, A. S. (2015). Emotional labor at a crossroads: Where do we go from here? *Annual Review of Organizational Psychology and Organizational Behavior, 2,* 323–349. https://doi.org/10.1146/annurev-orgpsych-032414-111400

Guerrero, E., Gomez, R., Moreno, J. M., Garcia-Baamonde, E., & Blazquez, M. (2011). Burnout syndrome, ways of coping and mental health in non-university teachers. *Behavioural Psychology: Psicologia Conductual*, *19*, 557–576.

Hackman, R. (2023). *Emotional labor: The invisible work shaping our lives and how to claim our power*. Flatiron Books.

Halbesleben, J. R. B. (2006). Sources of social support and burnout: A meta-analytic test of the conservation of resources model. *Journal of Applied Psychology, 91*(5), 1134–1145. https://doi.org/10.1037/0021-9010.91.5.1134

Hochschild, A. R. (1983). *The managed heart: Commercialization of human feeling*. University of California Press.

Jaggar, A. M. (1989). Love and knowledge: Emotion in feminist epistemology. *Inquiry, 32*(2), 151–176. https://doi.org/10.1080/00201748908602185

Kidger, J., Brockman, R., Tilling, K., Campbell, R., Ford, T., Araya, R., King, M., & Gunnell, D. (2016). Teachers' well-being and depressive symptoms, and associated risk factors: A large cross-sectional study in English secondary schools. *Journal of Affective Disorders*, *192*, 76–82. https://doi.org/10.1016/j.jad.2015.11.054

Kim, A., & Tsao, C. (2024). *The effects of prohibiting marriage bars: The case of US teachers* [Manuscript submitted for publication]. https://carolyntsao.github.io/website /marriage_bars.pdf

Lee, Y. H. (2019). Emotional labor, teacher burnout, and turnover intention in high-school physical education teaching. *European Physical Education Review, 25*(1), 236–253. https://doi.org/10.1177/1356336X17719559

Martin, S. E. (1999). Police force or police service? Gender and emotional labor. *The Annals of the American Academy of Political and Social Science*, *561*(1), 111–126. https://doi .org/10.1177/000271629956100l0

Molyneux, T. (2021). Preparing teachers for emotional labour: The missing piece in teacher education. *The Journal of Teaching and Learning, 15*(1), 39–56. https://doi.org/10.22329/ jtl.v15i1.6333

National Center for Education Statistics. (2021). *Characteristics of public school teachers.* Retrieved May 2021 from https://nces.ed.gov/programs/coe/indicator/clr

Neary, A., Gray, B. and O'Sullivan, M. (2016). A queer politics of emotion: Reimagining sexualities and schooling. *Gender and Education, 28*(2), 250–265. http://www .tandfonline.com/doi/abs/10.1080/09540253.2015.1114074?needAccess=true

Olson, R. E., McKenzie, J., Mills, K. A., Patulny, R., Bellocchi, A., & Caristo, F. (2019). Gendered emotion management and teacher outcomes in secondary school teaching: Review. *Teaching and Teacher Education, 80,* 128–144. https://doi.org/10.1016/j.tate.2019 .01.010

Pyles, L. (2020). Healing justice, transformative justice, and holistic self-care for social workers. *Social Work, 65*(2), 178–187. https://doi.org/10.1093/sw/swaa013

Raffo, S. (2019). *Healing justice: Building power, transforming movements.* Astraea Lesbian Foundation for Justice. https://astraeafoundation.org

Shaw, J., Amir, M., Lewin, T., Kemitare, J., Diop, A., Kithumbu, O., Mupotsa, D., & Odiase, S. (2022). *Contextualising healing justice as a feminist organising framework in Africa.* The Institute of Development Studies and Partner Organisations.

Stevenson, M. (2024). Understanding the emotional labor of English language teaching while Black in the United States. *TESOL Quarterly*, *58*(4), 1347–1371. https://doi.org/10.1002/ tesq.3274

Taxer, J. L., & Frenzel, A. C. (2015). Facets of teachers' emotional lives: A quantitative Investigation of teachers' genuine, faked, and hidden emotions. *Teaching and Teacher Education, 42,* 78–88. https://doi.org/10.1016/j.tate.2015.03.003

Taylor, S. G., Roberts, A. M., & Zarrett, N. (2021). A brief mindfulness-based intervention (bMBI) to reduce teacher stress and burnout. *Teaching and Teacher Education, 100*, 103284. https://doi.org/10.1016/j.tate.2021.103284

U.S. Department of Labor, Women's Bureau. (2024). *Most common occupations for women in the labor force*. U.S. Department of Labor. https://www.dol.gov/agencies/wb/data/occupations/most-common-occupations-women-labor-force

Yilmaz, K., Altinkurt, Y., Guner, M., & Sen, B. (2015). The relationship between teachers' emotional labor and burnout level. *Eurasian Journal of Educational Research, 59*, 75–90 http://dx.doi.org/10.14689/ejer.2015.59.5

Healing Teaching, Healing Ourselves

A Conversation With Amanda and Jeanette

Amanda Moreno and Jeanette Banashak reflect on their experiences of writing What Teachers Need *and consider unifying themes across chapters. There certainly remains much more to explore and wonder about and heal in education, but in this dialogue, the editors contemplate the scholarship and stories they have learned throughout the writing process and they dream about what could be.*

Learn something, for a reason, from someone!
Behind a desk in a classroom?
Or by the trees, watching the fish school?
How do we teach our children?
Equality in education they say!
But halve the gap for Indigenous children,
So what does that say about equality?
Are they not a united part of society?
Learn something, for a reason, from someone.
Is that someone you?

Halve the gap for Indigenous children.
Where is the equality?

—Ashwita Venkatesh (printed with permission from Manathunga et al., 2020)

I AM BECAUSE WE ARE

JB: Let's start with a question about process: Now that you are close to the end of the book project, what has been clarified for you in terms of initial questions and curiosities?

AM: Well, I think I was anticipating arguments from "both sides" in terms of putting together a book that was ostensibly "only" about teachers and their well-being, for its own sake. You saw some of this anticipatory defensiveness in the opening chapter when I referred to the obligation to improve teacher practice as "the price of admission," for teacher well-being. So we can invest in teacher well-being but only because it makes them better for their students, and I bristled against that. On the one hand, I was worried about readers who would be expecting a book more focused on students, and on the other hand, I was worried about our authors, and whether they would be openly, clearly, and boldly focused enough on the teachers in their approaches. And then I began thinking about two chapters that initially seemed like they are on these opposite sides of this continuum: On one "side" we have Alex Shevrin Venet's chapter, which is about teachers showing students unconditional positive regard. I remember when she first submitted her abstract, there was one brief phrase at the end that said she would demonstrate how showing unconditional positive regard for students was actually a wellness practice for teachers, and I was a bit skeptical. I wondered if it would be enough, if it would be another "price of admission" kind of argument, but then she submitted her full chapter and did such a gorgeous job with it, really convincingly showing, I thought, that what seemed like it was for the students was just as much, if not more, for themselves.

And then we have on the "other side," seemingly, Hillary Gourneau et al.'s chapter, which made the bold statement that their teacher intervention had absolutely nothing to do with student outcomes or making these tribal Head Start teachers into "better teachers." Originally, the Little Holy One intervention was directed toward the Native American families and children attending Head Start, giving them a space to recover from the trauma of colonialism, and to reconnect with their Tribal heritage, but the authors began to notice that since the teachers came from the same community as the children (which is a core principle of Head Start), the teachers were experiencing the same traumas, and that if anything, these teachers were overly self-sacrificing and never centering their own needs. They realized that the community as a whole could not heal unless teachers also had something that was just for themselves.

JB: I see, so on the one hand we have a practice that seems like it is only about nurturing students but it ends up being about a community-wide practice of moral alignment that is just as healing for teachers, and on the other hand we have a situation where it was realized that student and family healing could not take place if the teachers were unhealed.

AM: Yes, and they were so clear on this point—they made sure to *not* measure teacher practices or student outcomes! Their measures were things like depression, Tribal identity, resilience, and life satisfaction. Reading those two chapters in tandem helped me to realize that there are not actually "sides"—there is only one thing, which is wellness of the whole community. If you have an authentic, love-based approach, which all of the approaches in the book in effect are, you don't really have to worry about which particular population you're focusing on. By definition it will have ripple effects. It was important for this book to focus on teachers for their own sake because that calls attention to a harm that needed healing, but in the end, all methods that would satisfy the kind of conditions that we're considering are at their core community-based.

JB: Yes, this reminds me of the concept of *ubuntu* from South African philosophy, which means, "I am because we are" or "humanity toward others." In the transition from apartheid to majority rule in the nineties, *ubuntu* was one of the guiding ideals. There are so many similar concepts across cultures. There's the Mayan understanding, greeting, and ethical code, *In Lak'ech*, which is translated "You are my other me." Or, the worldview and prayer of the Lakota people, *Mitakuye Oyasin*, which means, "We are all related" or "All my relatives." These concepts and ways of being center our interconnection, collective identity, and reciprocity. Our authors pointed to these ways; those two chapters and all chapters in between, in one way or another made clear that healing teachers is healing the whole school community is healing the whole profession. I believe that this way of being challenges White intellectual superiority (Ewing, 2025) and the practices of individualism that pedestalize personal gain and self-sufficiency. Everyone's wellness is all of our wellness.

AM: Yes, and while we may have already known that on some level at the start, seeing all the different angles and approaches, even within a book purportedly focused on one population, affirmed this idea of "no wrong door" into healing teaching, healing education.

RETURNING TO THE BASICS

JB: I'm thinking about entry points into these authentic, love-based approaches to education. For example, how the expression of love looks different for new educators, midcareer educators, and late career educators.

AM: Say more about what you mean by these "levels" and how that relates to what you learned from our authors.

JB: There's a progression that learners go through when studying something. In education, for example, preservice teachers learn about the basics, the foundations of education, like pedagogy, teaching philosophy, a teacher's roles and responsibilities, etc. Eventually, they become eager to go beyond that level of competency to expand their abilities. I remember becoming skilled at an intermediate level after about three years of teaching. After several more years of teaching and leading, educators become ready to go beyond intermediate competencies to an advanced level where they develop more complex skills. But then, it kind of comes around full circle when advanced practitioners tend to go back to the basics, such as the foundations of curiosity and connection with their students. When I was a young teacher at 22, I was working with teachers who had been teaching for decades, and I saw how they returned to some of those foundational skills—many of those skills were relationship-based, like making authentic connections with students and peers and families/caregivers. As a new teacher, however, I wanted to incorporate all the fanciest tips and tricks that I had learned in undergrad.

AM: Got it, yes, I think of this similarly to the way I think of mindfulness. Toddlers are organically good at it, such as when they are absorbed in the present moment when they are playing in the mud or jumping in puddles, and then as they age, they lose that ease with staying in the moment. As adolescents or adults, we have to reteach ourselves how to become present. Right now, in the West, we struggle with authenticity. It's been squashed out of us through capitalism, individualism, and authoritarianism, and through neoliberalism, where things became outcome-based, like test scores. So right now, I'd consider any approach in a professional realm that is authentic and loving to be "advanced" because it means that the community has remained true to what really matters despite all the pulls in other directions.

JB: All of our authors return to the basics in their own ways: There are many more foundational skills and practices that are outlined by each author that are drawn from their unique relationships and contexts.

AM: Yes, and I've observed how the basics get usurped by our busy work lives, or fears about money, and so we humans become more mechanistic.

JB: Mechanistic and less human. And yet what I've learned from each of our authors are specific ways to be more human, more authentic. We are living in a time of so much uncertainty with decisions being made by global leaders that are impacting and harming babies and children, caregivers, the education system, and the environment. Some of the laws and policies attempt to separate humans from humans and humans from the natural world. But I believe that educators are in spaces to bring us together, no matter what context they are in, to practice and create policies that are basic to human and nature flourishing, like doing no harm and loving and respecting. Gary Nabhan (n.d., as cited in Kimmerer, 2013, p. 9) says, "We can't meaningfully proceed with healing, with restoration, without 're-story-ation.'" We hope readers can imagine other practices and policies that contribute to narratives of collaboration and coordination and challenge those that contribute to the illusion of separation. If we are not Indigenous, this may be a central developmental task of our life.

AM: And even though this sounds somewhat lofty, our authors were not suggesting pie-in-the-sky or unattainable approaches. They were very down-to-earth and foundational while not being overly prescriptive.

Each author provided specific enough ways to get back to what matters, that were visualizable and modifiable for their own settings.

THREADING THE NEEDLE BETWEEN INDIVIDUAL SELF-CARE AND SYSTEMS CHANGE

JB: When we first put out our invitation to authors our tagline was, "There are a lot of books about what teachers need *to do*; this book will be more about what teachers *need*." It was our way of succinctly explaining that we did not want this to be another book that just had a lot of *instructions* for teachers on how to stay sane despite the insanity. But at the same time, this wasn't a policy book either. We weren't asking teachers to wait around until the entire system became healed with better policies; we wanted to explore dynamic approaches happening right now to thread that needle, to explore that in-between space, to get teachers some answers that would make a difference in their lives without adding more to their load. Can you talk a bit about how we thought about threading that needle, for ourselves and with the chapter authors?

AM: It was a bit tricky for sure, but I think we settled on this notion of "creating conditions." So even if you were going to be focusing on building self-care skills, the question was, what were you going to recommend to at least "one level up" to create the conditions, to ease the path to that growth? My "formula" for that was if you are in a position to ask teachers to *do* something, to demand anything of them such as a change in practice (which would then include professional development facilitators who don't even work in the school building) then you are most likely *also* in a position to lighten their load or create the conditions for flourishing. Beyond individual self-care and skill-building are the conditions that allow new practices to be taken up more easily. This included suggestions we read about in the book such as professional development facilitators working closely with principals and teaching teams to provide the most targeted and current supports, providing reflective supervision in line with an articulated goal related to community well-being, and providing peer groups both within and across schools to share challenges and wins and learn about different approaches to solving problems. These seemingly basic ideas—like we were talking about earlier in terms of returning to the foundations—nevertheless take time and commitment, in the context of overfull days and maxed-out budgets. That's why it's so important that leaders, and the whole community for that matter, maintain a very high level of awareness that foundational or basic should not be mistaken for optional or expendable.

JB: I hear what you're saying, but then what would be the recommendation for individual teachers who might be reading this book, especially if they don't work in the context of an established statewide initiative or maybe they have a school leader who is OK but isn't necessarily focused on "creating the conditions for wellness"?

AM: There are a lot of lessons that an individual teacher can take with them, even into a school or system that isn't ready for broad-based change yet. The way we have framed this is to say that, at a minimum, the book should provide lots of good examples of "how I ought to be treated." Teachers have told us that even if they aren't yet treated that way, these models and approaches and visualizable examples are still helpful as a standard to work toward, and if nothing else, a simple affirmation that "No, you're not alone in thinking that ____ seems wrong" or "No, ______ is not too much to ask."

JB: And then of course, the same lessons about how change starts small, or the difference in a social dynamic that can be created by just one person shifting what they do or what they accept—all those same axioms apply here too. Start with a *What Teachers Need* book club among a few like-minded colleagues. Then add more teachers, and ideally, invite leadership too. Pick some practices to start with and commit to "implement them on Monday." Come back together, see how it's going, hold each other accountable in collegial ways—all of that good stuff. Ultimately, we should also include families, caregivers, and community stakeholders in the book club. Anyone who cares or needs to care about our education system and the humans involved in it.

AM: Thank you for including them. Yes, we all need to care about and consider ourselves responsible for teacher well-being.

THE SPARK OF ONE SESSION

JB: We spoke earlier about new awarenesses or sparks of inspiration that were conceptually related to the field, but what did you learn about yourself throughout this process?

AM: This is the first book that I've ever worked on—I've never even written a book chapter! I identify as a researcher, so my world has primarily been articles in scholarly journals that have been reporting on empirical studies. So it was a little bit strange for me to think about my very first venture into a book project being one that was really more for practitioners. As you know from our PD projects we have codesigned and coconducted, we have been responding to not only a post-COVID world, but from the beginning, we wanted the content to be a representation of folks' most current, out-of-the-box, humane, innovative approaches that were dynamically responding to the crises of the moment. When inviting authors, we used the example from our Hawai'i project, where the most recent cohort started just a couple of weeks after the Maui wildfires of 2023, and we described to them how we had to respond dynamically to that moment with changes to both the content and our approach. The climate crisis is speeding up natural disasters, which has unique effects on the educators and leaders who live in those places around the world and this was just one example of the changes coming fast and furious that don't stop at the schoolhouse door. With this book we wanted to know, what are people doing to help teachers out in response to this rapid onslaught, levels of chaos, and challenges that are being added on to a profession that was already in a satisfaction and retention crisis? We knew that if we waited for randomized controlled trials to know if these approaches were effective in creating healing, it might be too late.

JB: This is also why we wanted to make sure to incorporate various lenses into teacher support, from not just researchers but also theorists, higher ed faculty, PK–12 teachers, PD providers, leaders, and storytellers.

AM: Yes, so we knew that our authors' "proof of effectiveness" would not come in the form of randomized control trials or statistical significance (even if they were researchers), because that was not the time-scale we were interested in platforming. Instead, we asked them for real-time, concrete examples of healing and impact, and the authors really delivered! This may sound like it has nothing to do with what I learned about myself, but I promise I'm getting to that. When I read about the amazing examples of impact—changes that were unique to one individual, such as a teacher deciding to pursue a leadership pathway they wouldn't have otherwise, or a leader deciding to change from a militant disciplinary style to a more SEL-based, humanitarian style, or changes that would happen even after a brief intervention or even one session like you explained in your chapter about the dramatic impact of a single Nature Companionship experience—led me to this phrase that kept reoccurring in my mind: *the spark of one session.* And this is the kind of thing that traditional impact evaluations are just lousy at capturing. This was a welcome "jolt" to my identity as a researcher who is evidence-based, quantitatively based, and inclined to never overclaim results. But when the authors provided so many great examples of real, concrete impacts—from within the sessions themselves, or hearing about changes teachers made in their lives afterwards—I was as sure as I needed to be that these approaches were built on much more than good intentions and were making a real difference. I am grateful to our authors and to this experience for this awakening at this point in my career.

BE-LONG-ING

AM: What about you, what have you learned about yourself through this process?

JB: Early on, we knew that edited books are a "tough sell" in certain settings, but I have greatly appreciated the varied voices and perspectives in this book project. I've seen others' practices reflected in mine, which feels validating and invites me to continue doing some of the things I do. And of course, I've taken so many pearls from each chapter, so I'm looking forward to trying out some new-to-us ideas and seeing how they support the communities I'm teaching. I have also grown in trust and understanding of new colleagues in education, which is a community that I feel I belong to.

AM: Yes, I am unbelievably grateful for getting to intersect with these authors. I just felt so lucky all the time that they said yes to this project, and that we got to learn from them and work with them.

JB: Toko-pa Turner wrote, "At the very heart of 'belonging' is the word 'long.' To be-long to something is to stay with it for the long haul. It is an active choice we make to a relationship, to a place, to our body, to a life because we value it" (2017). I've learned about ways of connecting with myself, others, and the natural world toward unraveling fear and healing harms. I feel the way I hope our readers do: seen and heard. Another ripple effect for me is that I'm allowing myself to be touched by my students' questions and lives, by colleagues' struggles and learnings. The stories and scholarship in our book invite me to defend the students and my colleagues more deeply, to advocate for them more fiercely, and to celebrate them more bravely.

AM: I love that! There's a lot of bravery required in the teaching profession at the moment, for the teachers especially, and as we're reminded throughout the pages of this book, for those whose job it is to support them. I do want the principals, teacher education faculty, and professional development providers to take these appeals to act bravely as *demands* in the sense of being "called in"—in the same way that individuals with more privilege are called in to examine themselves and act with greater humility and responsibility.

JB: So much change is possible within community, let's take the next step toward cooperation and justice so that all children, teachers, and school leaders are more well. Dear educators, I believe we are the *someones* to do this work.

REFERENCES

Ewing, E. (2025). *Original sins: The (mis)education of Black and Native children and the construction of American racism.* One World.

Kimmerer, R. W. (2013). *Braiding sweetgrass: Indigenous wisdom, scientific knowledge, and the teachings of plants*. Milkweed Editions.

Manathunga, C., Davidow, S., Williams, P., Gilbey, K., Bunda, T., Raciti, M., & Stanton, S. (2020). Decolonisation through poetry: Building First Nations' voice and promoting truth-telling. *Education as Change, 24*(1), Article 7765. https://doi.org/10.25159/1947-9417/77

Turner, T. (2017). *Belonging: Remembering ourselves home*. Her Own Room Press.

Index

About the Editors and Contributors

Jeanette Banashak is a senior instructor and the program director for the online Master's in Early Childhood Education program with Leadership and Advocacy and SEL focus areas at Erikson Institute. She founded Forest Bathing Chicago and a training program for Nature Companionship, and dreams of a Chicago where every week, neighbors can participate in slow, mindful, playful nature immersion experiences right out their front door.

Amanda Moreno is an associate professor at Erikson Institute where she directs the doctoral program in child development and conducts research and professional learning projects in the areas of social and emotional learning, developmental neuroscience, embodied learning, and teacher wellness. She has been the PI or Co-PI of multiple federally funded grants, has published in and is on the editorial boards of journals such as *Early Childhood Research Quarterly*, and works to nurture and empower the next generation of liberatory educators.

Benelly Álvarez is a New York City public school educator focusing on bilingual and special education and language equity and access. She has experience teaching in elementary school classrooms where she prioritizes advocating for students and their families' needs. She also has experience as an educational administrator where she supports teachers and school leaders in creating equitable school systems and structures. She is a coauthor of the book, *Reading, Writing, and Talk: Teaching for Equity and Justice in the Early Grades*, which focuses on the importance of language equity in early childhood classrooms.

Ivette Marlenne Alvarez is a doctoral student and researcher at Erikson Institute, studying how professional learning environments foster bilingual teachers' healing and leadership. She teaches K–5th grade bilingual social–emotional learning at a Chicago Public School, where she also leads the school's social-emotional support efforts. With over a decade of experience, she has taught pre-K students and Spanish-speaking parents, and facilitated bilingual professional development. She is committed to cocreating spaces that are rooted in radical healing and love.

Teresa N. Brockie is a member of the A'aninin Nation from the Fort Belknap Reservation and an associate professor at Johns Hopkins University. In collaboration with Tribal members on the Fort Peck Reservation she codesigned and adapted a 12-component intervention called Wakȟáŋyeža (Little Holy One). It aims to instill traditional values in children to prevent adolescent suicide and substance use, to teach caregivers methods for coping with trauma and stress, and promote positive parenting practices.

Kamilah Drummond is the founder of KDRUMM Consulting LLC, a nationally recognized expert in transformative SEL and equity. She partners with schools and organizations to design strategic, equity-centered professional learning. A 2023 CASEL award recipient, keynote speaker, and published writer, Kamilah also facilitates with the National SEED Project. Kamilah is the board chair for SEL4MA, serves on the Boston Arts Academy board, and is a sought-after speaker and consultant committed to adult SEL, justice, and healing-centered education.

Addison Duane is an assistant professor of child & adolescent development in the College of Education at Sacramento State University. As a former elementary school teacher, she conducts community-based research to investigate trauma and transformation in schools. She earned an MA in curriculum & instruction with a focus on critical pedagogy from the University of Colorado, a PhD in educational psychology from Wayne State University, and completed a postdoctoral fellowship with UC Berkeley's Innovations for Youth.

Hilary Gourneau is a member of the Fort Peck Assiniboine and Sioux Tribes and is the Fort Peck Tribes Head Start Director. She obtained a master in counselor education degree with a certificate in trauma-informed services at Portland State University. She believes in order for success to be possible within schools, Native students and their families need to feel connected, respected, supported, and reflected at all levels.

Tara Hofkens is an education researcher at RAND and visiting scholar at the University of Virginia where she studies social and affective processes involved in teaching and learning. She is currently working on school-based interventions that support active and experiential learning funded by the Department of Education, the National Science Foundation, the LEGO Foundation, and the Overdeck Foundation. She also consults with public and independent school systems on how to support student motivation, engagement, and well-being.

Rebeca Itzkowich was a teacher education faculty member at Erikson Institute for over 25 years. Her research focuses on how issues of bilingualism and biliteracy impact identity and learning in the United States. As an immigrant from Mexico, her passion and commitment have been to support immigrant children and their families, first as a teacher in Head Start and public schools in New York City, Oklahoma, and Illinois, and then as a teacher educator. She is a founding member of the Early Math Collaborative and RJEM (Racial Justice in Early Mathematics) at Erikson Institute.

Patricia A. Jennings is a professor at the University of Virginia School of Education and Human Development. She is a leader in the field of social and emotional learning and mindfulness in education and has developed and evaluated effective programs to support educator and student well-being. She is the author of four books and multiple peer reviewed articles and chapters. Previously she spent 22 years as a teacher and school leader.

Mai Xi Lee is the social emotional learning director at the Sacramento County Office of Education, where she leads the California statewide CalHOPE Student Support project. Mai Xi believes in the power of a more humanized educational ecosystem and has spent the last decade-plus leading systemic and transformative SEL implementation efforts across large school systems in CA. She remains committed to ensuring that schools become places and spaces for healing and thriving for all.

Brent Malicote is an Associate Superintendent at the Sacramento County Office of Education (SCOE). He is involved in a variety of programs that support student needs across the county. He also advocates for SEL with his work at CalHOPE, a community that helps children integrate back into learning after experiencing trauma. He has held multiple administrative and leadership positions where he prioritizes creating inclusive learning environments.

Jessica Martell is a New York City public school educator who focuses on curating inclusive classrooms with an emphasis on practices rooted in restorative justice. She has worked alongside students and their parents for over 25 years to disrupt educational inequities. She is also an instructor and doctoral candidate at Teachers College, Columbia University, emphasizing culturally responsive teaching practices with preservice teachers. She is a coauthor of the book *Reading, Writing, and Talk: Teaching for Equity and Justice in the Early Grades,* which focuses on the importance of language equity in early childhood classrooms.

Lorea Martínez is the award-winning founder of HEART in Mind, a company dedicated to helping schools and organizations integrate SEL in their practices, products, and learning communities. A global educator, Dr. Martínez is a Columbia University Teachers College faculty member, educating aspiring principals in emotional intelligence. Her book, *Teaching with the HEART in Mind*, was selected as and here a teacher favorite by the Greater Good Science Center at UC Berkeley. Dr. Martínez is passionate about strengthening adult social and emotional capacity and currently focuses on the implementation of her Growing Your HEART Skills program for educators.

Ashley N. Metzger is a postdoctoral research fellow at the SHIFT Research Institute at the University of California, Berkeley. She studies the behavioral health of neurodivergent children and youth in schools and the processes of school transformation to promote well-being. As a Fellow, she works on the research and evaluation team for CalHOPE Student Support. Ashley received a William T. Grant Foundation Officers' Research Grant to help understand educators' use of research evidence to improve the lives of young people and transform schools.

Kamryn S. Morris is an assistant professor of social work at the University of Washington. After working in classroom and out-of-school settings, she earned her PhD in family & human development from Arizona State University. She is a prevention scientist and investigates culturally relevant practices for supporting school belonging, the pervasiveness of racism, and equitable school transformation. Kamryn completed her postdoctoral training with the SHIFT Research Institute at the University of California, Berkeley.

Micia Mosely is the founder and director of The Black Teacher Project (BTP). She received her PhD in education, with an emphasis on social and cultural studies from the University of California at Berkeley. Micia has been a leader in educational equity as a high school teacher and in her work with the Bay Area Coalition of Equitable Schools, The Posse Foundation, and The National Equity Project. In 2015 she founded BTP, which supports the leadership and wellness of Black teachers. Micia is also an accomplished actress and stand-up comedian.

Alexander Enrique Parker is a doctoral candidate at the Johns Hopkins University School of Education, as well as a public educator, with over 10 years of experience as a 4th grade teacher. He researches burnout and emotional labor in K–12 educators, focusing on gender dynamics and affective challenges for teachers of color. In addition, he explores restorative justice and other means of reducing exclusionary disciplinary practices in U.S. schools.

Roberto Rivera is the cofounder and CEO of CADRE LLC, a Chicago-based company that creates culturally relevant tools and technologies to improve individual and collective well-being. A global leader in education and youth development, Dr. Rivera brings over 25 years of experience working with school communities across the United States and internationally. Once labeled an "at-risk" student, he transformed adversity into purpose with his work, which sits at the intersection of hip-hop, healing, social justice, and educational innovation, and is featured in the permanent "Upstander" exhibit at the Illinois Holocaust Museum. A CASEL research collaborator and national speaker, Roberto's mission is to build thriving ecosystems where students, educators, and communities are affirmed and empowered.

Valerie B. Shapiro is an associate professor at UC Berkeley. She is a translation scientist who studies system-level strategies to overcome the persistent gap between rigorous research and the routines of educational practice as it relates to the promotion of mental, emotional, and behavioral well-being of children and youth. Valerie serves as the scientific director and special project advisor to CalHOPE Student Support. In this work, she and her partners were recognized with the 2024 Chancellor's Award for Campus Community Partnerships at UC Berkeley, and also honored by the Society for Prevention Research with their 2024 Public Service Award for putting lessons from research into practice.

Mariana Souto-Manning is a distinguished, award-winning scholar and leader in early childhood teaching and teacher education, and president of Erikson Institute. A first-generation immigrant from Brazil, her work centers justice, belonging, and the dismantling of systemic inequities. She draws on community-rooted pedagogies and epistemologies to advance collective healing and transformation. Author of 12 books and over 100 articles, she partners with educators, families, and communities to reimagine education as a site of liberation.

Sara Staley is an assistant professor of Teacher Learning, Research, and Practice at the University of Colorado Boulder. She codirects A Queer Endeavor, a nationally recognized center for gender and sexual diversity in education that works in partnership with districts and school communities to organize learning environments in which LGBTQ+ youth can thrive. Her work has appeared in journals such as *Research in the Teaching of English* and the *Harvard Educational Review*.

Maurice Swinney is the chief innovation officer at Chicago Beyond, where he creates more equitable systems for young people and communities. He served as Chicago Public Schools' (CPS) first chief equity officer and interim chief education officer. Here, Maurice led the creation of the district's first equity framework and shifted funding to underserved schools, making over 20 policies more equitable. His accomplishments stem from his 21 years of varied experience in education.

Eseta Tualaulelei is an associate professor at the University of Southern Queensland in Australia. She teaches literacy education and intercultural communication to early years preservice teachers. She is passionate about equitable education for children with diverse cultural and linguistic backgrounds, and her research is focused on intercultural education and teacher professional learning and development. Her research is informed by Bourdieu, indigenous Pacific Islands' research approaches, and critical education theories.

Alex Shevrin Venet is an educator, author, and professional development facilitator based in Vermont. She teaches graduate teacher education at Vermont State

University and Antioch University. Previously, she was a teacher and leader at an alternative therapeutic school, community college instructor, and after-school teacher in the upper elementary grades. Alex's work focuses on trauma-informed education practices with a focus on empowering teachers to create systemic change. She is the author of the bestselling book *Equity-Centered Trauma-Informed Education* and *Becoming an Everyday Changemaker.*

Dody Wibowo is a scholar-practitioner in peace education with over two decades of experience. He serves as lecturer and quality assurance coordinator for the master's degree in peace and conflict resolution at Universitas Gadjah Mada, Indonesia, and as Director of Advocacy and Community Empowerment at the Sukma Foundation. Holding a PhD from the University of Otago, his work focuses on supporting teachers in delivering peace education.

Deborah H. Wilson has worked as a registered nurse internationally for the last 30 years and obtained a PhD from Johns Hopkins University. Her research uses community-based participatory research to work with Native American communities to adapt, implement and evaluate sustainable, culturally informed interventions to promote and strengthen Native early childhood education teachers' health and well-being. Wilson currently works as a senior lecturer at Auckland University of Technology, New Zealand.